MARVEL FUTURE FIGHT FIRSTS

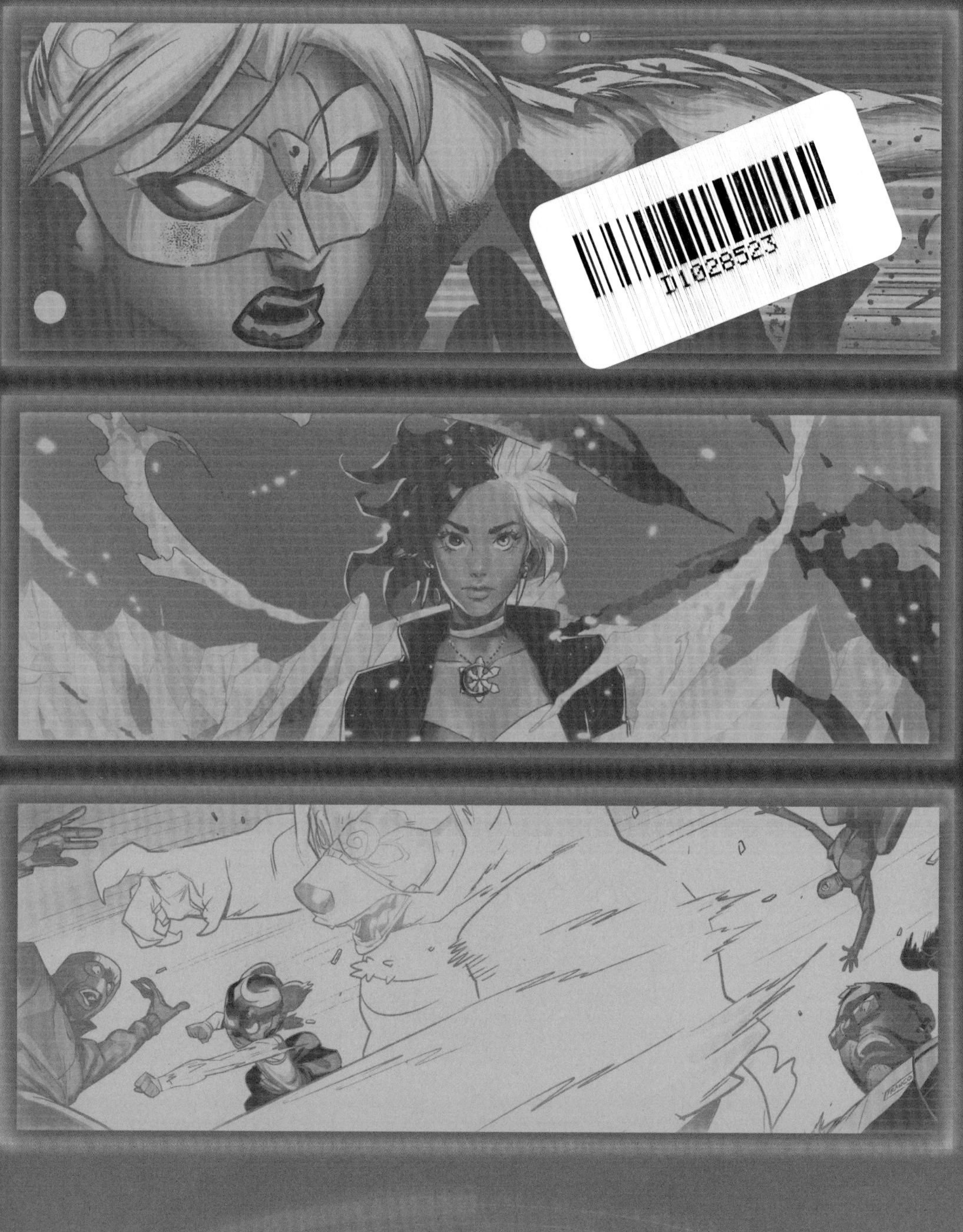

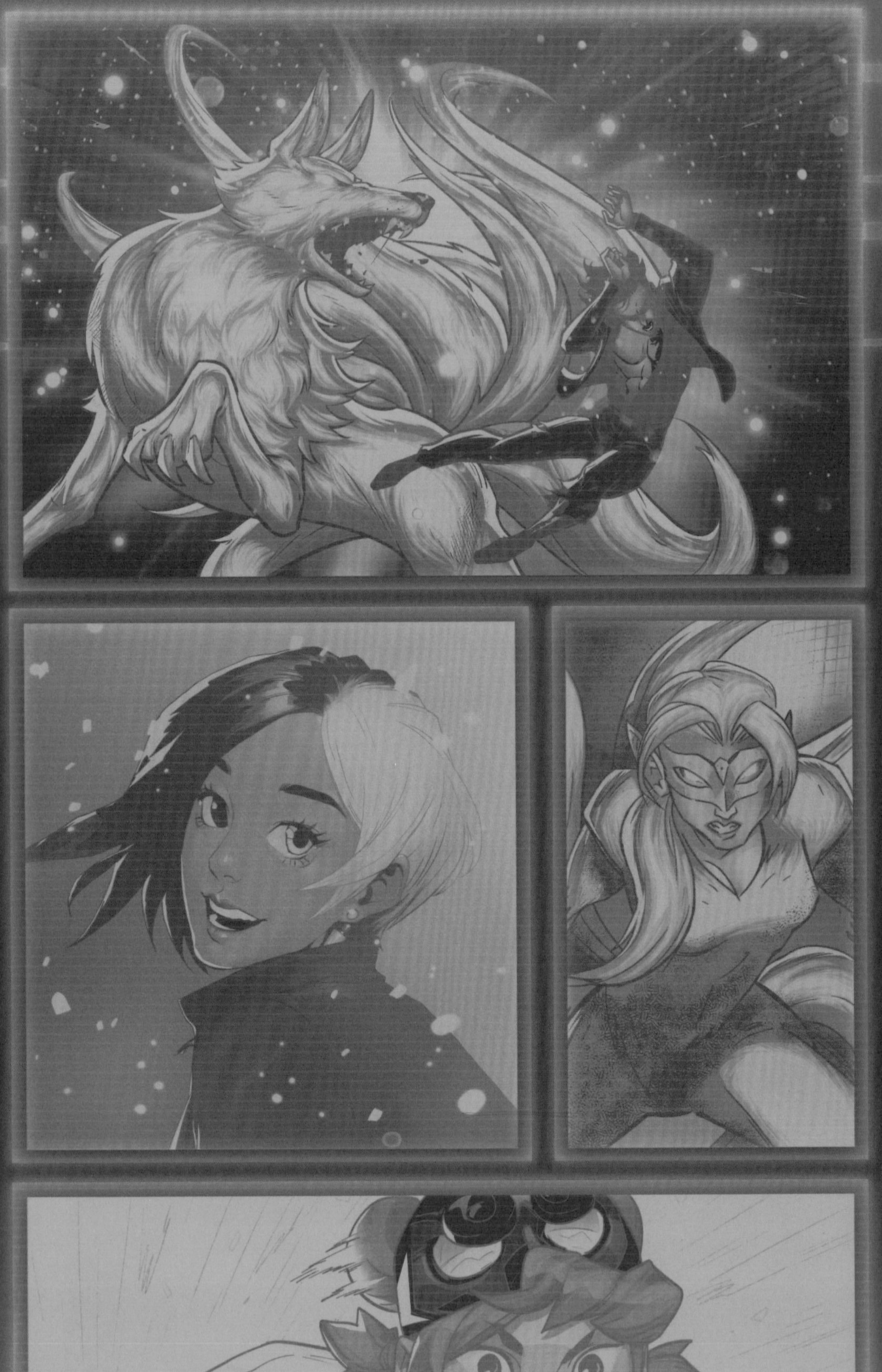

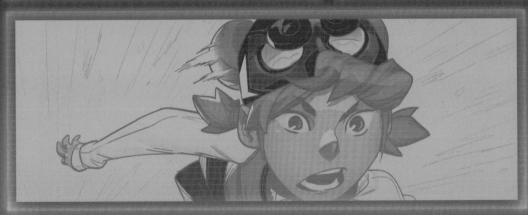

WRITER
ALYSSA WONG

ARTISTS
KEVIN LIBRANDA, GEOFFO, GANG HYUK LIM, JON LAM & ALÉ GARZA WITH CORY HAMSCHER

COLOR ARTISTS
ISRAEL SILVA, GANG HYUK LIM, PARIS ALLEYNE & DONO SÁNCHEZ-ALMARA WITH PROTOBUNKER

LETTERER
VC's JOE SABINO

COVER ART
INHYUK LEE

ASSISTANT EDITORS
LINDSEY COHICK & TOM GRONEMAN

EDITOR
MARK PANICCIA

SPECIAL THANKS TO
DANNY KOO & BILL ROSEMANN

COLLECTION EDITOR **JENNIFER GRÜNWALD**
ASSISTANT MANAGING EDITOR **MAIA LOY**
ASSISTANT MANAGING EDITOR **LISA MONTALBANO**
EDITOR, SPECIAL PROJECTS **MARK D. BEAZLEY**
VP PRODUCTION & SPECIAL PROJECTS **JEFF YOUNGQUIST**
BOOK DESIGNERS **STACIE ZUCKER** with **NICK RUSSELL**
SVP PRINT, SALES & MARKETING **DAVID GABRIEL**
EDITOR IN CHIEF **C.B. CEBULSKI**

FUTURE FIGHT FIRSTS. Contains material originally published in magazine form as FUTURE FIGHT FIRSTS: CRESCENT AND IO (2019) #1, FUTURE FIGHT FIRSTS: LUNA SNOW (2019) #1 and FUTURE FIGHT FIRSTS: WHITE FOX (2019) #1. First printing 2020. ISBN 978-1-302-92300-6. Published by MARVEL WORLDWIDE, INC., a subsidiary of MARVEL ENTERTAINMENT, LLC. OFFICE OF PUBLICATION: 1290 Avenue of the Americas, New York, NY 10104. © 2020 MARVEL No similarity between any of the names, characters, persons, and/or institutions in this magazine with those of any living or dead person or institution is intended, and any such similarity which may exist is purely coincidental. **Printed in Canada.** KEVIN FEIGE, Chief Creative Officer; DAN BUCKLEY, President, Marvel Entertainment; JOHN NEE, Publisher; JOE QUESADA, EVP & Creative Director; TOM BREVOORT, SVP of Publishing; DAVID BOGART, Associate Publisher & SVP of Talent Affairs; Publishing & Partnership; DAVID GABRIEL, VP of Print & Digital Publishing; JEFF YOUNGQUIST, VP of Production & Special Projects; DAN CARR, Executive Director of Publishing Technology; ALEX MORALES, Director of Publishing Operations; DAN EDINGTON, Managing Editor; SUSAN CRESPI, Production Manager; STAN LEE, Chairman Emeritus. For information regarding advertising in Marvel Comics or on Marvel.com, please contact Vit DeBellis, Custom Solutions & Integrated Advertising Manager, at vdebellis@marvel.com. For Marvel subscription inquiries, please call 888-511-5480. **Manufactured between 1/31/2020 and 3/3/2020 by SOLISCO PRINTERS, SCOTT, QC, CANADA.**

10 9 8 7 6 5 4 3 2 1

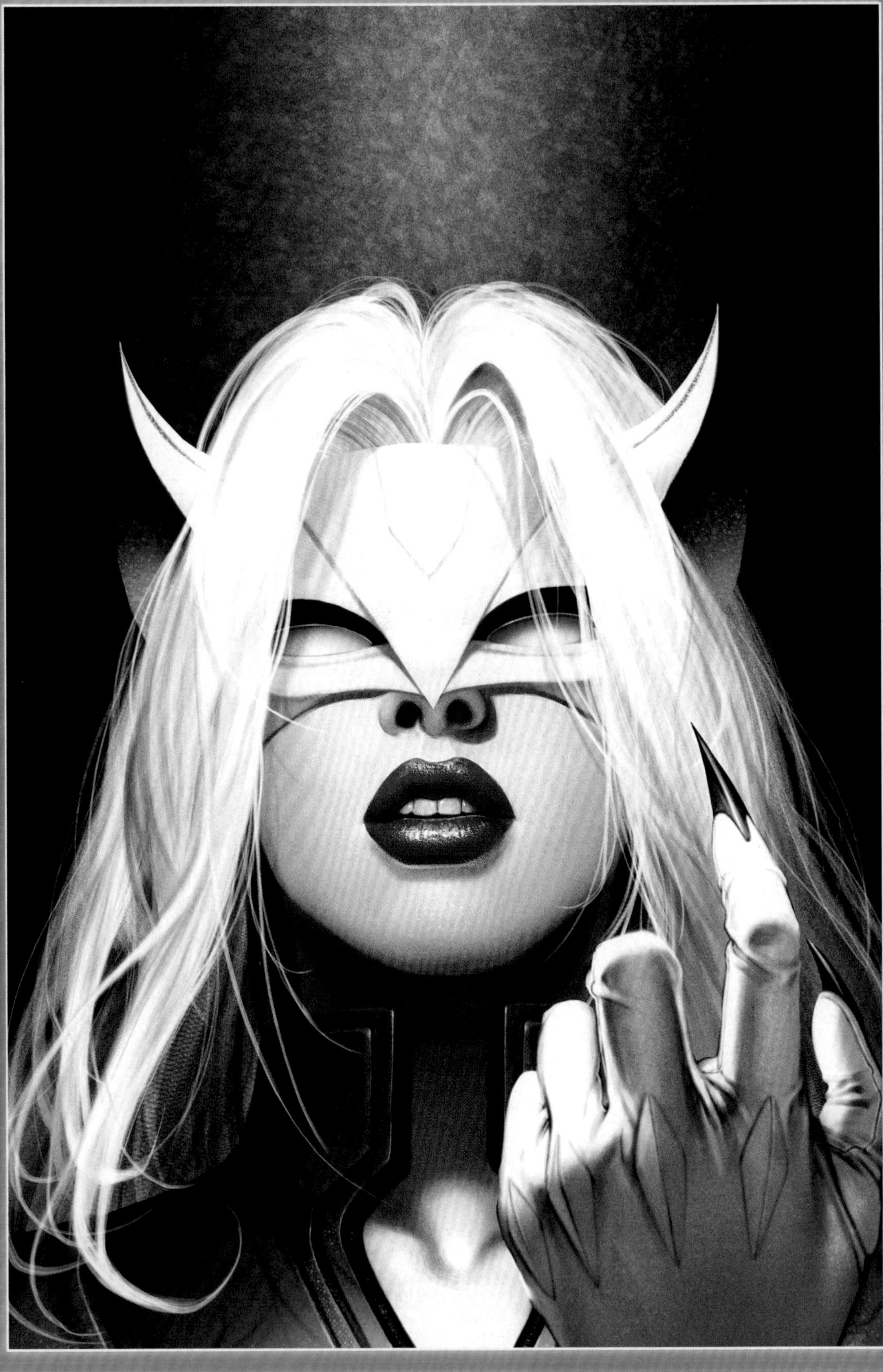

FUTURE FIGHT FIRSTS
WHITE FOX

MARVEL FUTURE FIGHT FIRSTS

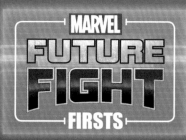

Ami Han is an operative in the South Korean National Intelligence Service. But she is also the last of the kumiho, a mystical race of shape-shifters, and the super hero known as

WHITE FOX

As White Fox, she's fought alongside many heroes — including the Avengers and Jimmy Woo's new Agents of Atlas team. But who was she before she became White Fox? And what happened to the rest of the kumiho?

WRITER
ALYSSA WONG

ARTISTS
KEVIN LIBRANDA & GEOFFO

COLORIST
ISRAEL SILVA

LETTERER
VC's JOE SABINO

COVER ARTIST
INHYUK LEE

LOGO DESIGN
ADAM DEL RE

ASSISTANT EDITORS
LINDSEY COHICK & TOM GRONEMAN

EDITOR
MARK PANICCIA

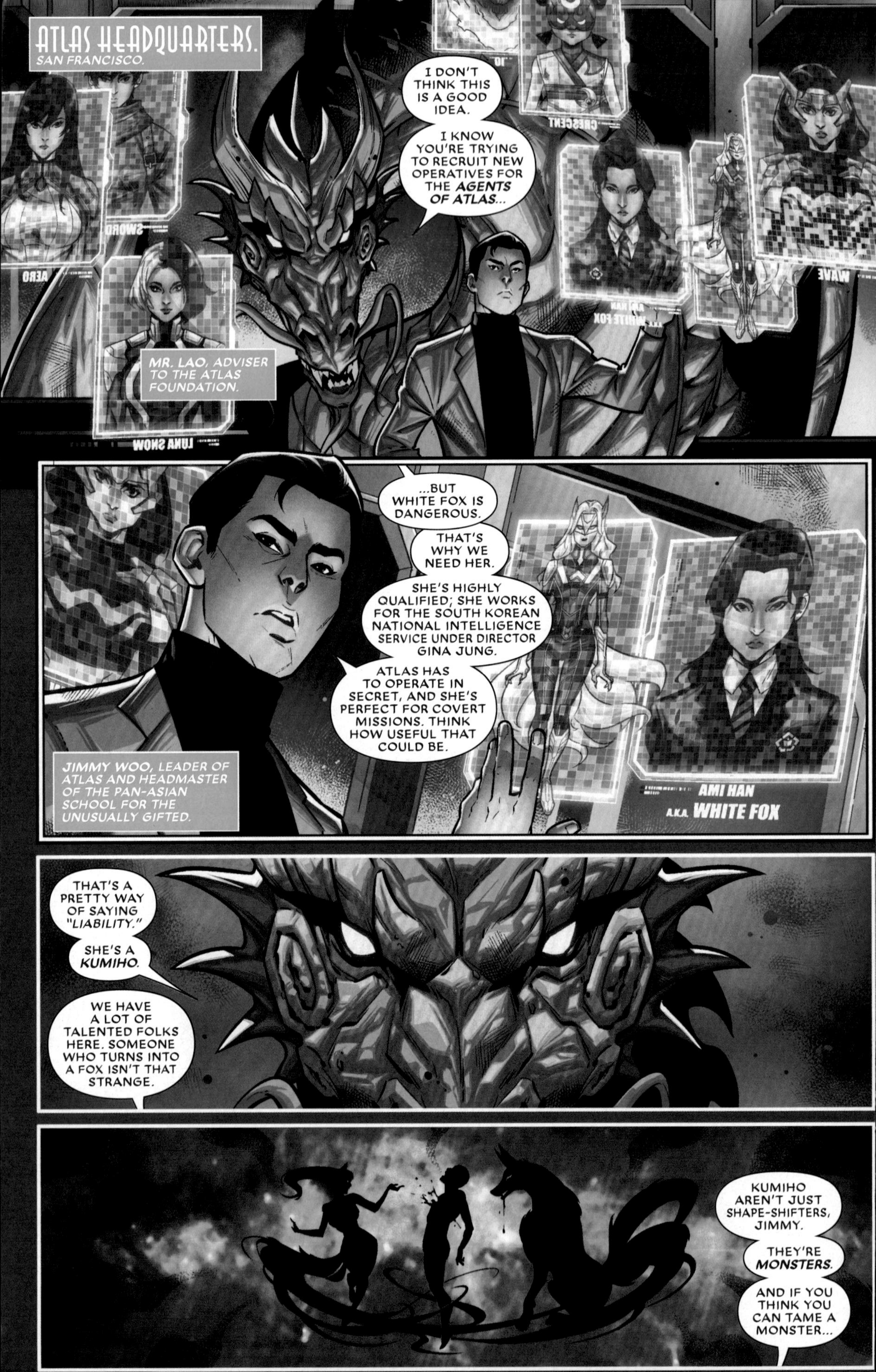
ATLAS HEADQUARTERS.
SAN FRANCISCO.
I DON'T THINK THIS IS A GOOD IDEA.
I KNOW YOU'RE TRYING TO RECRUIT NEW OPERATIVES FOR THE AGENTS OF ATLAS...
MR. LAO, ADVISER TO THE ATLAS FOUNDATION.
...BUT WHITE FOX IS DANGEROUS.
THAT'S WHY WE NEED HER.
SHE'S HIGHLY QUALIFIED; SHE WORKS FOR THE SOUTH KOREAN NATIONAL INTELLIGENCE SERVICE UNDER DIRECTOR GINA JUNG.
ATLAS HAS TO OPERATE IN SECRET, AND SHE'S PERFECT FOR COVERT MISSIONS. THINK HOW USEFUL THAT COULD BE.
JIMMY WOO, LEADER OF ATLAS AND HEADMASTER OF THE PAN-ASIAN SCHOOL FOR THE UNUSUALLY GIFTED.
AMI HAN
A.K.A. WHITE FOX
THAT'S A PRETTY WAY OF SAYING "LIABILITY."
SHE'S A KUMIHO.
WE HAVE A LOT OF TALENTED FOLKS HERE. SOMEONE WHO TURNS INTO A FOX ISN'T THAT STRANGE.
KUMIHO AREN'T JUST SHAPE-SHIFTERS, JIMMY.
THEY'RE MONSTERS.
AND IF YOU THINK YOU CAN TAME A MONSTER...

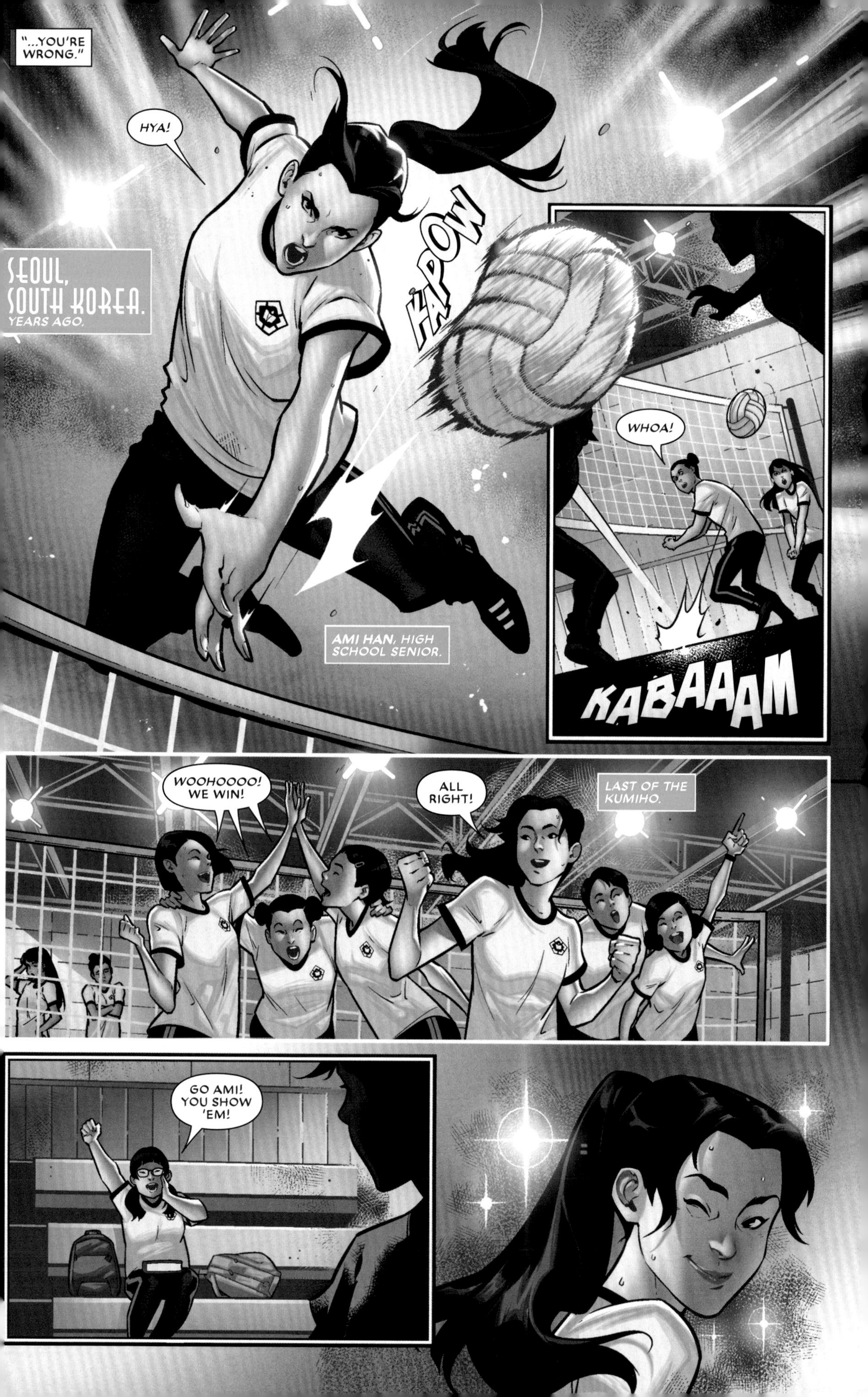
"...YOU'RE WRONG."
HYA!
SEOUL, SOUTH KOREA.
YEARS AGO.
KAPOW
AMI HAN, HIGH SCHOOL SENIOR.
WHOA!
KABAAAAM
WOOHOOOO! WE WIN!
ALL RIGHT!
LAST OF THE KUMIHO.
GO AMI! YOU SHOW 'EM!

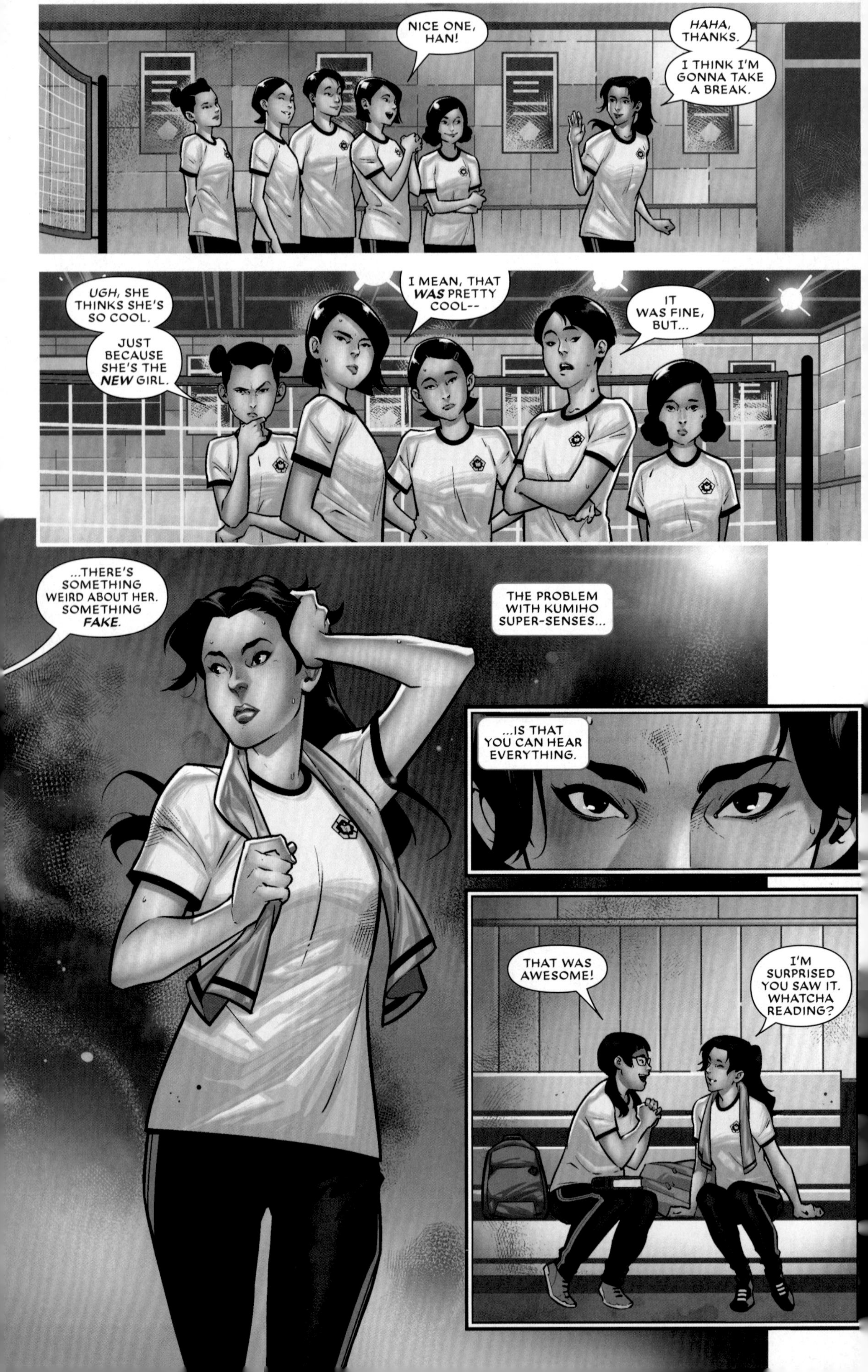
NICE ONE, HAN!
HAHA, THANKS.
I THINK I'M GONNA TAKE A BREAK.
UGH, SHE THINKS SHE'S SO COOL.
JUST BECAUSE SHE'S THE ***NEW*** GIRL.
I MEAN, THAT ***WAS*** PRETTY COOL--
IT WAS FINE, BUT...
...THERE'S SOMETHING WEIRD ABOUT HER. SOMETHING ***FAKE***.
THE PROBLEM WITH KUMIHO SUPER-SENSES...
...IS THAT YOU CAN HEAR EVERYTHING.
THAT WAS AWESOME!
I'M SURPRISED YOU SAW IT. WHATCHA READING?

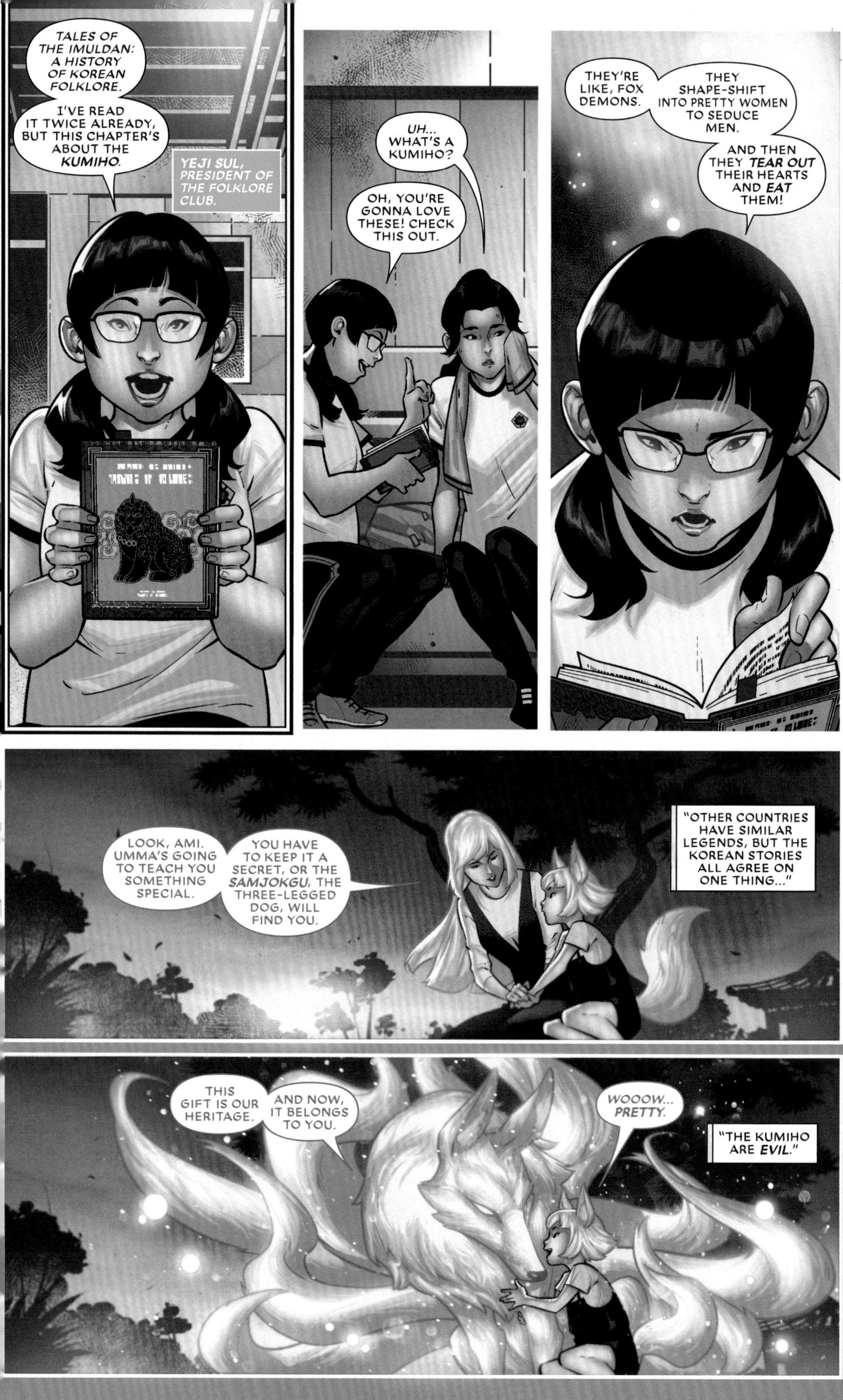
TALES OF THE IMULDAN: A HISTORY OF KOREAN FOLKLORE.
I'VE READ IT TWICE ALREADY, BUT THIS CHAPTER'S ABOUT THE *KUMIHO*.
YEJI SUL, PRESIDENT OF THE FOLKLORE CLUB.
UH... WHAT'S A KUMIHO?
OH, YOU'RE GONNA LOVE THESE! CHECK THIS OUT.
THEY'RE LIKE, FOX DEMONS.
THEY SHAPE-SHIFT INTO PRETTY WOMEN TO SEDUCE MEN.
AND THEN THEY ***TEAR OUT*** THEIR HEARTS AND ***EAT*** THEM!
"OTHER COUNTRIES HAVE SIMILAR LEGENDS, BUT THE KOREAN STORIES ALL AGREE ON ONE THING..."
LOOK, AMI. UMMA'S GOING TO TEACH YOU SOMETHING SPECIAL.
YOU HAVE TO KEEP IT A SECRET, OR THE ***SAMJOKGU***, THE THREE-LEGGED DOG, WILL FIND YOU.
THIS GIFT IS OUR HERITAGE.
AND NOW, IT BELONGS TO YOU.
*WOOOW... **PRETTY**.*
"THE KUMIHO ARE ***EVIL***."

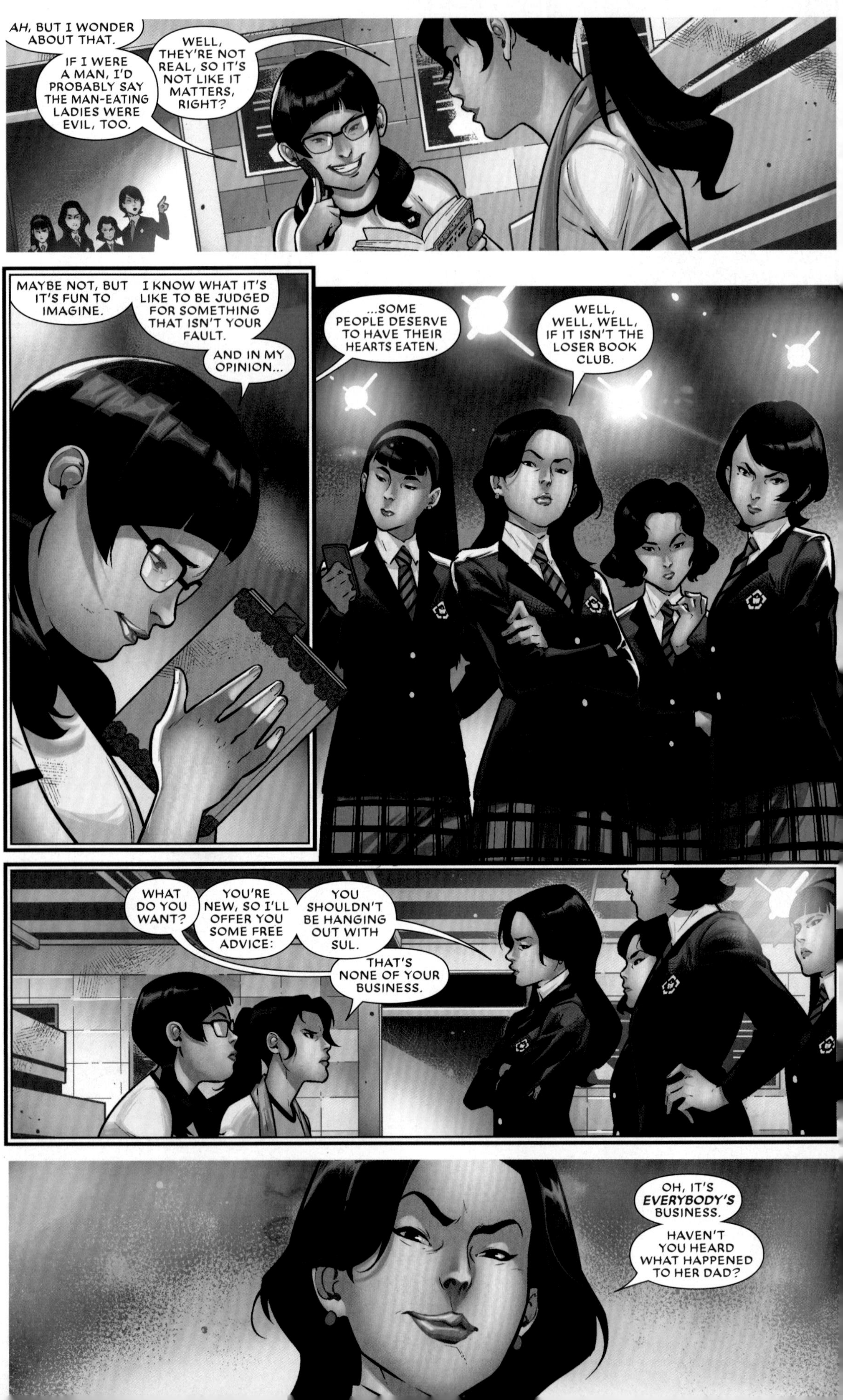
AH, BUT I WONDER ABOUT THAT.
IF I WERE A MAN, I'D PROBABLY SAY THE MAN-EATING LADIES WERE EVIL, TOO.
WELL, THEY'RE NOT REAL, SO IT'S NOT LIKE IT MATTERS, RIGHT?
MAYBE NOT, BUT IT'S FUN TO IMAGINE.
I KNOW WHAT IT'S LIKE TO BE JUDGED FOR SOMETHING THAT ISN'T YOUR FAULT.
AND IN MY OPINION...
...SOME PEOPLE DESERVE TO HAVE THEIR HEARTS EATEN.
WELL, WELL, WELL, IF IT ISN'T THE LOSER BOOK CLUB.
WHAT DO YOU WANT?
YOU'RE NEW, SO I'LL OFFER YOU SOME FREE ADVICE:
YOU SHOULDN'T BE HANGING OUT WITH SUL.
THAT'S NONE OF YOUR BUSINESS.
OH, IT'S *EVERYBODY'S* BUSINESS.
HAVEN'T YOU HEARD WHAT HAPPENED TO HER DAD?

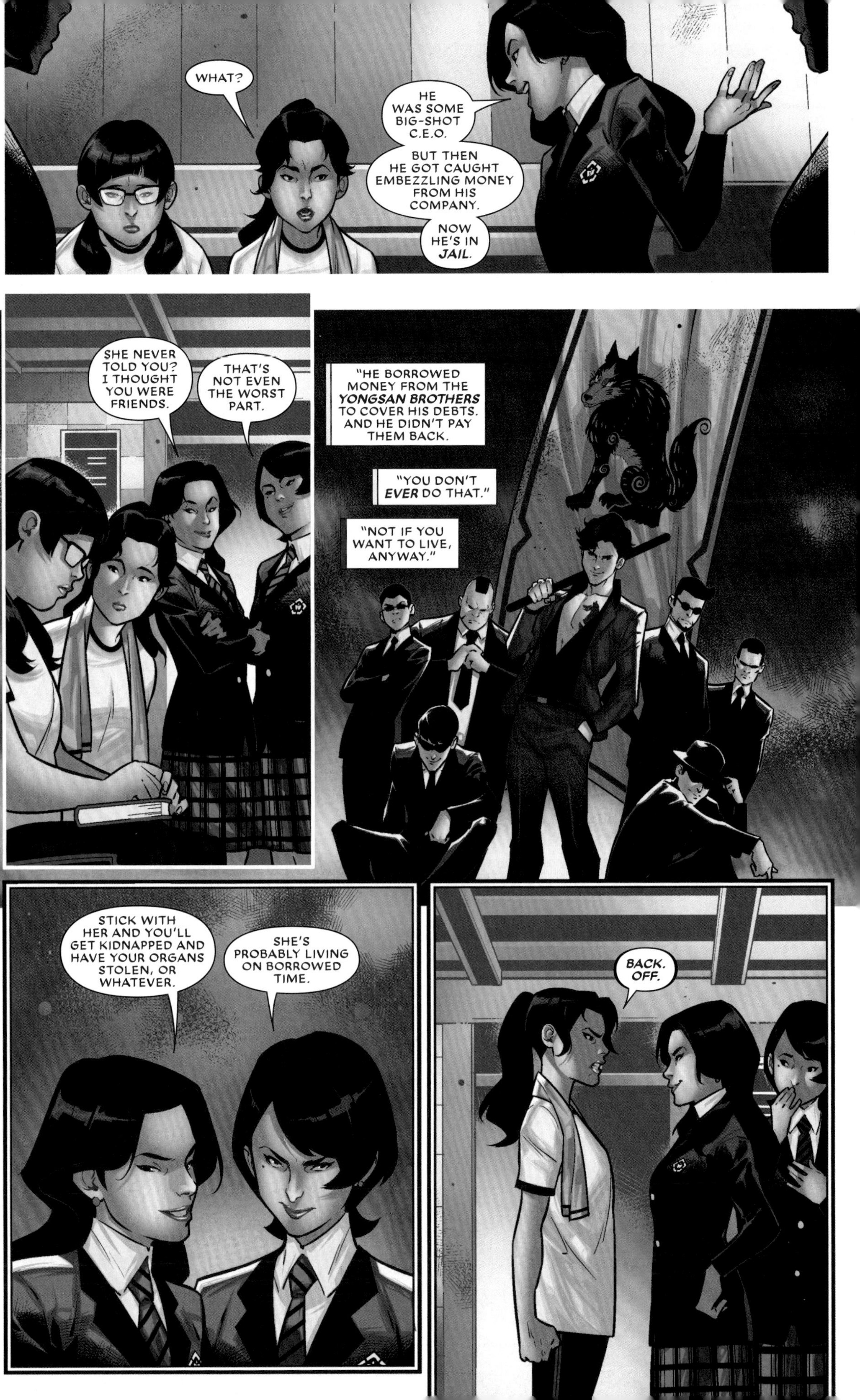
WHAT?
HE WAS SOME BIG-SHOT C.E.O.
BUT THEN HE GOT CAUGHT EMBEZZLING MONEY FROM HIS COMPANY.
NOW HE'S IN *JAIL*.
SHE NEVER TOLD YOU? I THOUGHT YOU WERE FRIENDS.
THAT'S NOT EVEN THE WORST PART.
"HE BORROWED MONEY FROM THE *YONGSAN BROTHERS* TO COVER HIS DEBTS. AND HE DIDN'T PAY THEM BACK.
"YOU DON'T *EVER* DO THAT."
"NOT IF YOU WANT TO LIVE, ANYWAY."
STICK WITH HER AND YOU'LL GET KIDNAPPED AND HAVE YOUR ORGANS STOLEN, OR WHATEVER.
SHE'S PROBABLY LIVING ON BORROWED TIME.
BACK. OFF.

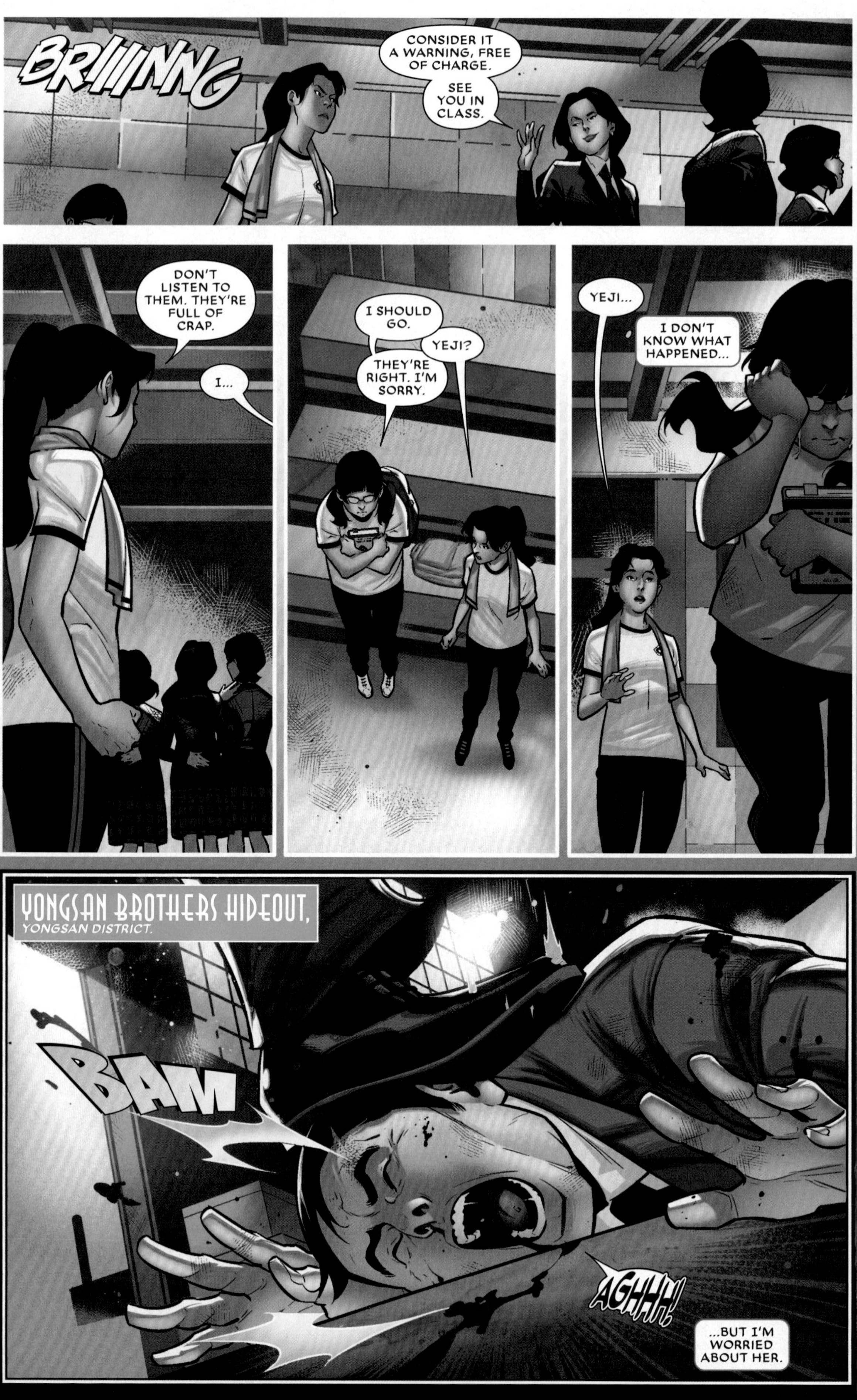
BRIIINNG
CONSIDER IT A WARNING, FREE OF CHARGE.
SEE YOU IN CLASS.
DON'T LISTEN TO THEM. THEY'RE FULL OF CRAP.
I...
I SHOULD GO.
THEY'RE RIGHT. I'M SORRY.
YEJI?
YEJI...
I DON'T KNOW WHAT HAPPENED...
YONGSAN BROTHERS HIDEOUT,
YONGSAN DISTRICT.
BAM
AGHHH!
...BUT I'M WORRIED ABOUT HER.

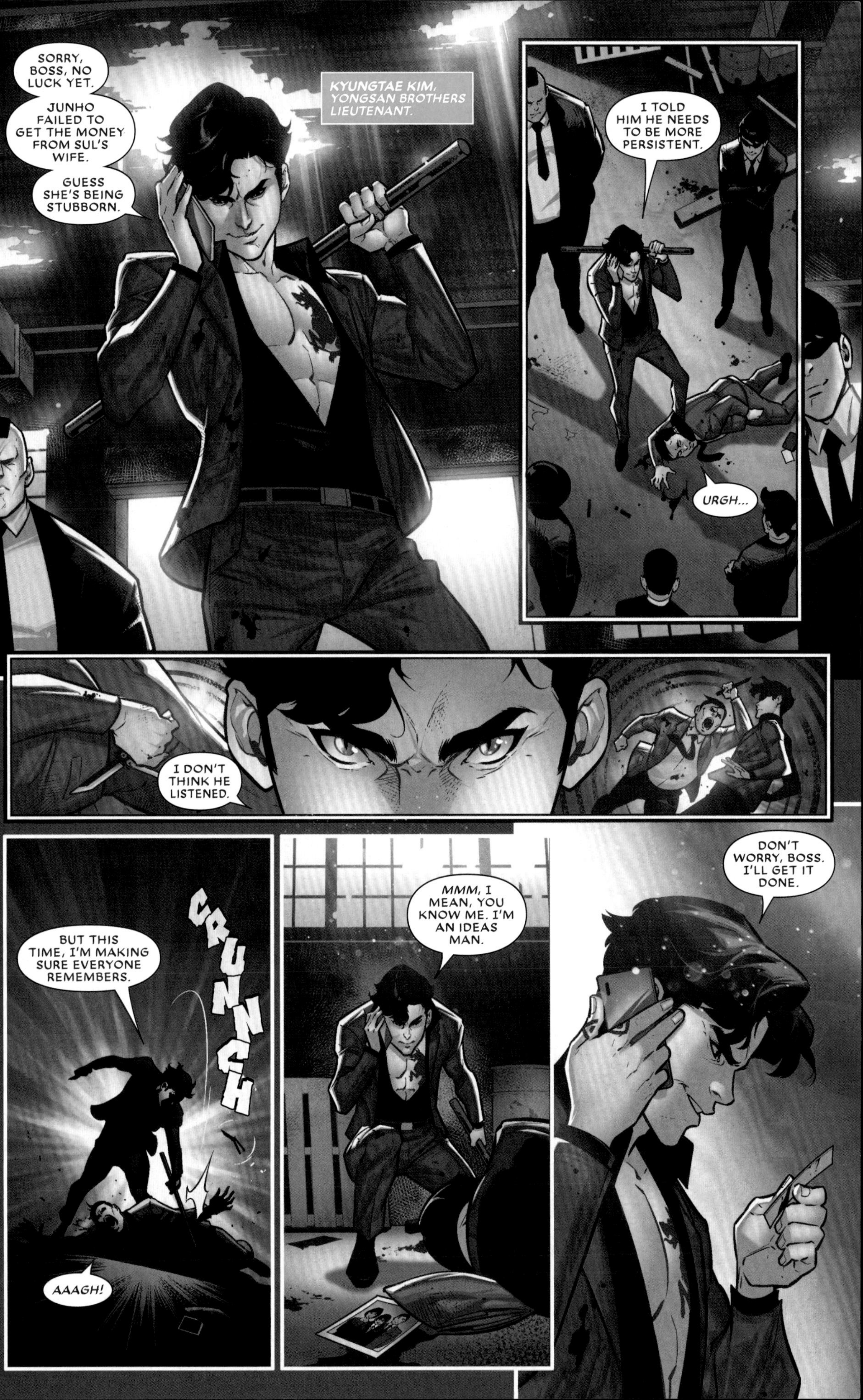
SORRY, BOSS, NO LUCK YET.
JUNHO FAILED TO GET THE MONEY FROM SUL'S WIFE.
GUESS SHE'S BEING STUBBORN.
KYUNGTAE KIM, YONGSAN BROTHERS LIEUTENANT.
I TOLD HIM HE NEEDS TO BE MORE PERSISTENT.
URGH...
I DON'T THINK HE LISTENED.
BUT THIS TIME, I'M MAKING SURE EVERYONE REMEMBERS.
CRUNCH
AAAGH!
MMM, I MEAN, YOU KNOW ME. I'M AN IDEAS MAN.
DON'T WORRY, BOSS. I'LL GET IT DONE.

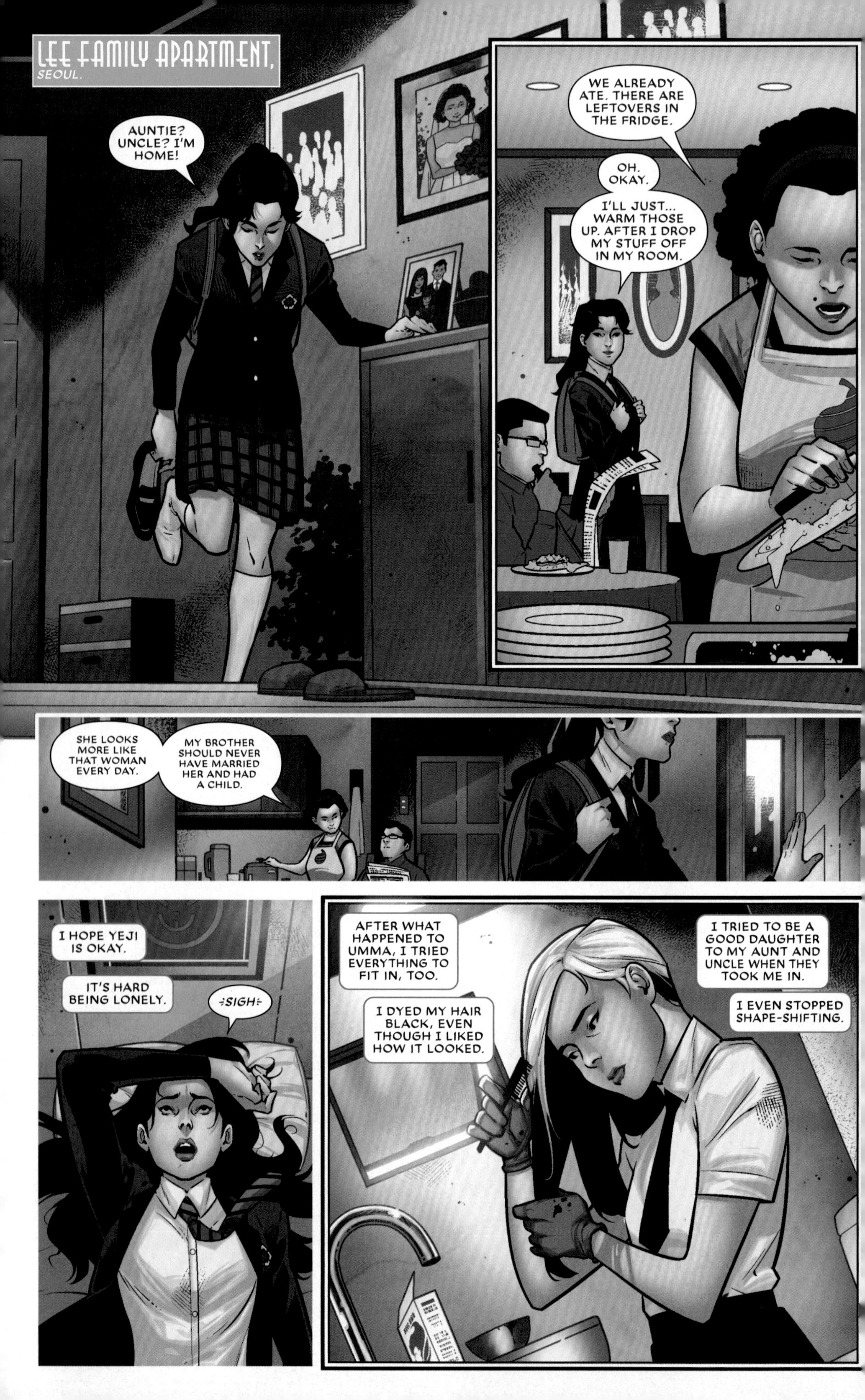
LEE FAMILY APARTMENT, SEOUL.
AUNTIE? UNCLE? I'M HOME!
WE ALREADY ATE. THERE ARE LEFTOVERS IN THE FRIDGE.
OH. OKAY.
I'LL JUST... WARM THOSE UP. AFTER I DROP MY STUFF OFF IN MY ROOM.
SHE LOOKS MORE LIKE THAT WOMAN EVERY DAY.
MY BROTHER SHOULD NEVER HAVE MARRIED HER AND HAD A CHILD.
I HOPE YEJI IS OKAY.
IT'S HARD BEING LONELY.
≑SIGH≑
AFTER WHAT HAPPENED TO UMMA, I TRIED EVERYTHING TO FIT IN, TOO.
I DYED MY HAIR BLACK, EVEN THOUGH I LIKED HOW IT LOOKED.
I TRIED TO BE A GOOD DAUGHTER TO MY AUNT AND UNCLE WHEN THEY TOOK ME IN.
I EVEN STOPPED SHAPE-SHIFTING.

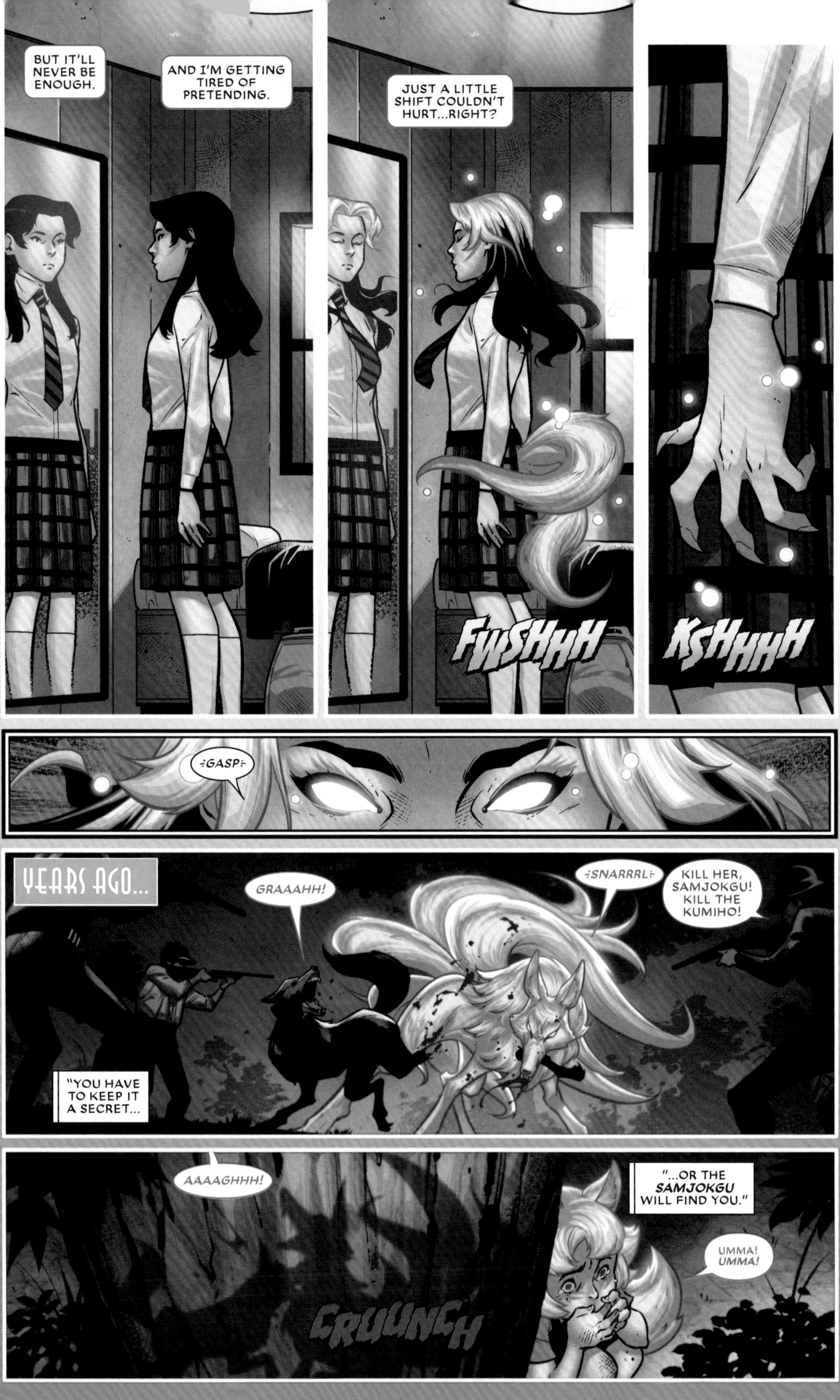
BUT IT'LL NEVER BE ENOUGH.
AND I'M GETTING TIRED OF PRETENDING.
JUST A LITTLE SHIFT COULDN'T HURT...RIGHT?
FWSHHH
KSHHHH
GASP
YEARS AGO...
GRAAAHH!
SNARRRL
KILL HER, SAMJOKGU! KILL THE KUMIHO!
"YOU HAVE TO KEEP IT A SECRET...
AAAAGHHH!
"...OR THE SAMJOKGU WILL FIND YOU."
UMMA! UMMA!
CRUUNCH

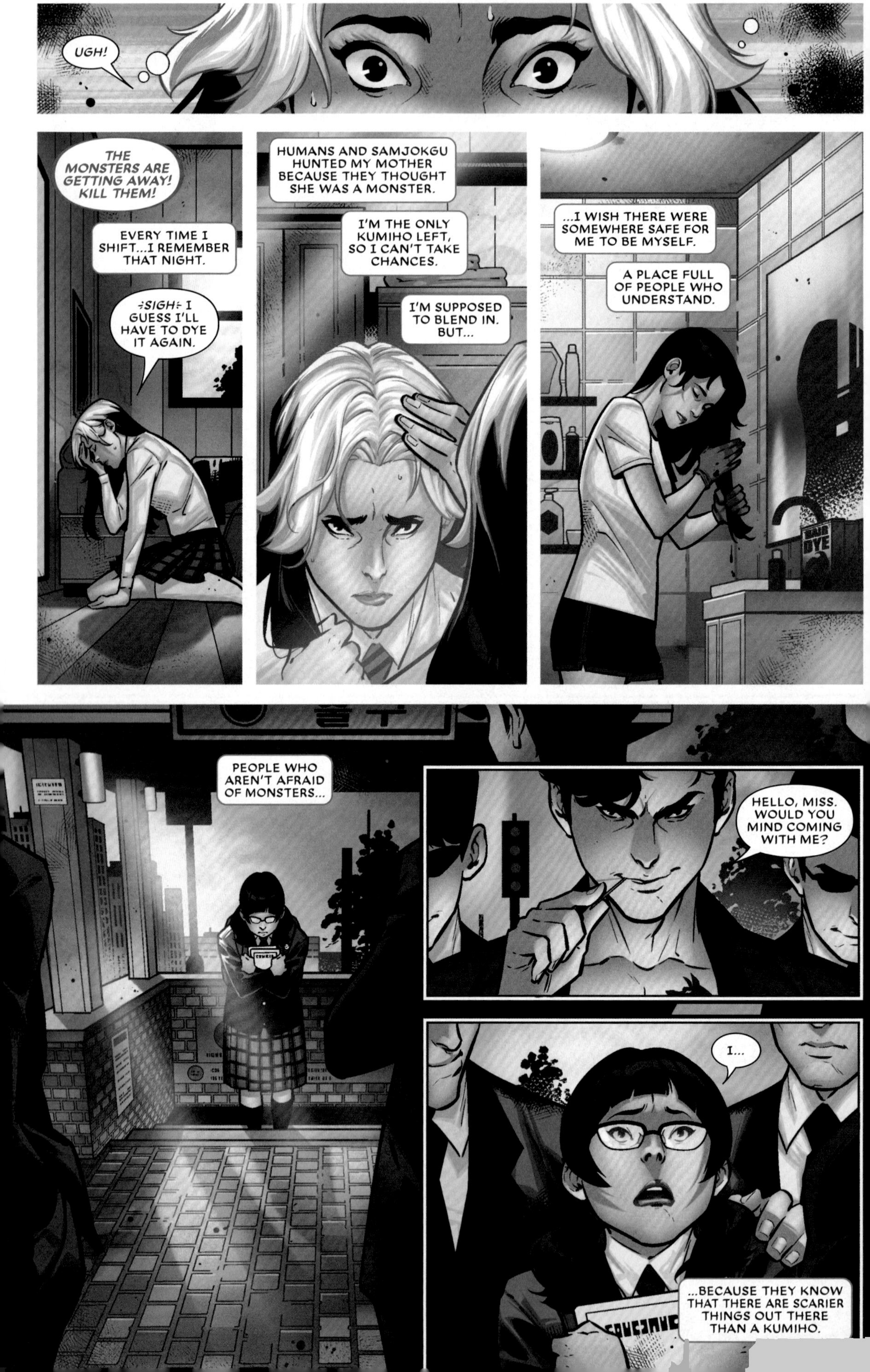
UGH!
THE MONSTERS ARE GETTING AWAY! KILL THEM!
EVERY TIME I SHIFT...I REMEMBER THAT NIGHT.
⁼SIGH⁼ I GUESS I'LL HAVE TO DYE IT AGAIN.
HUMANS AND SAMJOKGU HUNTED MY MOTHER BECAUSE THEY THOUGHT SHE WAS A MONSTER.
I'M THE ONLY KUMIHO LEFT, SO I CAN'T TAKE CHANCES.
I'M SUPPOSED TO BLEND IN. BUT...
...I WISH THERE WERE SOMEWHERE SAFE FOR ME TO BE MYSELF.
A PLACE FULL OF PEOPLE WHO UNDERSTAND.
HAIR DYE
PEOPLE WHO AREN'T AFRAID OF MONSTERS...
HELLO, MISS. WOULD YOU MIND COMING WITH ME?
I...
...BECAUSE THEY KNOW THAT THERE ARE SCARIER THINGS OUT THERE THAN A KUMIHO.

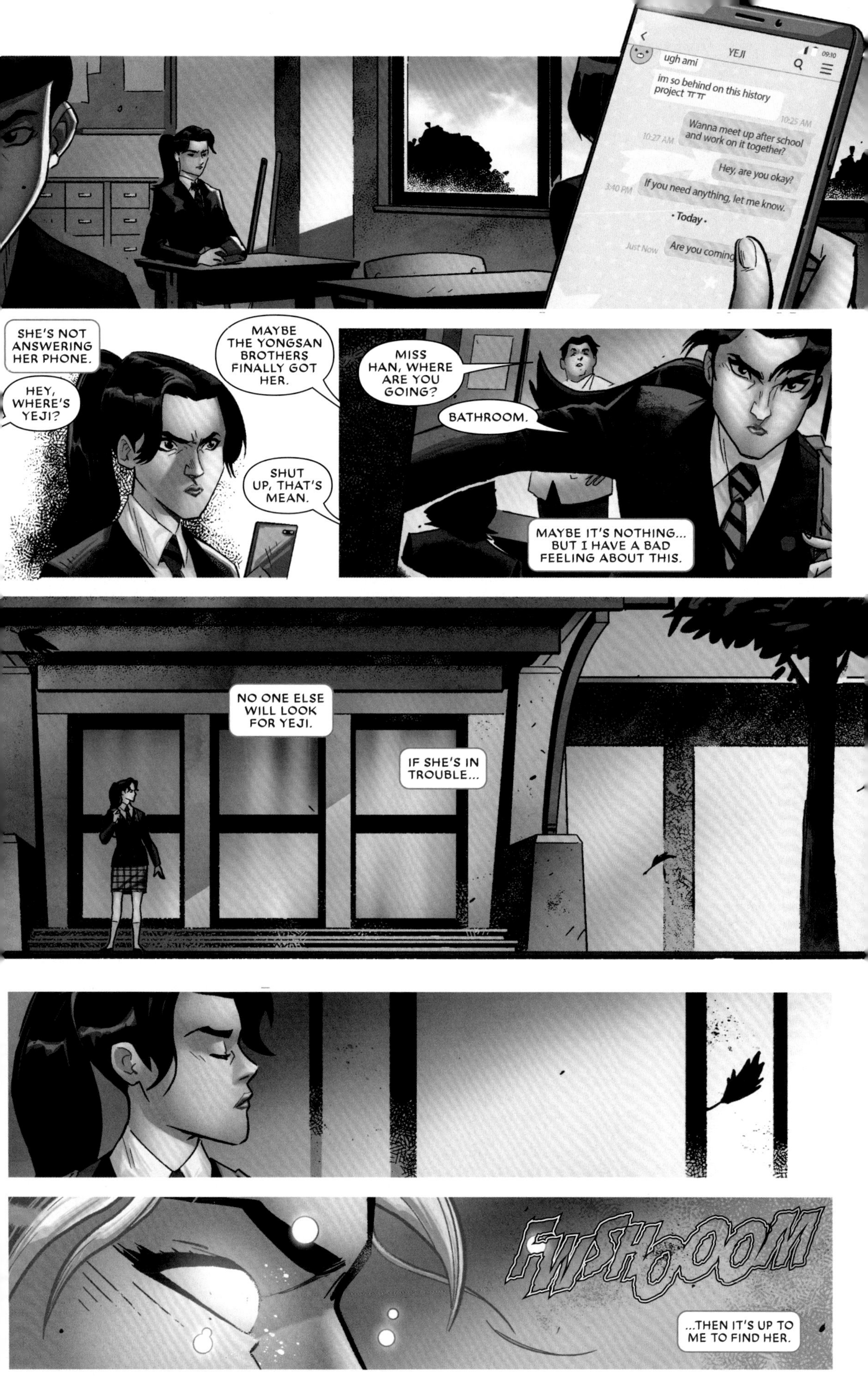
YEJI
ugh ami
im so behind on this history project ㅠㅠ
10:25 AM
Wanna meet up after school and work on it together?
10:27 AM
Hey, are you okay?
3:40 PM
If you need anything, let me know.
• Today •
Just Now
Are you coming
SHE'S NOT ANSWERING HER PHONE.
HEY, WHERE'S YEJI?
MAYBE THE YONGSAN BROTHERS FINALLY GOT HER.
SHUT UP, THAT'S MEAN.
MISS HAN, WHERE ARE YOU GOING?
BATHROOM.
MAYBE IT'S NOTHING... BUT I HAVE A BAD FEELING ABOUT THIS.
NO ONE ELSE WILL LOOK FOR YEJI.
IF SHE'S IN TROUBLE...
FWSHOOOM
...THEN IT'S UP TO ME TO FIND HER.

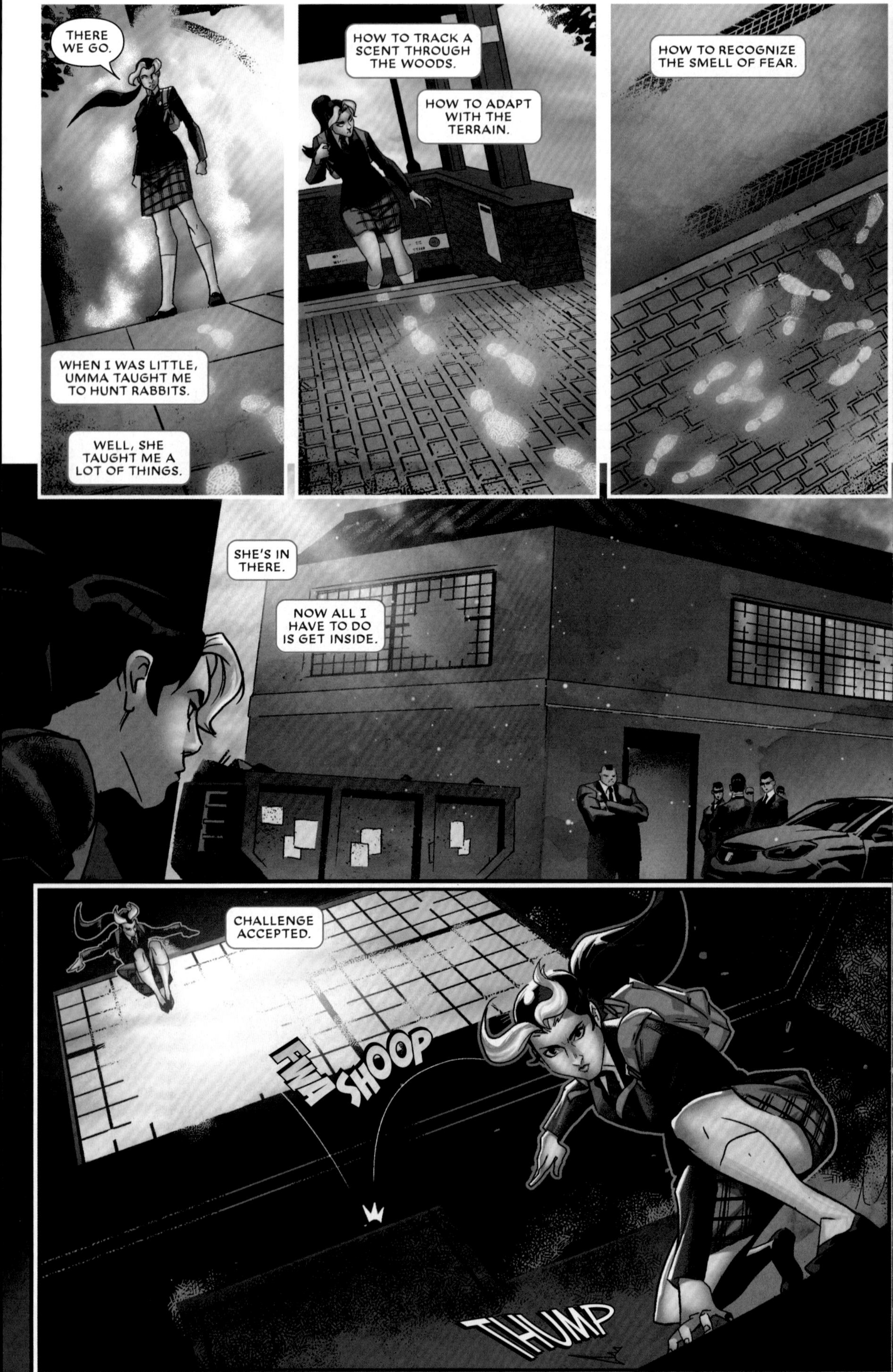
THERE WE GO.
WHEN I WAS LITTLE, UMMA TAUGHT ME TO HUNT RABBITS.
WELL, SHE TAUGHT ME A LOT OF THINGS.
HOW TO TRACK A SCENT THROUGH THE WOODS.
HOW TO ADAPT WITH THE TERRAIN.
HOW TO RECOGNIZE THE SMELL OF FEAR.
SHE'S IN THERE.
NOW ALL I HAVE TO DO IS GET INSIDE.
CHALLENGE ACCEPTED.
FWA SHOOP
THUMP

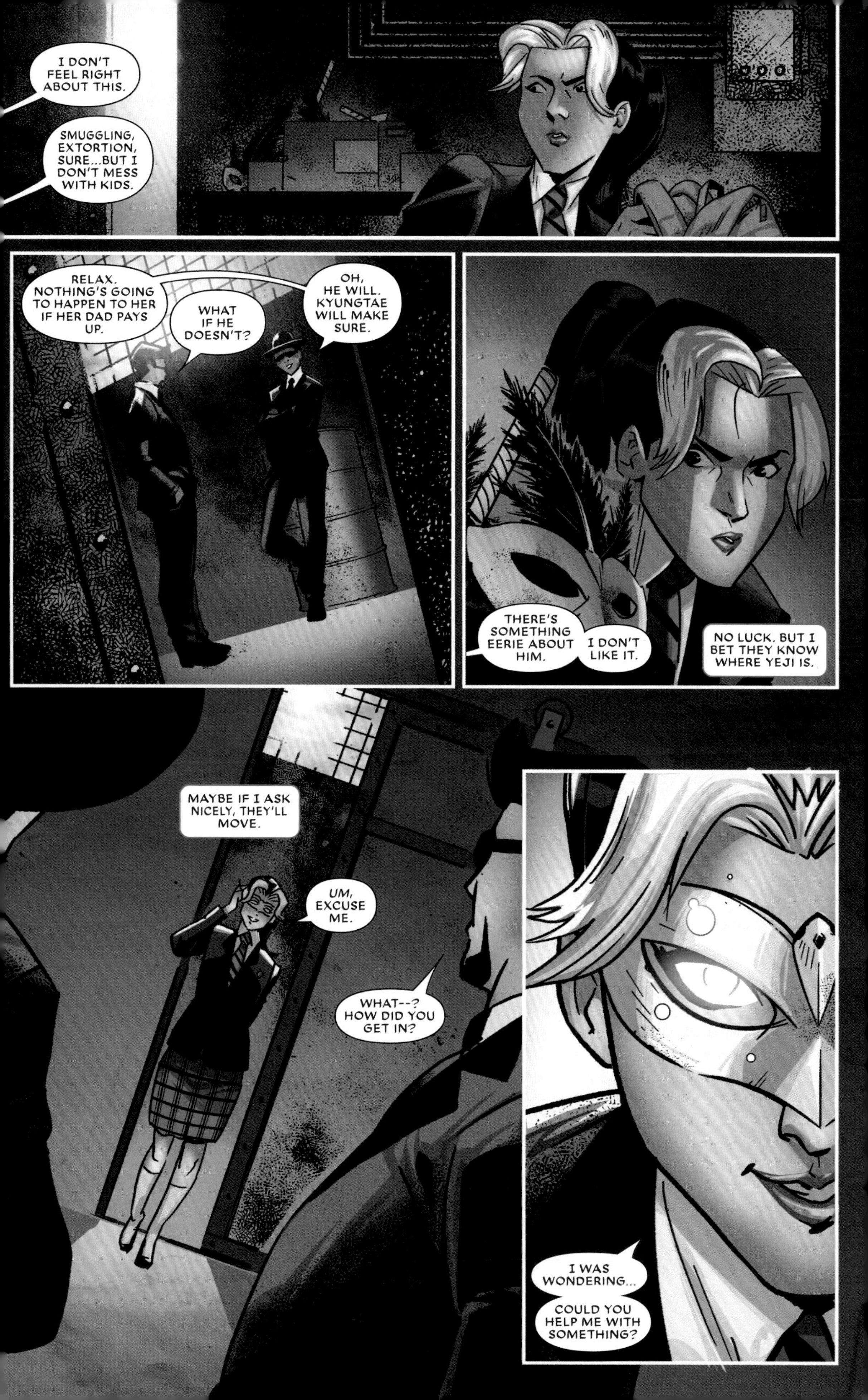
I DON'T FEEL RIGHT ABOUT THIS.
SMUGGLING, EXTORTION, SURE...BUT I DON'T MESS WITH KIDS.
RELAX. NOTHING'S GOING TO HAPPEN TO HER IF HER DAD PAYS UP.
WHAT IF HE DOESN'T?
OH, HE WILL. KYUNGTAE WILL MAKE SURE.
THERE'S SOMETHING EERIE ABOUT HIM.
I DON'T LIKE IT.
NO LUCK. BUT I BET THEY KNOW WHERE YEJI IS.
MAYBE IF I ASK NICELY, THEY'LL MOVE.
UM, EXCUSE ME.
WHAT--? HOW DID YOU GET IN?
I WAS WONDERING...
COULD YOU HELP ME WITH SOMETHING?

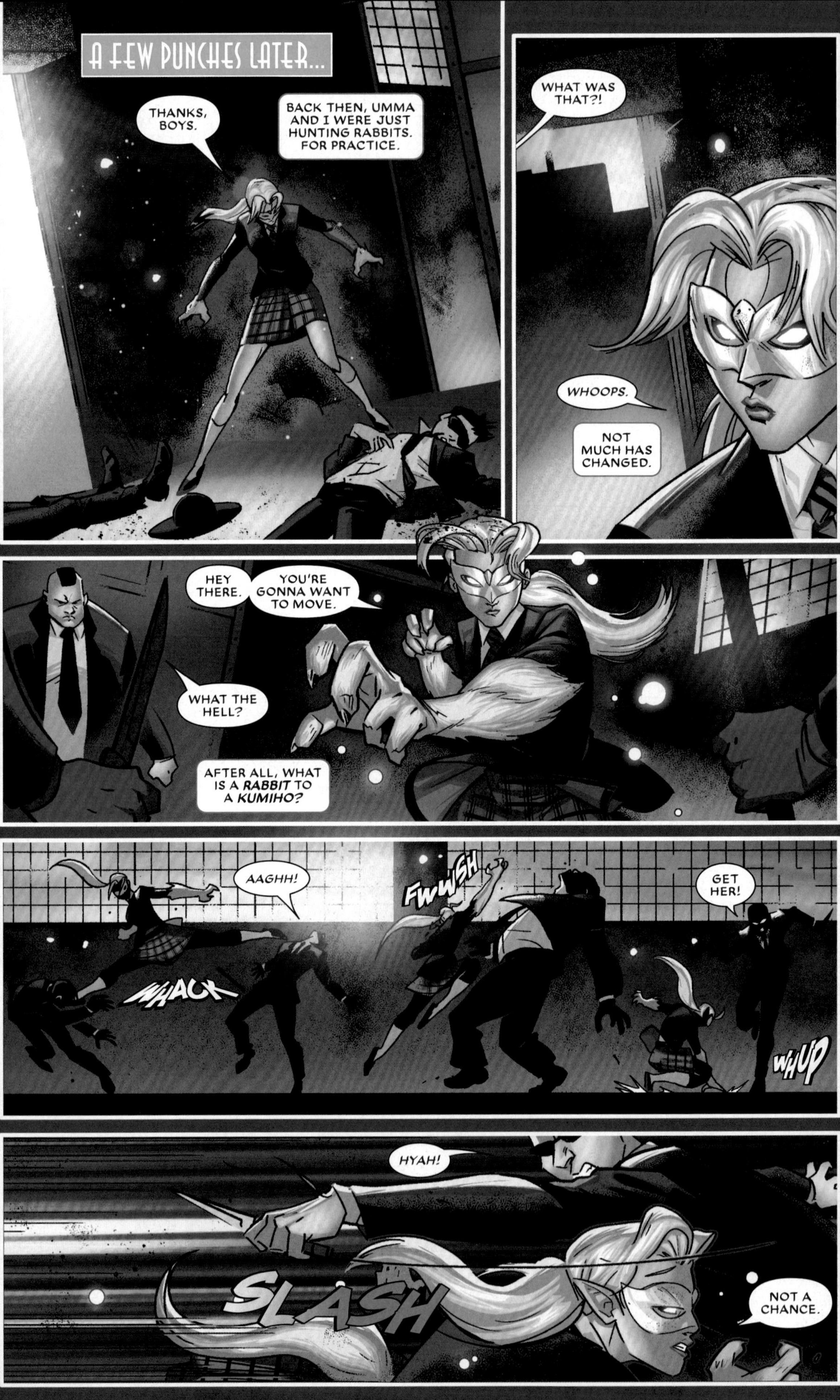
A FEW PUNCHES LATER...
THANKS, BOYS.
BACK THEN, UMMA AND I WERE JUST HUNTING RABBITS. FOR PRACTICE.
WHAT WAS THAT?!
WHOOPS.
NOT MUCH HAS CHANGED.
HEY THERE.
YOU'RE GONNA WANT TO MOVE.
WHAT THE HELL?
AFTER ALL, WHAT IS A *RABBIT* TO A *KUMIHO?*
AAGHH!
WHACK
FWWSH
GET HER!
WHUP
HYAH!
SLASH
NOT A CHANCE.

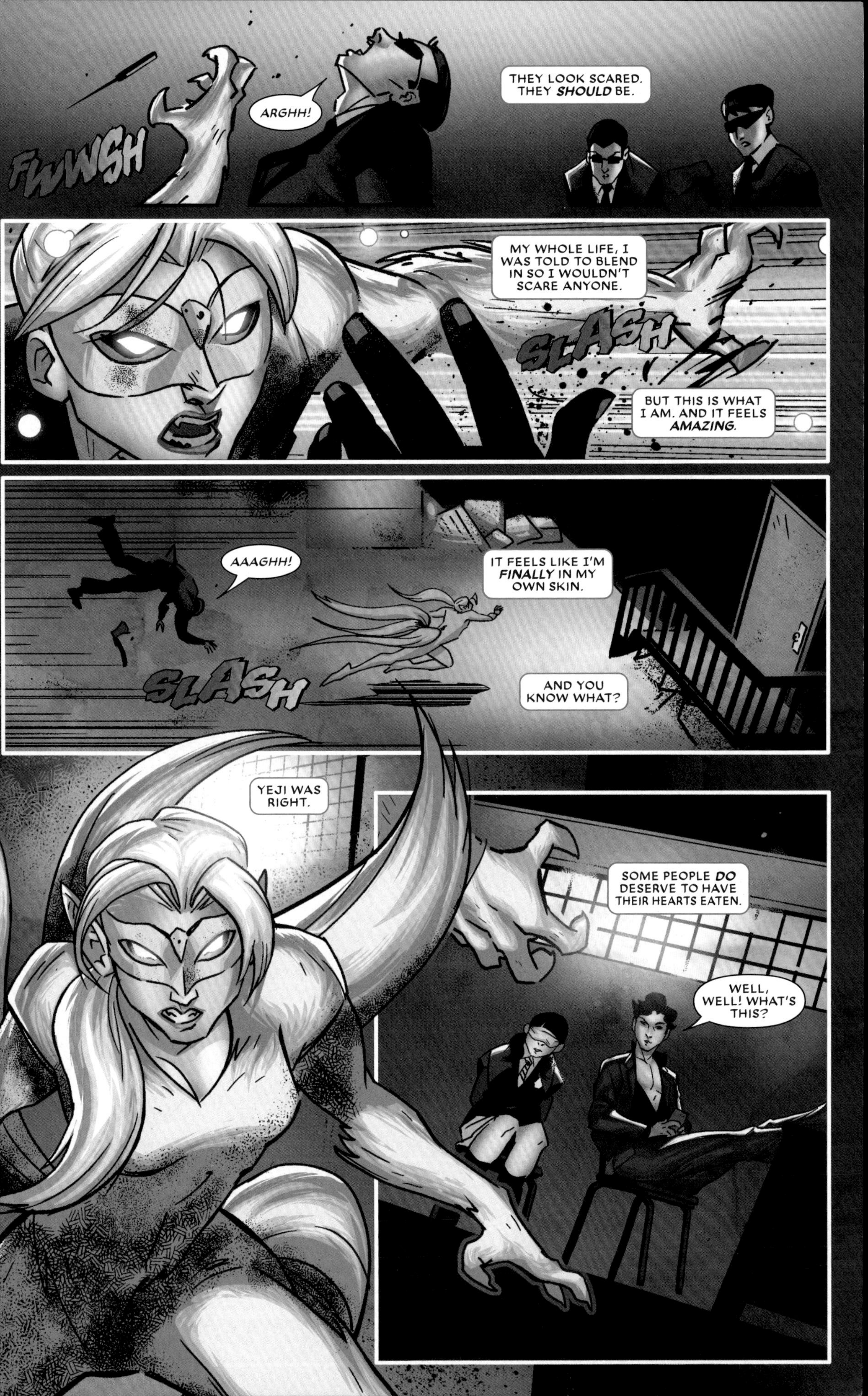
FWWSH
ARGHH!
THEY LOOK SCARED. THEY SHOULD BE.
MY WHOLE LIFE, I WAS TOLD TO BLEND IN SO I WOULDN'T SCARE ANYONE.
SLASH
BUT THIS IS WHAT I AM. AND IT FEELS AMAZING.
AAAGHH!
IT FEELS LIKE I'M FINALLY IN MY OWN SKIN.
SLASH
AND YOU KNOW WHAT?
YEJI WAS RIGHT.
SOME PEOPLE DO DESERVE TO HAVE THEIR HEARTS EATEN.
WELL, WELL! WHAT'S THIS?

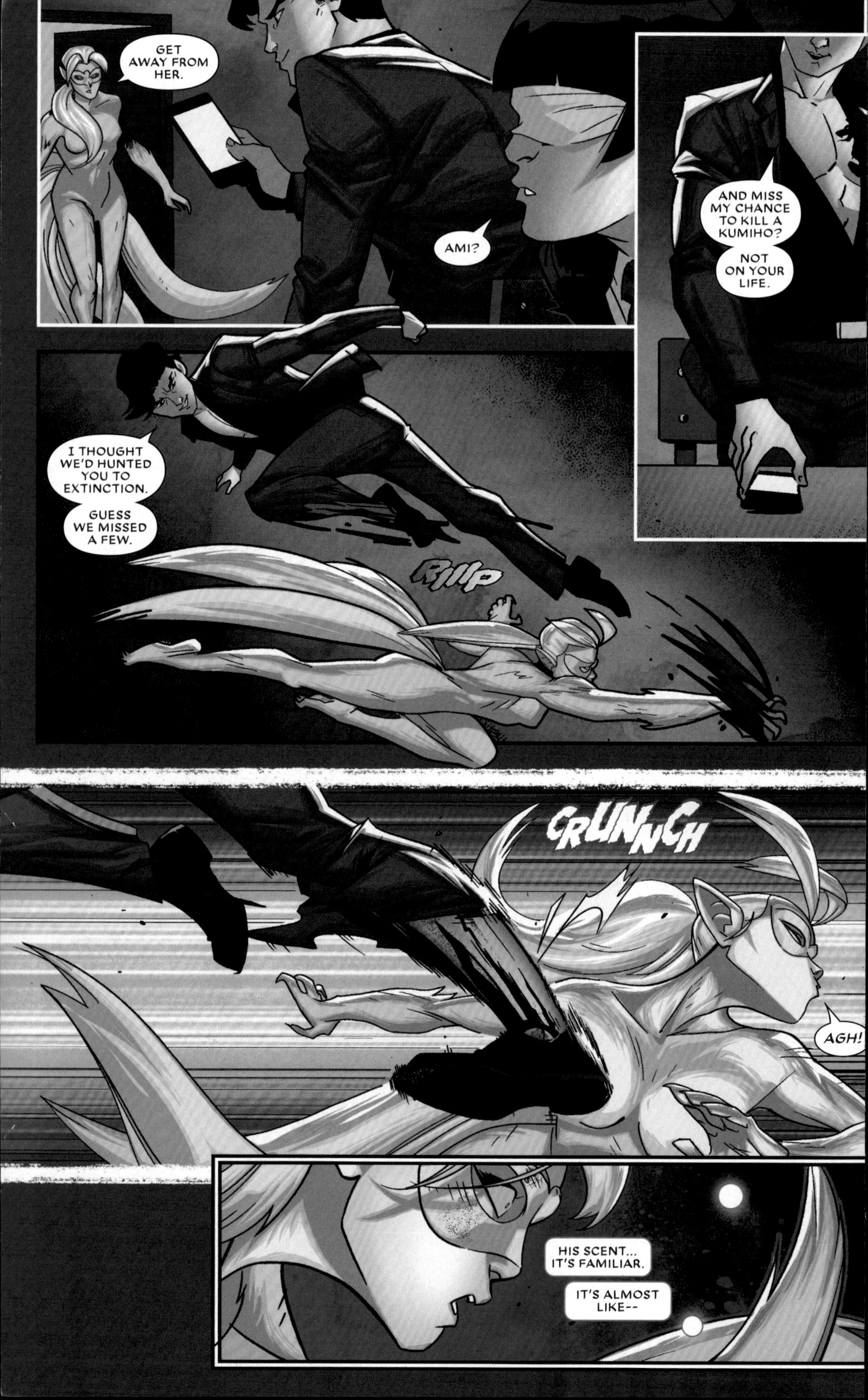

GET AWAY FROM HER.
AMI?
AND MISS MY CHANCE TO KILL A KUMIHO?
NOT ON YOUR LIFE.
I THOUGHT WE'D HUNTED YOU TO EXTINCTION.
GUESS WE MISSED A FEW.
RIIIP
CRUNNCH
AGH!
HIS SCENT... IT'S FAMILIAR.
IT'S ALMOST LIKE--

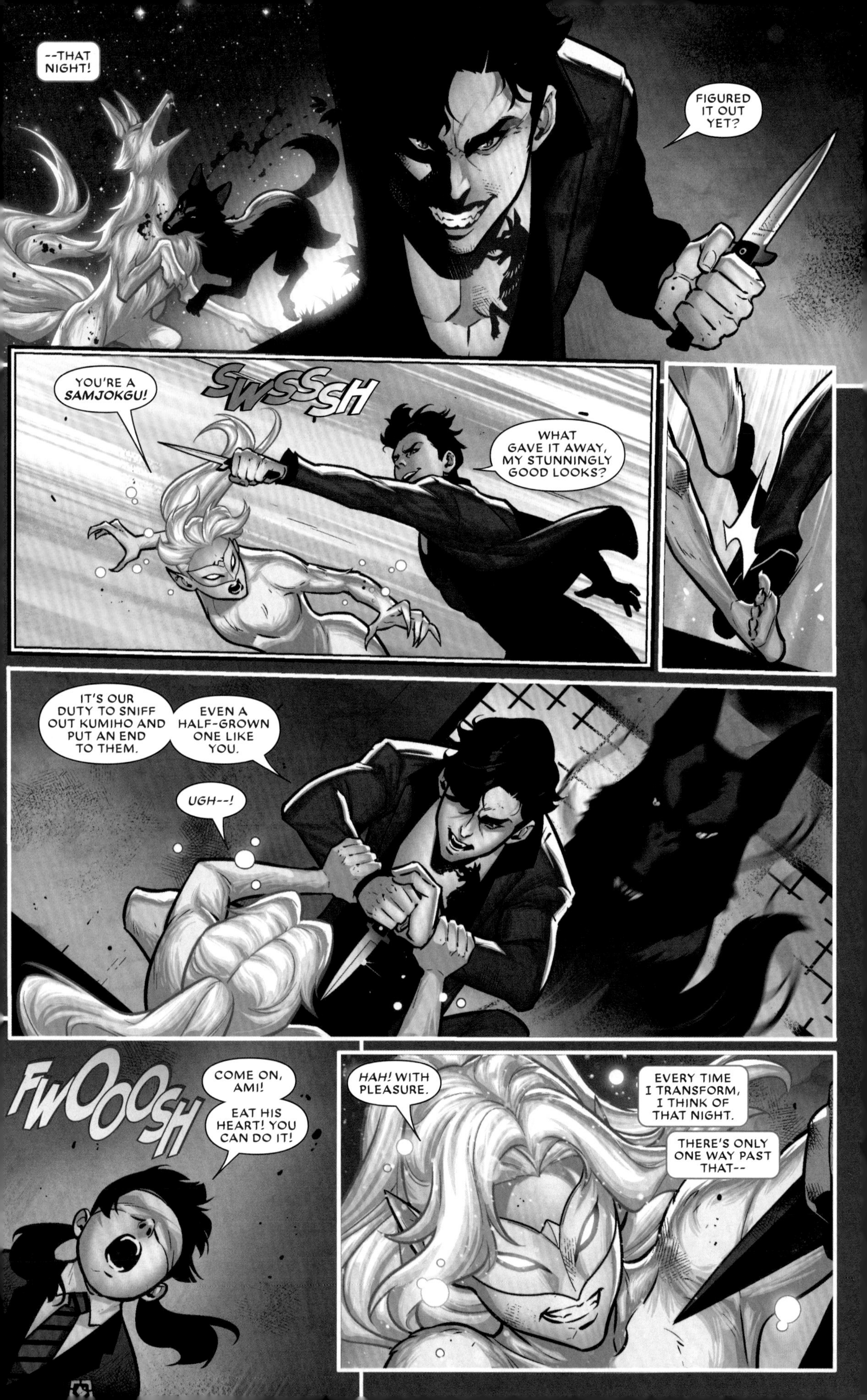
--THAT NIGHT!
FIGURED IT OUT YET?
YOU'RE A *SAMJOKGU!*
SWSSSH
WHAT GAVE IT AWAY, MY STUNNINGLY GOOD LOOKS?
IT'S OUR DUTY TO SNIFF OUT KUMIHO AND PUT AN END TO THEM.
EVEN A HALF-GROWN ONE LIKE YOU.
UGH--!
FWOOOSH
COME ON, AMI!
EAT HIS HEART! YOU CAN DO IT!
HAH! WITH PLEASURE.
EVERY TIME I TRANSFORM, I THINK OF THAT NIGHT.
THERE'S ONLY ONE WAY PAST THAT--

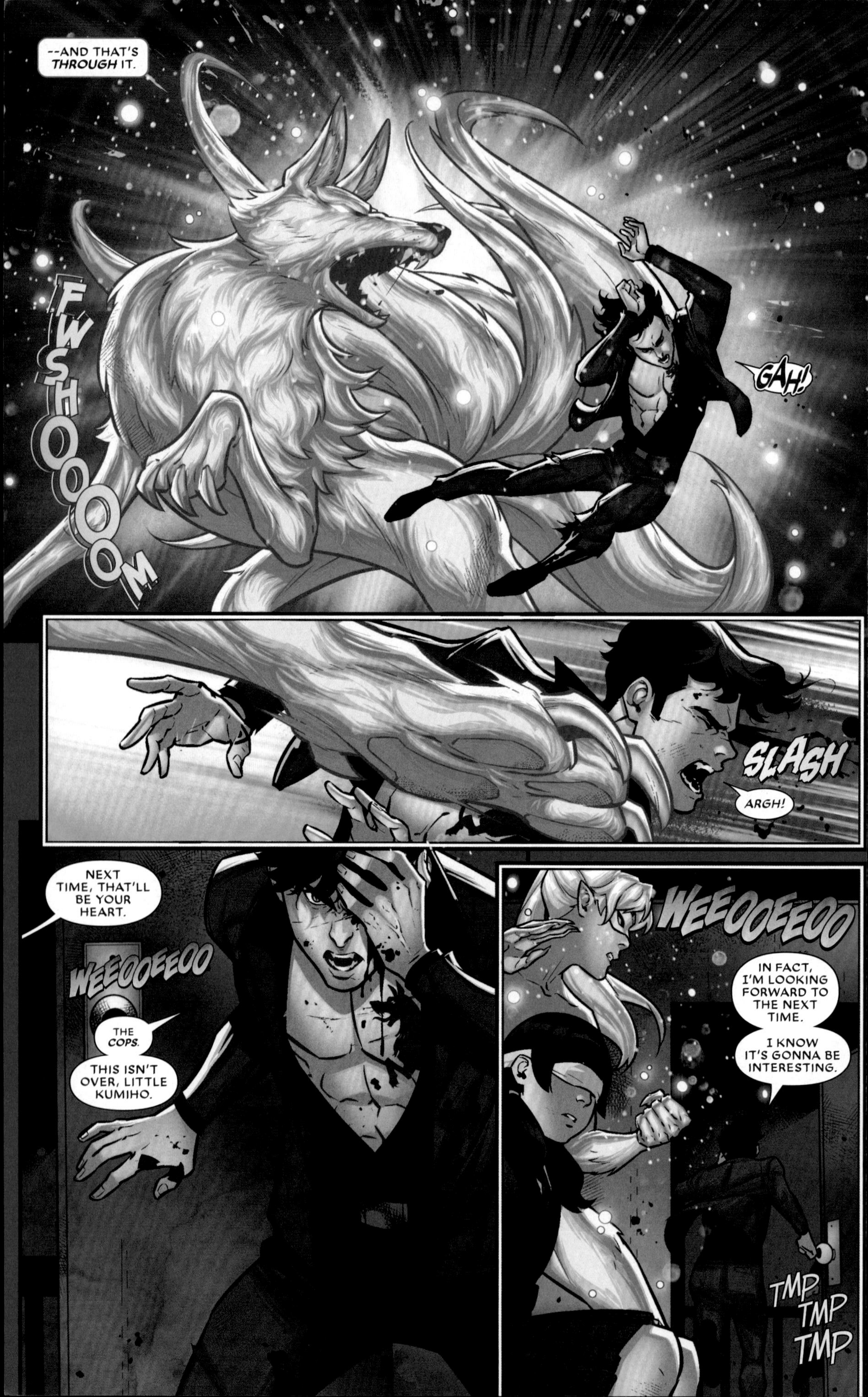
--AND THAT'S *THROUGH* IT.
FWSHOOOOOM
GAH!
SLASH
ARGH!
NEXT TIME, THAT'LL BE YOUR HEART.
WEEOOEEOO
THE *COPS.*
THIS ISN'T OVER, LITTLE KUMIHO.
WEEOOEEOO
IN FACT, I'M LOOKING FORWARD TO THE NEXT TIME.
I KNOW IT'S GONNA BE INTERESTING.
TMP TMP TMP

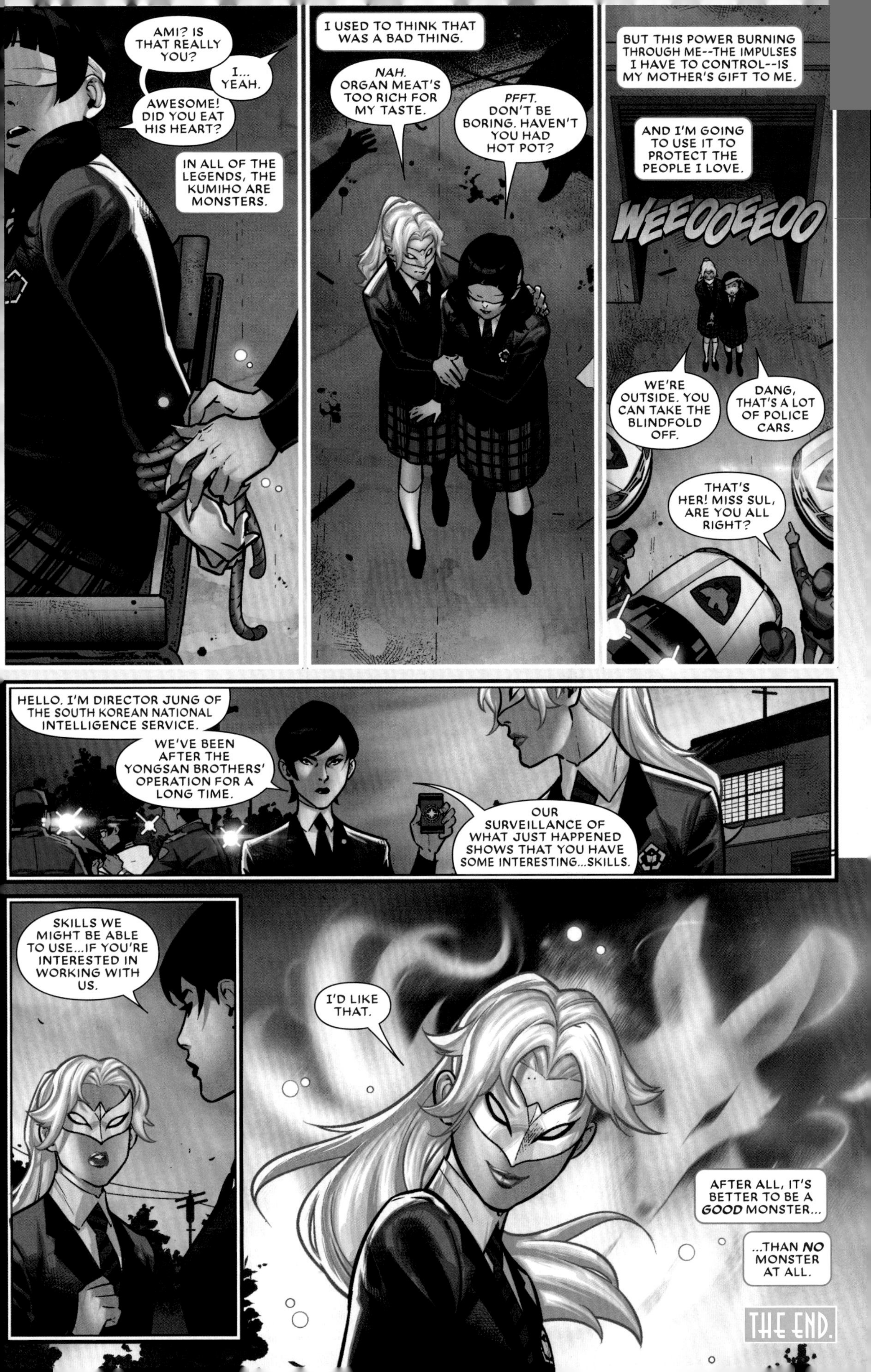
AMI? IS THAT REALLY YOU?
I... YEAH.
AWESOME! DID YOU EAT HIS HEART?
IN ALL OF THE LEGENDS, THE KUMIHO ARE MONSTERS.
I USED TO THINK THAT WAS A BAD THING.
NAH. ORGAN MEAT'S TOO RICH FOR MY TASTE.
PFFT. DON'T BE BORING. HAVEN'T YOU HAD HOT POT?
BUT THIS POWER BURNING THROUGH ME--THE IMPULSES I HAVE TO CONTROL--IS MY MOTHER'S GIFT TO ME.
AND I'M GOING TO USE IT TO PROTECT THE PEOPLE I LOVE.
WEEOOEEOO
WE'RE OUTSIDE. YOU CAN TAKE THE BLINDFOLD OFF.
DANG, THAT'S A LOT OF POLICE CARS.
THAT'S HER! MISS SUL, ARE YOU ALL RIGHT?
HELLO. I'M DIRECTOR JUNG OF THE SOUTH KOREAN NATIONAL INTELLIGENCE SERVICE.
WE'VE BEEN AFTER THE YONGSAN BROTHERS' OPERATION FOR A LONG TIME.
OUR SURVEILLANCE OF WHAT JUST HAPPENED SHOWS THAT YOU HAVE SOME INTERESTING...SKILLS.
SKILLS WE MIGHT BE ABLE TO USE...IF YOU'RE INTERESTED IN WORKING WITH US.
I'D LIKE THAT.
AFTER ALL, IT'S BETTER TO BE A GOOD MONSTER...
...THAN NO MONSTER AT ALL.
THE END.

re: WHITE FOX

First of all, thank you for picking up this comic! I want to introduce you to YongJoon Cho, Marvel Future Fight's art director from the Netmarble Monster team. We collaborated and are working extremely hard to design awesome new "lifestyle" costumes for our Future Fight mobile game fans.

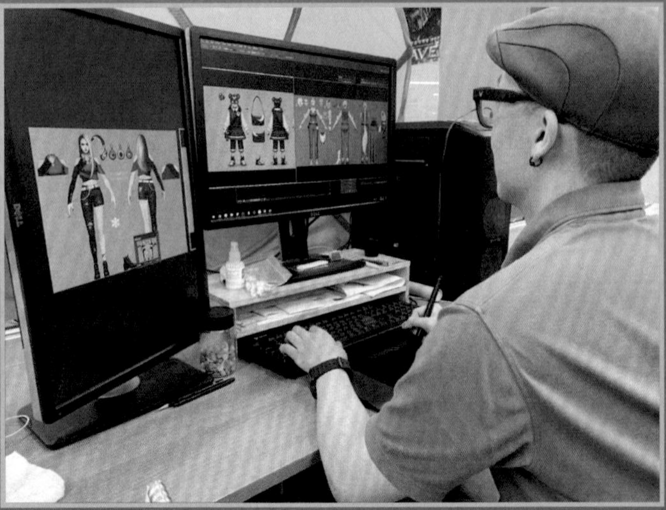

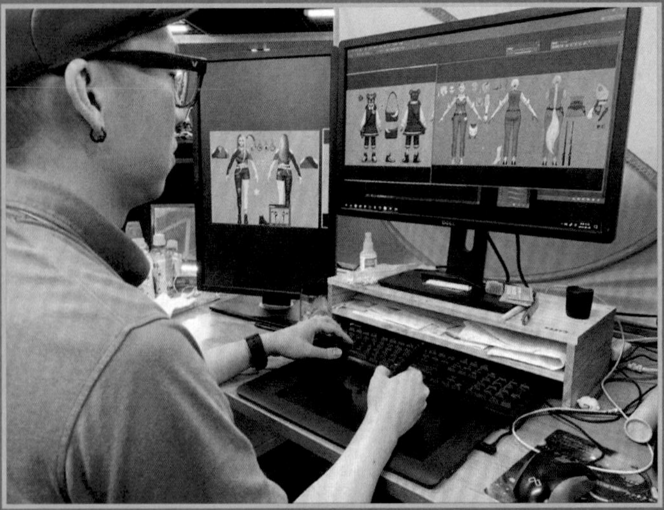

Did you know White Fox is originally from South Korea? We are extremely happy to feature her in the game alongside other *Future Fight*-original characters from South Korea—Luna Snow, and Crescent and Io! If you haven't played Marvel Future Fight, download for free and give it a spin!

— Danny Koo,
Marvel Games Senior Producer,
Asia.

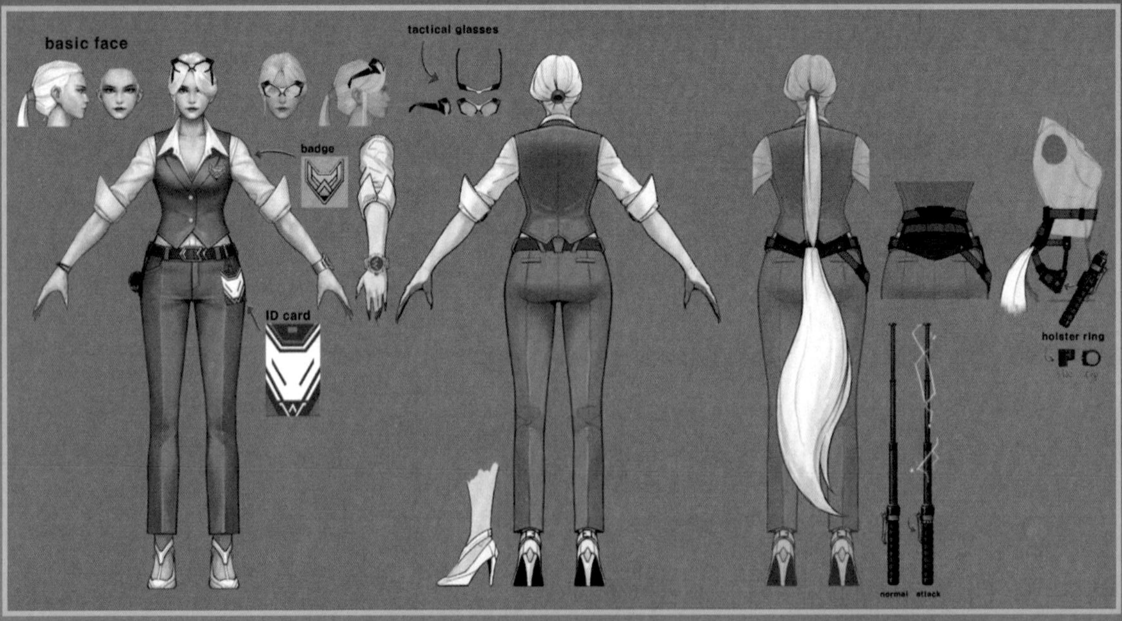
basic face
tactical glasses
badge
ID card
holster ring
normal
attack

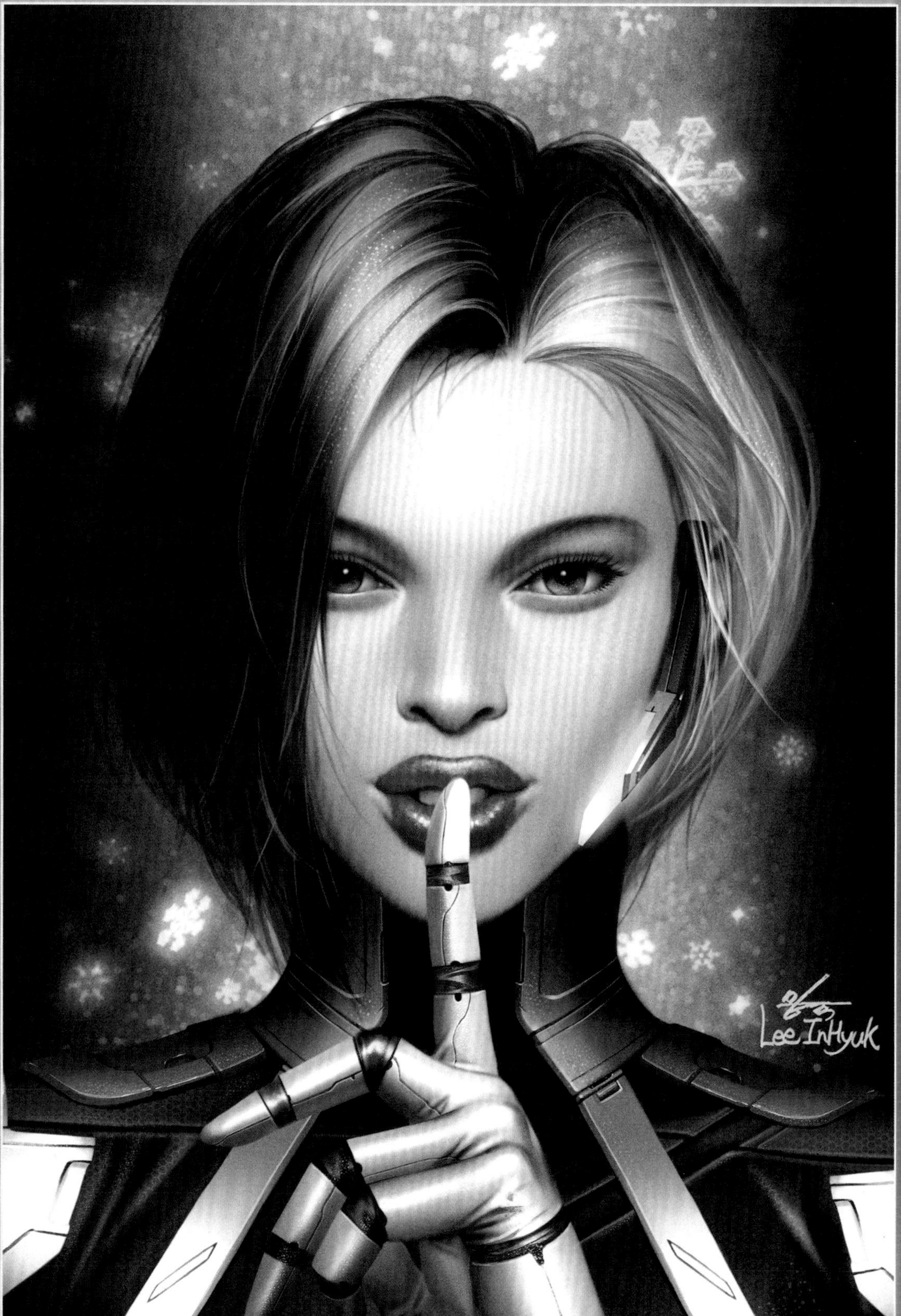
Lee InHyuk

FUTURE FIGHT FIRSTS
LUNA SNOW

MARVEL
FUTURE
FIGHT
FIRSTS

Seol Hee is the international singing sensation and super hero known as

LUNA SNOW

With her elemental ice powers, Luna Snow protects her home country of South Korea and battles global threats with Jimmy Woo's new Agents of Atlas. But how did Luna get her powers and rise to superstardom?

WRITER
ALYSSA WONG

ARTIST
GANG HYUK LIM

LETTERER
VC's JOE SABINO

COVER ARTIST
INHYUK LEE

LOGO DESIGN
**JAY BOWEN &
ADAM DEL RE**

ASSISTANT EDITORS
**LINDSEY COHICK
& TOM GRONEMAN**

EDITOR
**MARK
PANICCIA**

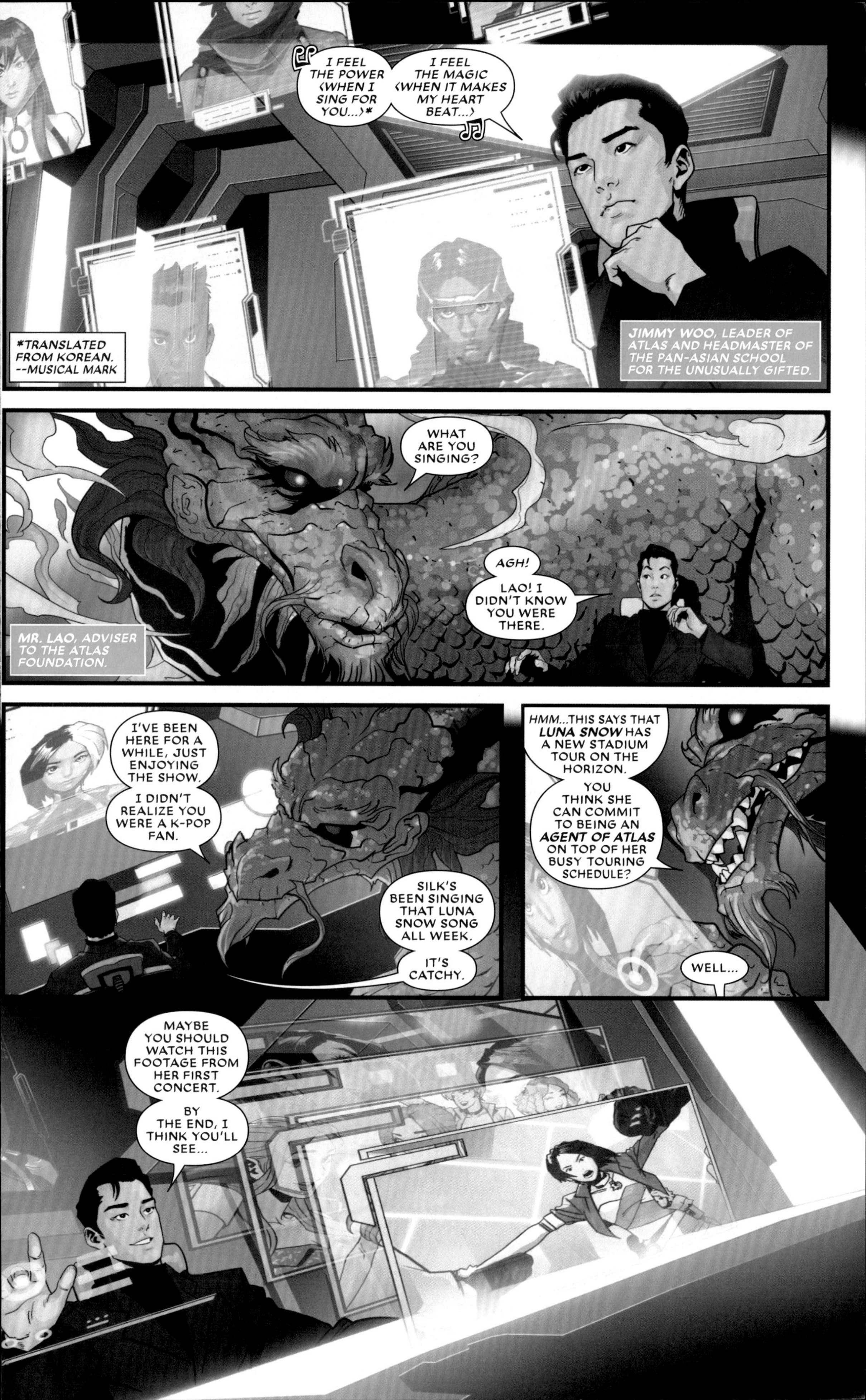

I FEEL THE POWER ‹WHEN I SING FOR YOU...›*
I FEEL THE MAGIC ‹WHEN IT MAKES MY HEART BEAT...›
*TRANSLATED FROM KOREAN. --MUSICAL MARK
JIMMY WOO, LEADER OF ATLAS AND HEADMASTER OF THE PAN-ASIAN SCHOOL FOR THE UNUSUALLY GIFTED.
WHAT ARE YOU SINGING?
AGH!
LAO! I DIDN'T KNOW YOU WERE THERE.
MR. LAO, ADVISER TO THE ATLAS FOUNDATION.
I'VE BEEN HERE FOR A WHILE, JUST ENJOYING THE SHOW.
I DIDN'T REALIZE YOU WERE A K-POP FAN.
SILK'S BEEN SINGING THAT LUNA SNOW SONG ALL WEEK.
IT'S CATCHY.
HMM...THIS SAYS THAT LUNA SNOW HAS A NEW STADIUM TOUR ON THE HORIZON.
YOU THINK SHE CAN COMMIT TO BEING AN AGENT OF ATLAS ON TOP OF HER BUSY TOURING SCHEDULE?
WELL...
MAYBE YOU SHOULD WATCH THIS FOOTAGE FROM HER FIRST CONCERT.
BY THE END, I THINK YOU'LL SEE...

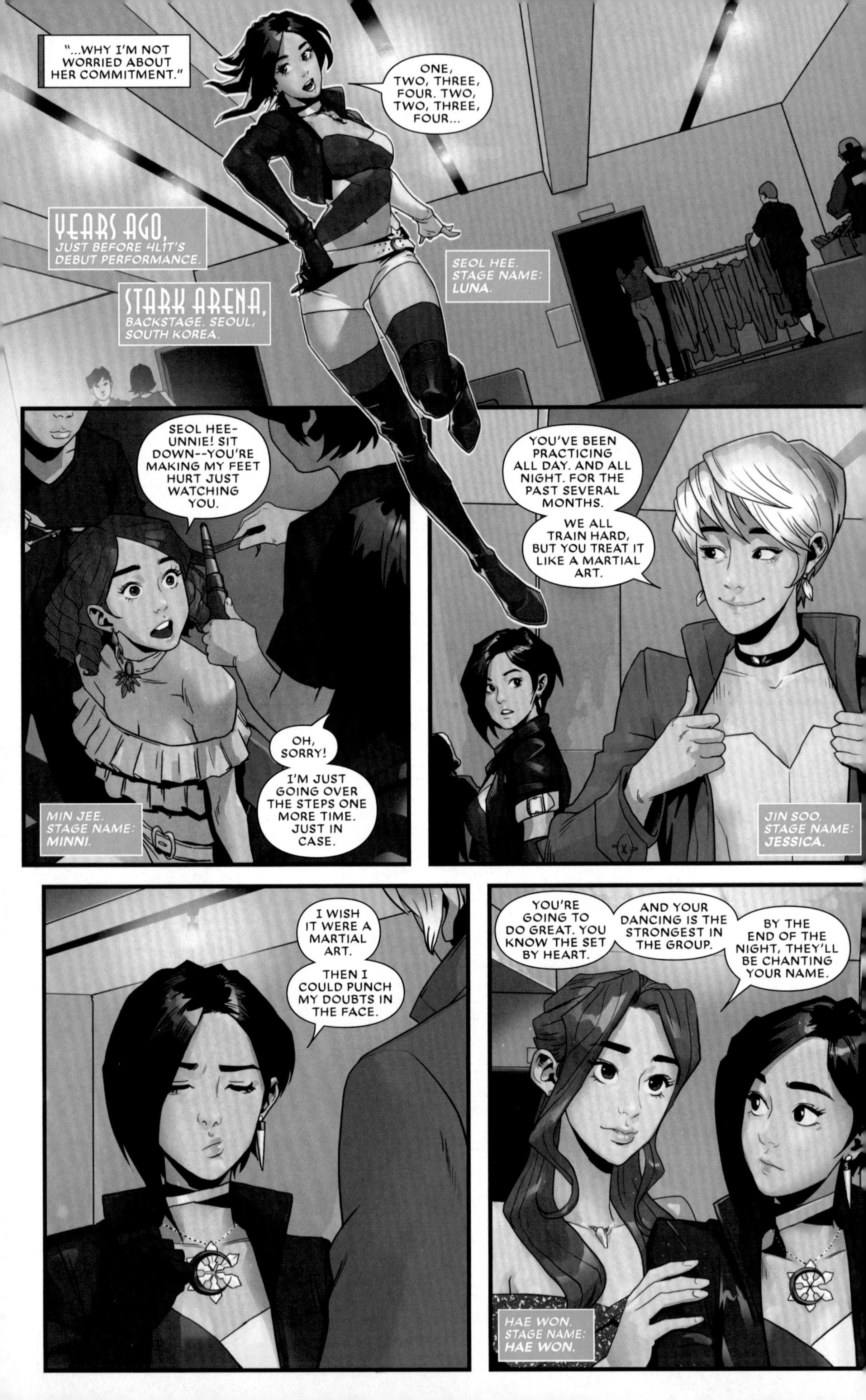
"...WHY I'M NOT WORRIED ABOUT HER COMMITMENT."
ONE, TWO, THREE, FOUR. TWO, TWO, THREE, FOUR...
YEARS AGO, JUST BEFORE 4L1T'S DEBUT PERFORMANCE.
STARK ARENA, BACKSTAGE. SEOUL, SOUTH KOREA.
SEOL HEE. STAGE NAME: LUNA.
SEOL HEE-UNNIE! SIT DOWN--YOU'RE MAKING MY FEET HURT JUST WATCHING YOU.
OH, SORRY!
I'M JUST GOING OVER THE STEPS ONE MORE TIME. JUST IN CASE.
MIN JEE. STAGE NAME: MINNI.
YOU'VE BEEN PRACTICING ALL DAY. AND ALL NIGHT. FOR THE PAST SEVERAL MONTHS.
WE ALL TRAIN HARD, BUT YOU TREAT IT LIKE A MARTIAL ART.
JIN SOO. STAGE NAME: JESSICA.
I WISH IT WERE A MARTIAL ART.
THEN I COULD PUNCH MY DOUBTS IN THE FACE.
YOU'RE GOING TO DO GREAT. YOU KNOW THE SET BY HEART.
AND YOUR DANCING IS THE STRONGEST IN THE GROUP.
BY THE END OF THE NIGHT, THEY'LL BE CHANTING YOUR NAME.
HAE WON. STAGE NAME: HAE WON.

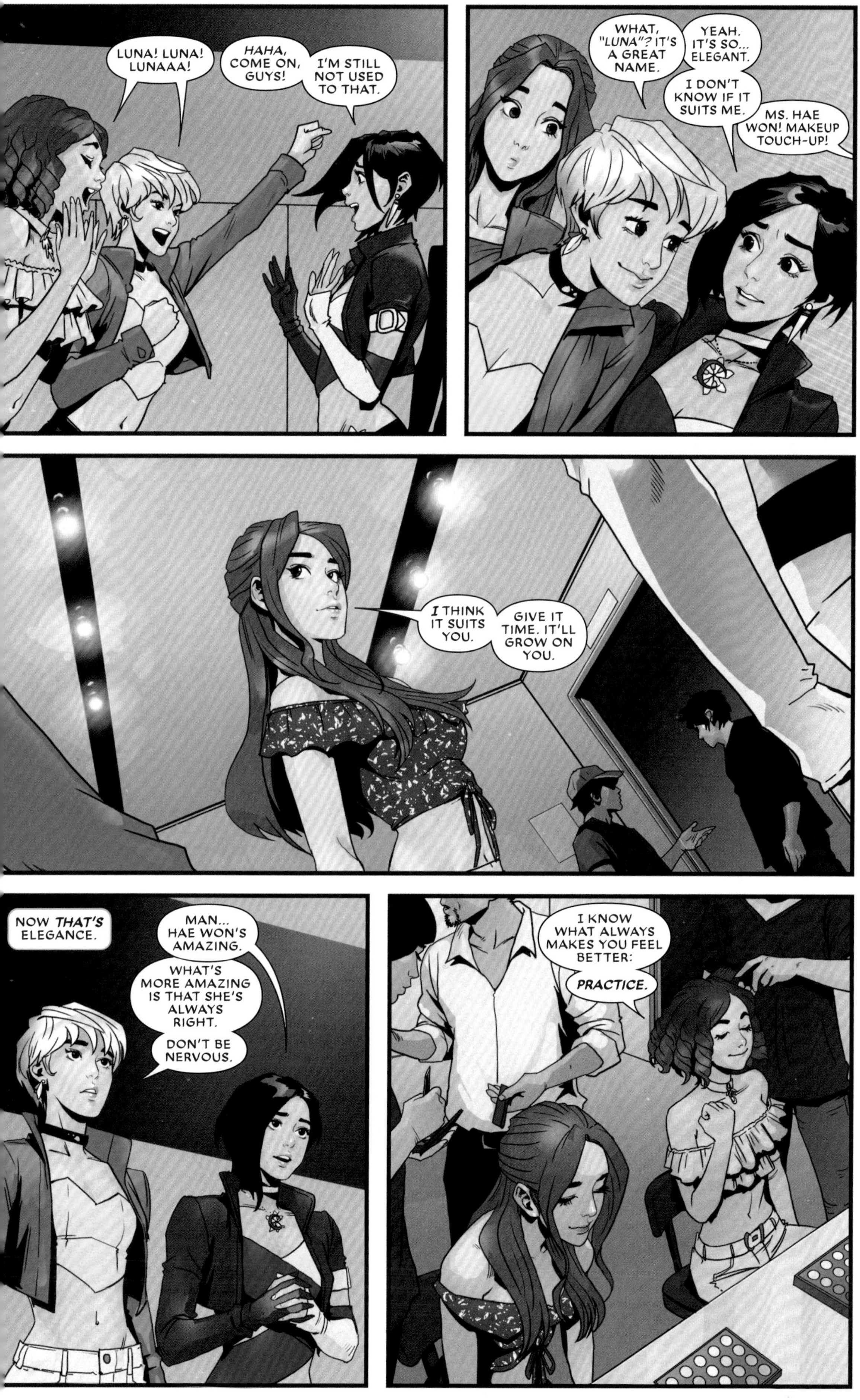
LUNA! LUNA! LUNAAA!
HAHA, COME ON, GUYS!
I'M STILL NOT USED TO THAT.
WHAT, "LUNA"? IT'S A GREAT NAME.
YEAH. IT'S SO... ELEGANT.
I DON'T KNOW IF IT SUITS ME.
MS. HAE WON! MAKEUP TOUCH-UP!
I THINK IT SUITS YOU.
GIVE IT TIME. IT'LL GROW ON YOU.
NOW THAT'S ELEGANCE.
MAN... HAE WON'S AMAZING.
WHAT'S MORE AMAZING IS THAT SHE'S ALWAYS RIGHT.
DON'T BE NERVOUS.
I KNOW WHAT ALWAYS MAKES YOU FEEL BETTER:
PRACTICE.

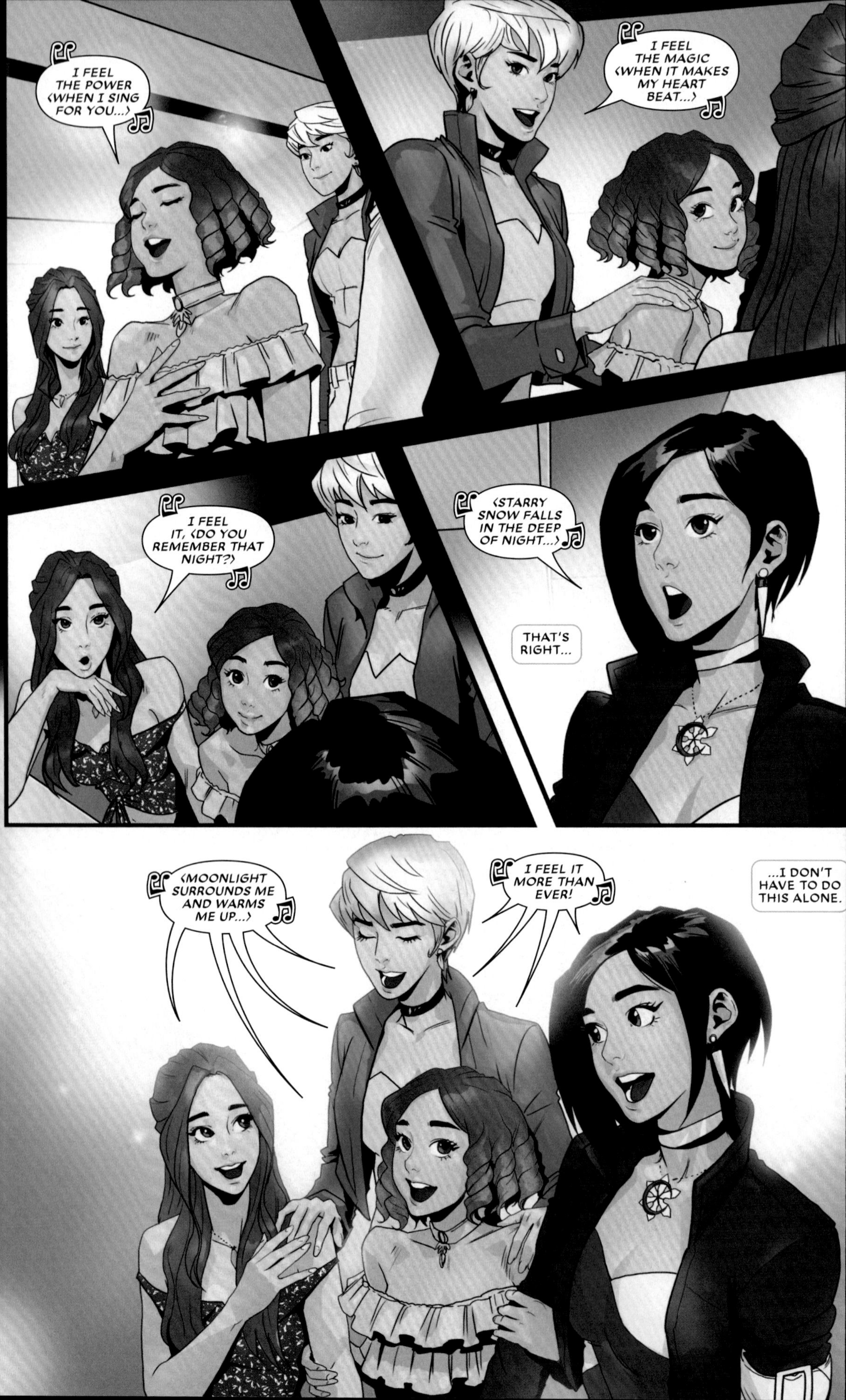
I FEEL THE POWER ‹WHEN I SING FOR YOU...›
I FEEL THE MAGIC ‹WHEN IT MAKES MY HEART BEAT...›
I FEEL IT, ‹DO YOU REMEMBER THAT NIGHT?›
‹STARRY SNOW FALLS IN THE DEEP OF NIGHT...›
THAT'S RIGHT...
‹MOONLIGHT SURROUNDS ME AND WARMS ME UP...›
I FEEL IT MORE THAN EVER!
...I DON'T HAVE TO DO THIS ALONE.

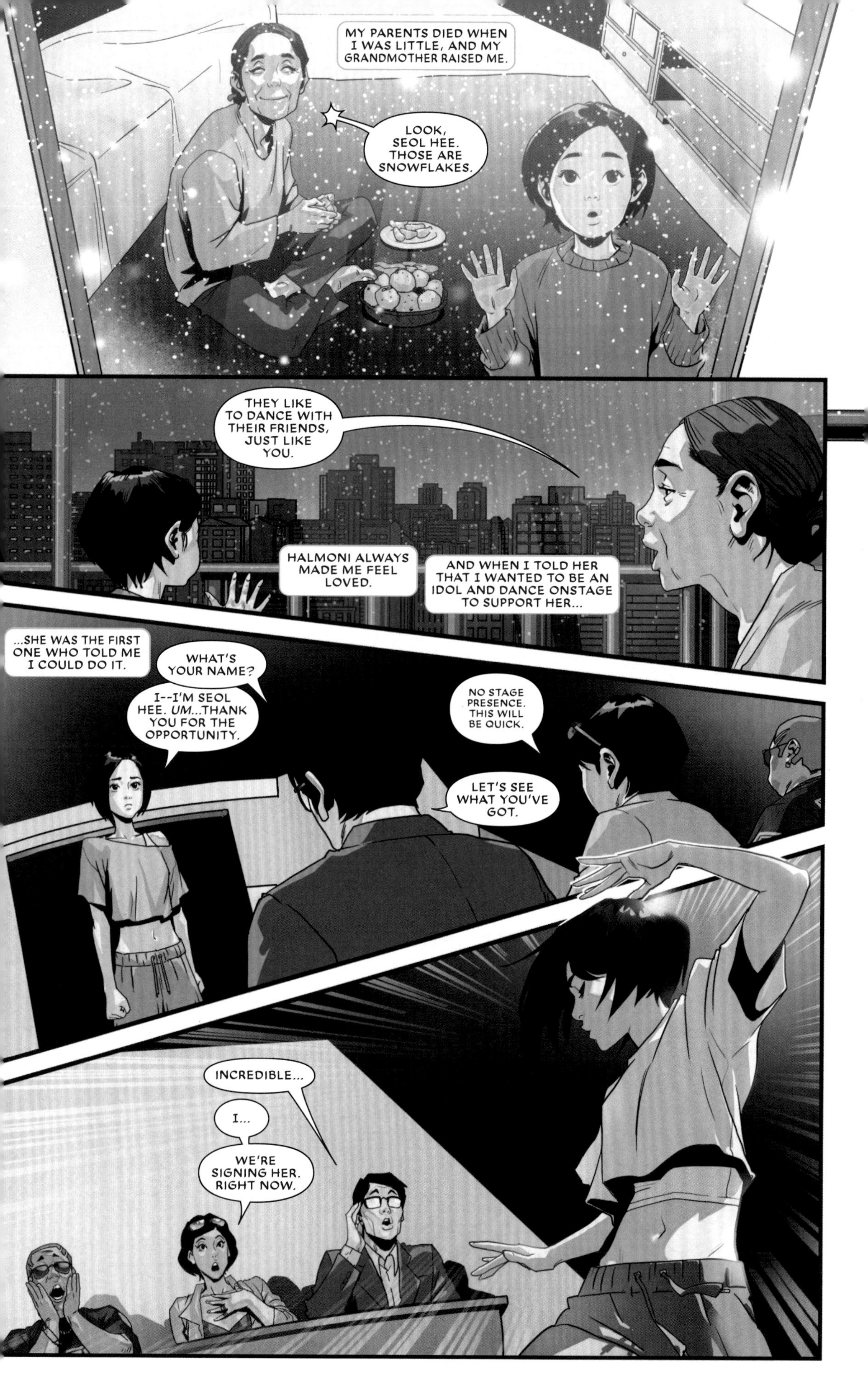
MY PARENTS DIED WHEN I WAS LITTLE, AND MY GRANDMOTHER RAISED ME.
LOOK, SEOL HEE. THOSE ARE SNOWFLAKES.
THEY LIKE TO DANCE WITH THEIR FRIENDS, JUST LIKE YOU.
HALMONI ALWAYS MADE ME FEEL LOVED.
AND WHEN I TOLD HER THAT I WANTED TO BE AN IDOL AND DANCE ONSTAGE TO SUPPORT HER...
...SHE WAS THE FIRST ONE WHO TOLD ME I COULD DO IT.
WHAT'S YOUR NAME?
I--I'M SEOL HEE. *UM*...THANK YOU FOR THE OPPORTUNITY.
NO STAGE PRESENCE. THIS WILL BE QUICK.
LET'S SEE WHAT YOU'VE GOT.
INCREDIBLE...
I...
WE'RE SIGNING HER. RIGHT NOW.

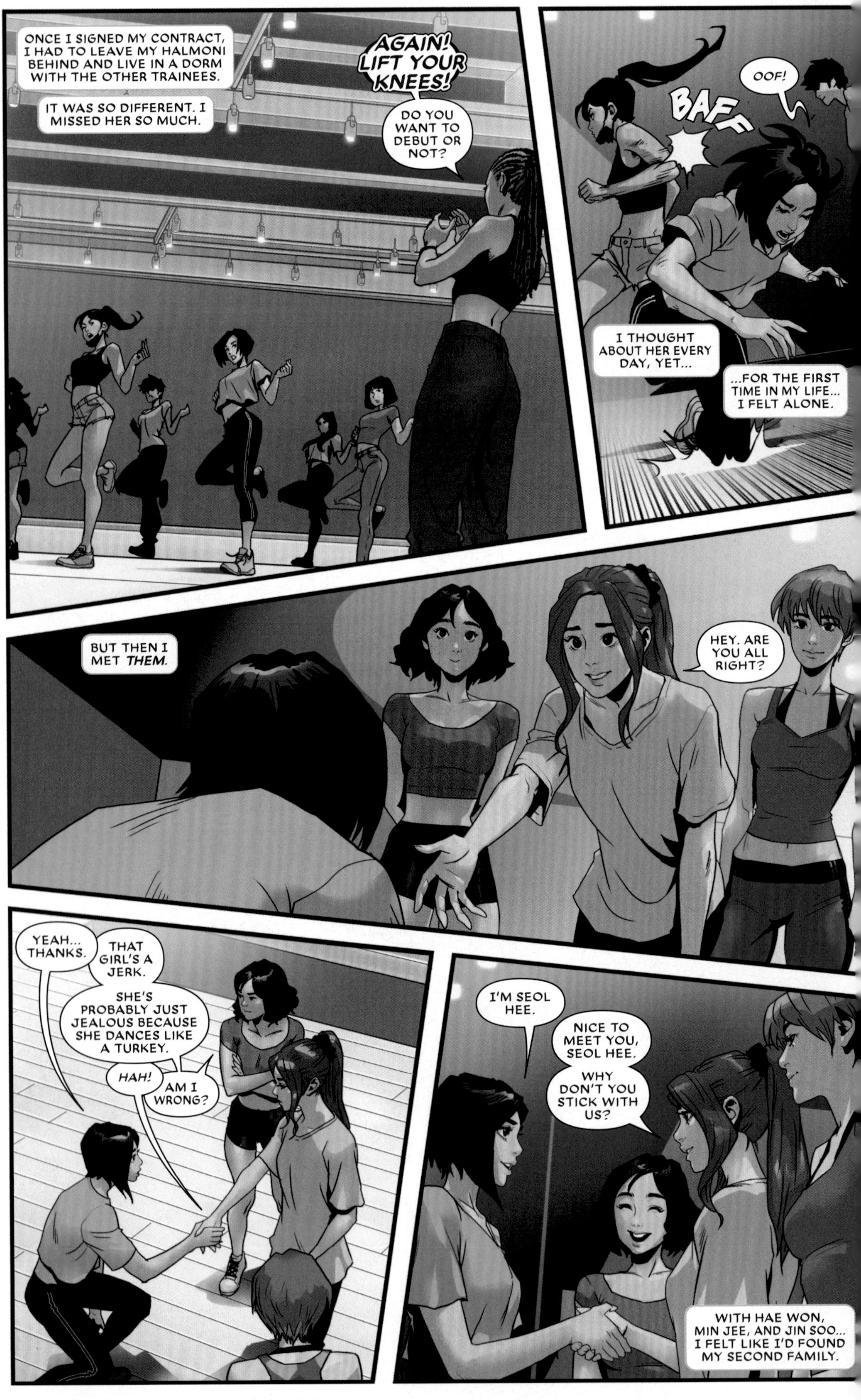
ONCE I SIGNED MY CONTRACT, I HAD TO LEAVE MY HALMONI BEHIND AND LIVE IN A DORM WITH THE OTHER TRAINEES.
IT WAS SO DIFFERENT. I MISSED HER SO MUCH.
AGAIN! LIFT YOUR KNEES!
DO YOU WANT TO DEBUT OR NOT?
BAFF
OOF!
I THOUGHT ABOUT HER EVERY DAY, YET...
...FOR THE FIRST TIME IN MY LIFE... I FELT ALONE.
BUT THEN I MET *THEM*.
HEY. ARE YOU ALL RIGHT?
YEAH... THANKS.
THAT GIRL'S A JERK.
SHE'S PROBABLY JUST JEALOUS BECAUSE SHE DANCES LIKE A TURKEY.
HAH!
AM I WRONG?
I'M SEOL HEE.
NICE TO MEET YOU, SEOL HEE.
WHY DON'T YOU STICK WITH US?
WITH HAE WON, MIN JEE, AND JIN SOO... I FELT LIKE I'D FOUND MY SECOND FAMILY.

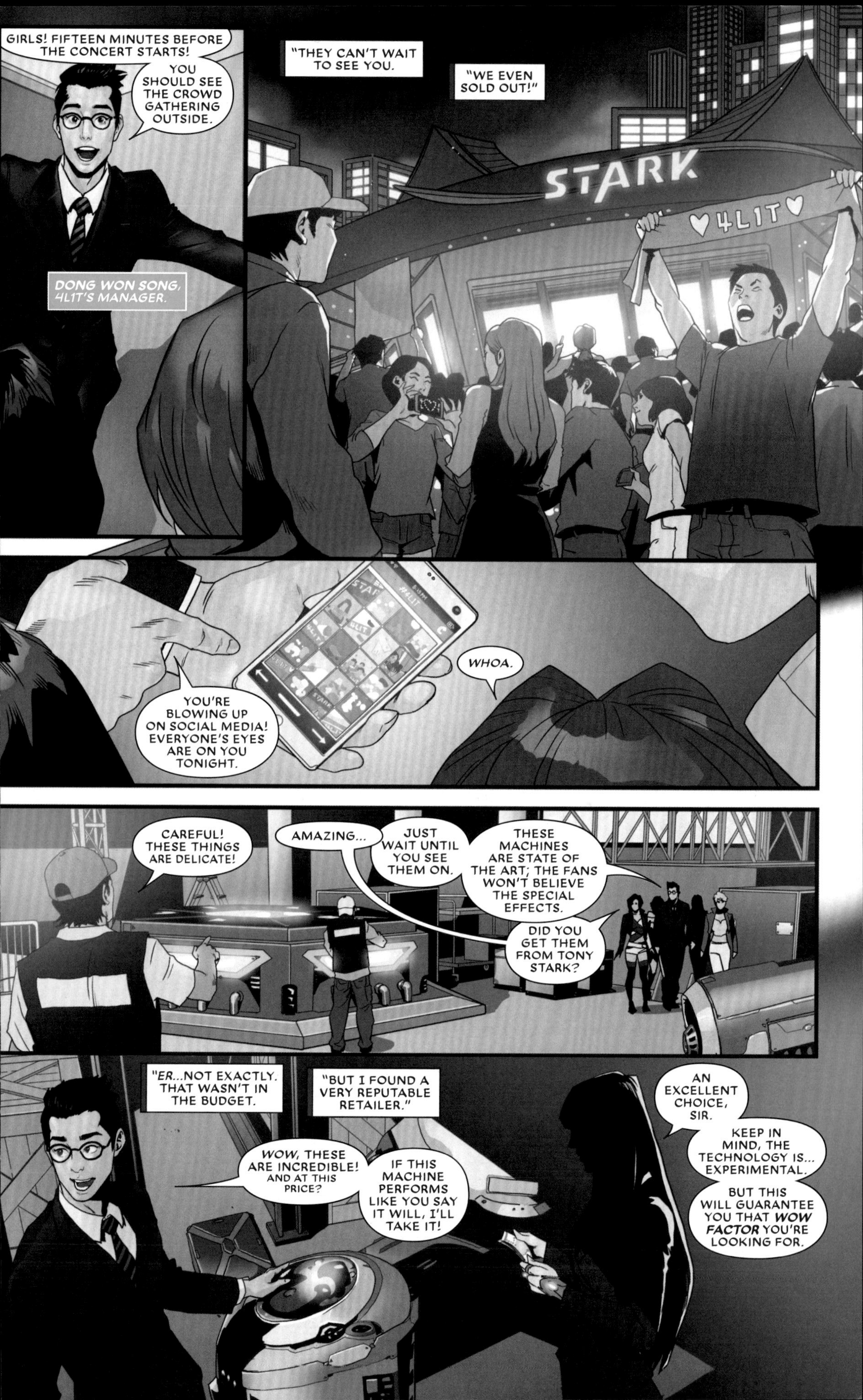
GIRLS! FIFTEEN MINUTES BEFORE THE CONCERT STARTS!
YOU SHOULD SEE THE CROWD GATHERING OUTSIDE.
DONG WON SONG, 4L1T'S MANAGER.
"THEY CAN'T WAIT TO SEE YOU.
"WE EVEN SOLD OUT!"
STARK
4L1T
YOU'RE BLOWING UP ON SOCIAL MEDIA! EVERYONE'S EYES ARE ON YOU TONIGHT.
WHOA.
CAREFUL! THESE THINGS ARE DELICATE!
AMAZING...
JUST WAIT UNTIL YOU SEE THEM ON.
THESE MACHINES ARE STATE OF THE ART; THE FANS WON'T BELIEVE THE SPECIAL EFFECTS.
DID YOU GET THEM FROM TONY STARK?
"ER...NOT EXACTLY. THAT WASN'T IN THE BUDGET.
"BUT I FOUND A VERY REPUTABLE RETAILER."
WOW, THESE ARE INCREDIBLE! AND AT THIS PRICE?
IF THIS MACHINE PERFORMS LIKE YOU SAY IT WILL, I'LL TAKE IT!
AN EXCELLENT CHOICE, SIR.
KEEP IN MIND, THE TECHNOLOGY IS... EXPERIMENTAL.
BUT THIS WILL GUARANTEE YOU THAT WOW FACTOR YOU'RE LOOKING FOR.

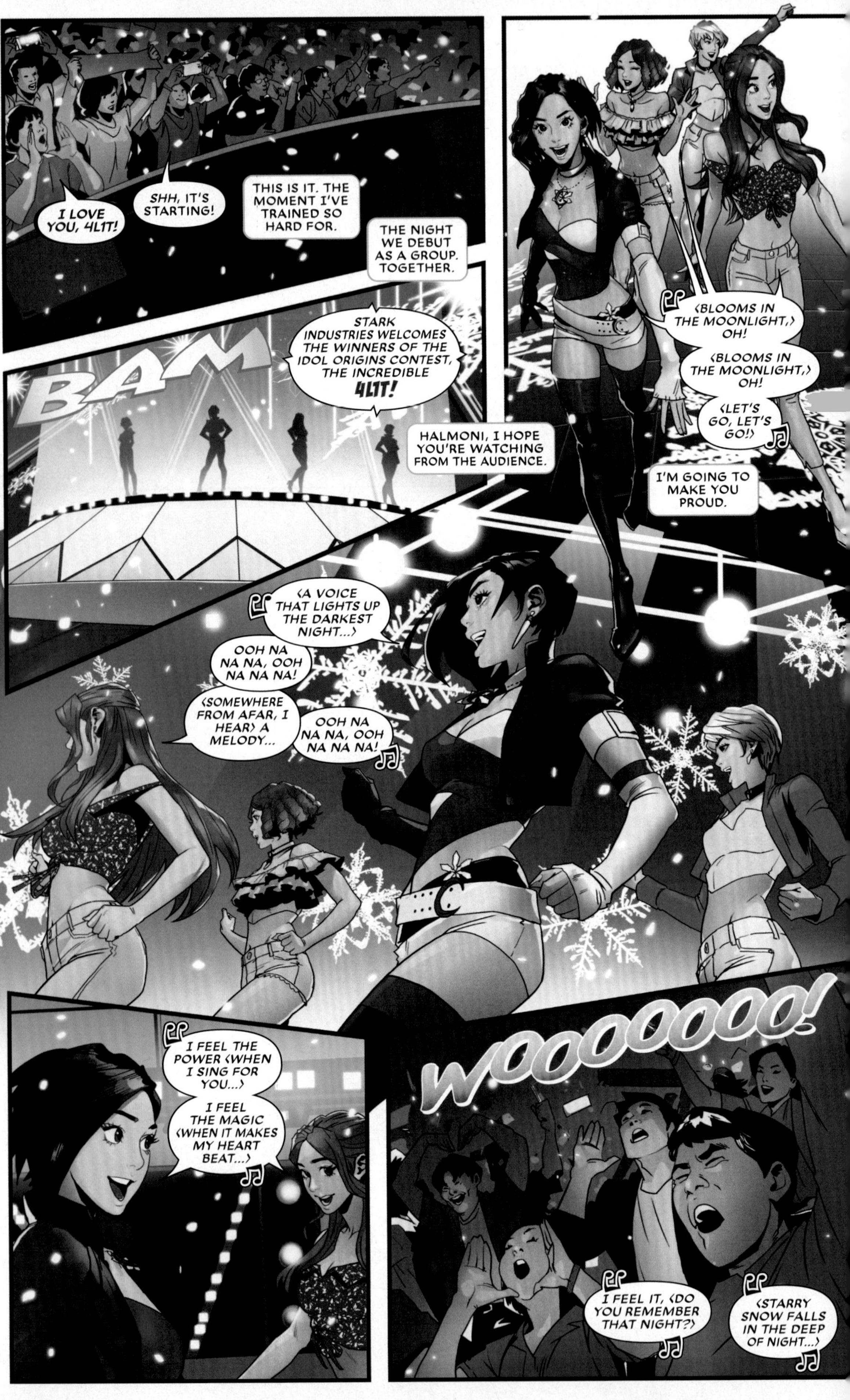
I LOVE YOU, 4L1T!
SHH, IT'S STARTING!
THIS IS IT. THE MOMENT I'VE TRAINED SO HARD FOR.
THE NIGHT WE DEBUT AS A GROUP. TOGETHER.
BAM
STARK INDUSTRIES WELCOMES THE WINNERS OF THE IDOL ORIGINS CONTEST, THE INCREDIBLE 4L1T!
HALMONI, I HOPE YOU'RE WATCHING FROM THE AUDIENCE.
‹BLOOMS IN THE MOONLIGHT,› OH!
‹BLOOMS IN THE MOONLIGHT,› OH!
‹LET'S GO, LET'S GO!›
I'M GOING TO MAKE YOU PROUD.
‹A VOICE THAT LIGHTS UP THE DARKEST NIGHT...›
OOH NA NA NA, OOH NA NA NA!
‹SOMEWHERE FROM AFAR, I HEAR› A MELODY...
OOH NA NA NA, OOH NA NA NA!
I FEEL THE POWER ‹WHEN I SING FOR YOU...›
I FEEL THE MAGIC ‹WHEN IT MAKES MY HEART BEAT...›
WOOOOOOOO!
I FEEL IT, ‹DO YOU REMEMBER THAT NIGHT?›
‹STARRY SNOW FALLS IN THE DEEP OF NIGHT...›

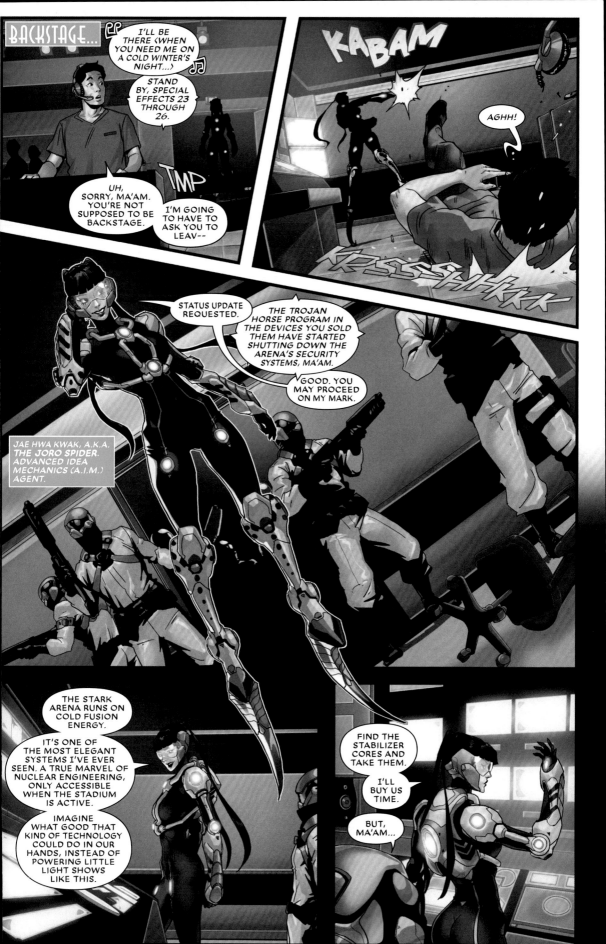

BACKSTAGE...

I'LL BE THERE ‹WHEN YOU NEED ME ON A COLD WINTER'S NIGHT...› ♪

STAND BY, SPECIAL EFFECTS 23 THROUGH 26.

TMP

UH, SORRY, MA'AM. YOU'RE NOT SUPPOSED TO BE BACKSTAGE.

I'M GOING TO HAVE TO ASK YOU TO LEAV--

KABAM

AGHH!

KRSSSHKK

STATUS UPDATE REQUESTED.

THE TROJAN HORSE PROGRAM IN THE DEVICES YOU SOLD THEM HAVE STARTED SHUTTING DOWN THE ARENA'S SECURITY SYSTEMS, MA'AM.

GOOD. YOU MAY PROCEED ON MY MARK.

JAE HWA KWAK, A.K.A. *THE JORO SPIDER.* ADVANCED IDEA MECHANICS (A.I.M.) AGENT.

THE STARK ARENA RUNS ON COLD FUSION ENERGY.

IT'S ONE OF THE MOST ELEGANT SYSTEMS I'VE EVER SEEN. A TRUE MARVEL OF NUCLEAR ENGINEERING, ONLY ACCESSIBLE WHEN THE STADIUM IS ACTIVE.

IMAGINE WHAT GOOD THAT KIND OF TECHNOLOGY COULD DO IN OUR HANDS, INSTEAD OF POWERING LITTLE LIGHT SHOWS LIKE THIS.

FIND THE STABILIZER CORES AND TAKE THEM.

I'LL BUY US TIME.

BUT, MA'AM...

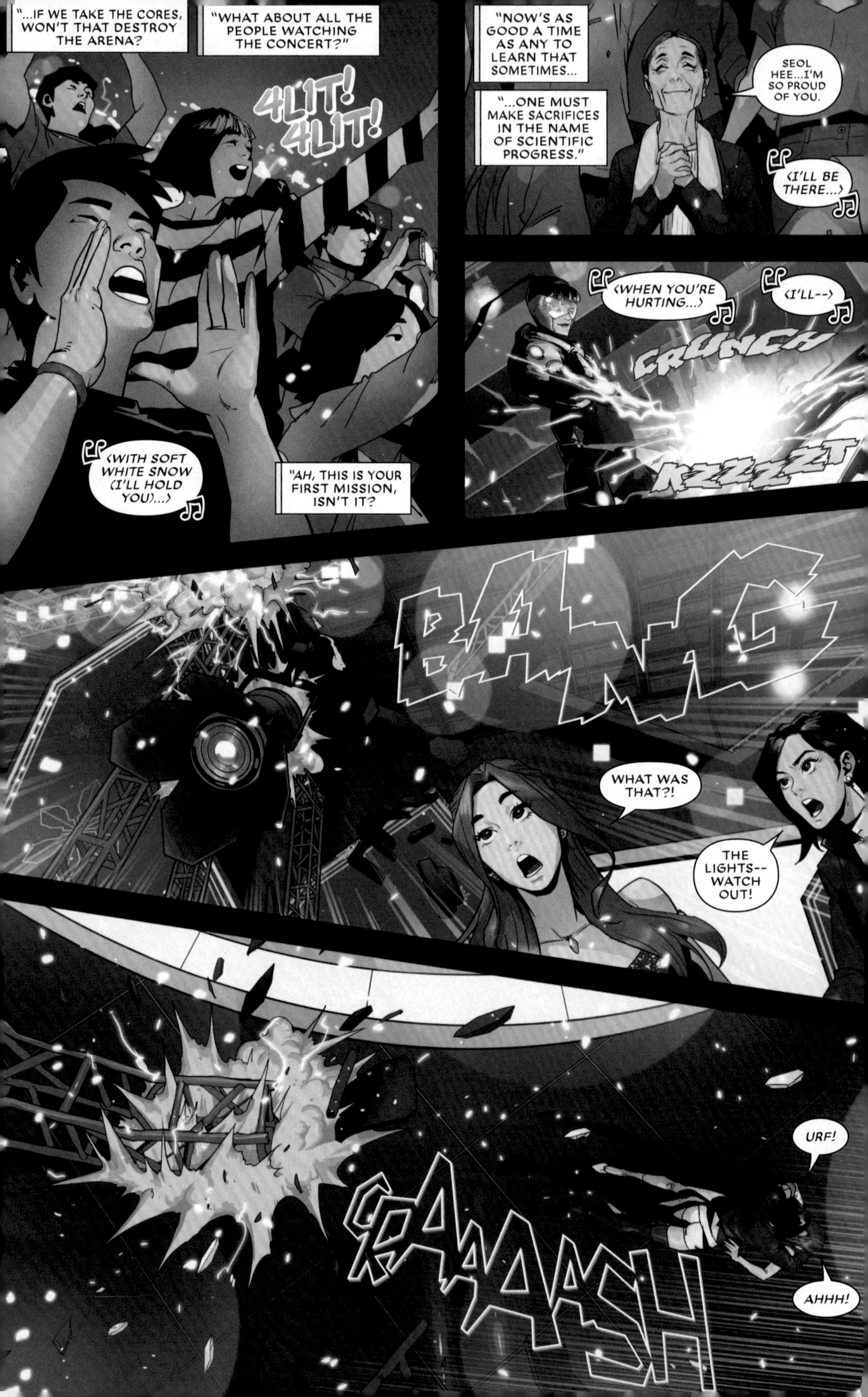
"...IF WE TAKE THE CORES, WON'T THAT DESTROY THE ARENA?
"WHAT ABOUT ALL THE PEOPLE WATCHING THE CONCERT?"
4LIT! 4LIT!
‹WITH SOFT WHITE SNOW (I'LL HOLD YOU)...›
"AH, THIS IS YOUR FIRST MISSION, ISN'T IT?
"NOW'S AS GOOD A TIME AS ANY TO LEARN THAT SOMETIMES...
"...ONE MUST MAKE SACRIFICES IN THE NAME OF SCIENTIFIC PROGRESS."
SEOL HEE...I'M SO PROUD OF YOU.
‹I'LL BE THERE...›
‹WHEN YOU'RE HURTING...›
‹I'LL--›
CRUNCH
KZZZZZT
BANG
WHAT WAS THAT?!
THE LIGHTS-- WATCH OUT!
CRAAASH
URF!
AHHH!

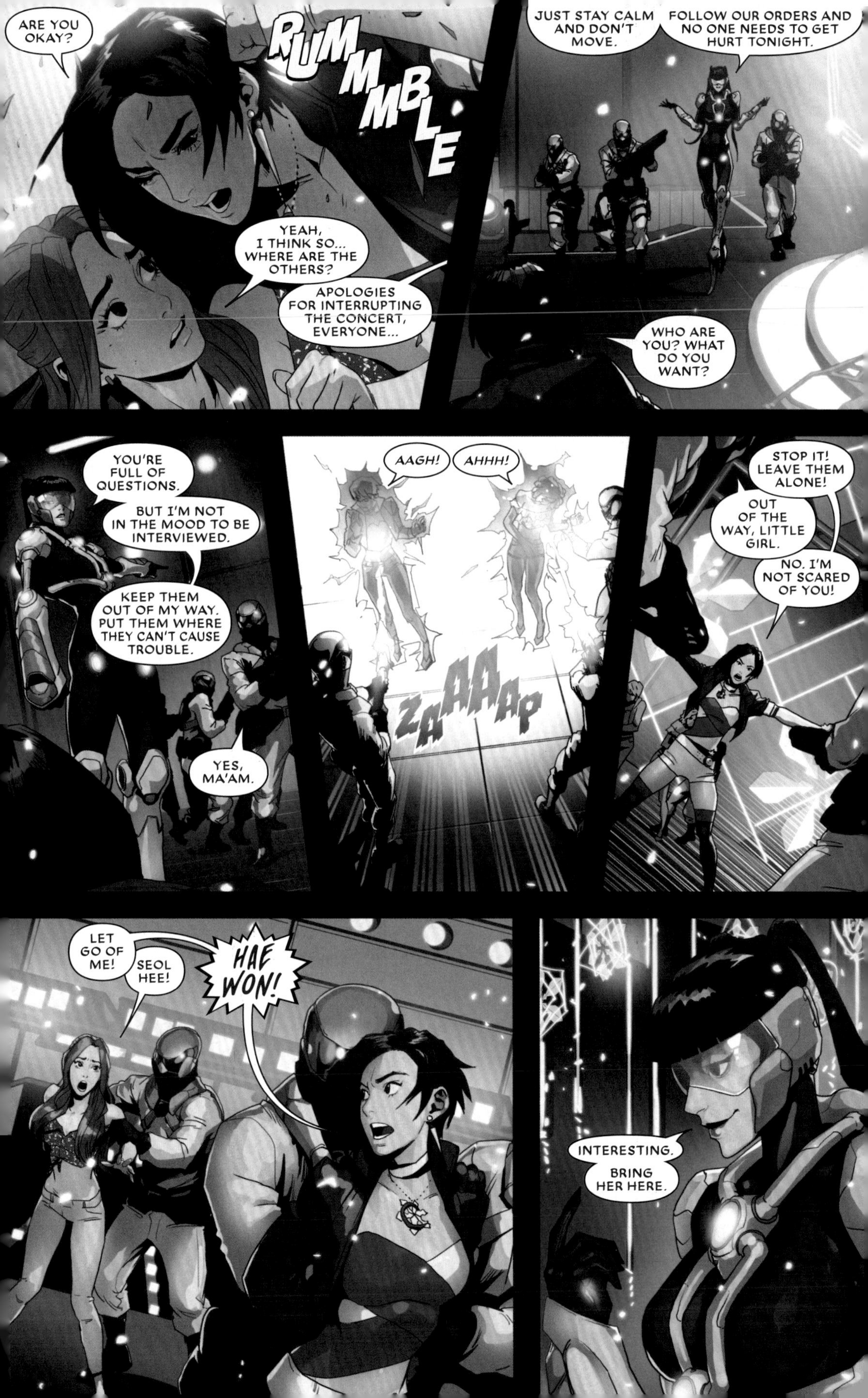
ARE YOU OKAY?
RUMMMBLE
YEAH, I THINK SO... WHERE ARE THE OTHERS?
APOLOGIES FOR INTERRUPTING THE CONCERT, EVERYONE...
JUST STAY CALM AND DON'T MOVE.
FOLLOW OUR ORDERS AND NO ONE NEEDS TO GET HURT TONIGHT.
WHO ARE YOU? WHAT DO YOU WANT?
YOU'RE FULL OF QUESTIONS.
BUT I'M NOT IN THE MOOD TO BE INTERVIEWED.
KEEP THEM OUT OF MY WAY. PUT THEM WHERE THEY CAN'T CAUSE TROUBLE.
YES, MA'AM.
AAGH!
AHHH!
ZAAAAP
STOP IT! LEAVE THEM ALONE!
OUT OF THE WAY, LITTLE GIRL.
NO. I'M NOT SCARED OF YOU!
LET GO OF ME!
SEOL HEE!
HAE WON!
INTERESTING.
BRING HER HERE.

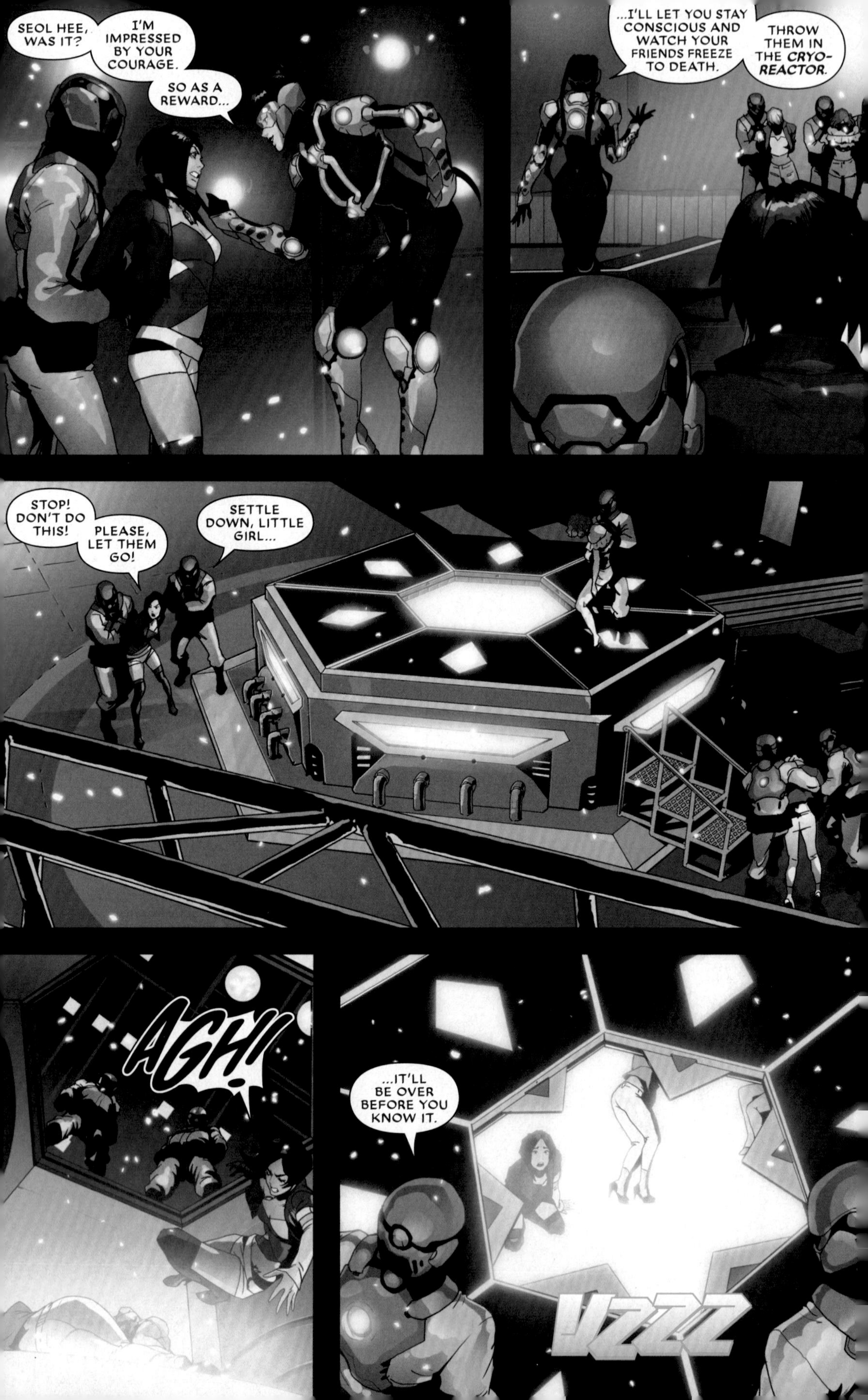
SEOL HEE, WAS IT?
I'M IMPRESSED BY YOUR COURAGE.
SO AS A REWARD...
...I'LL LET YOU STAY CONSCIOUS AND WATCH YOUR FRIENDS FREEZE TO DEATH.
THROW THEM IN THE CRYO-REACTOR.
STOP! DON'T DO THIS!
PLEASE, LET THEM GO!
SETTLE DOWN, LITTLE GIRL...
AGH!
...IT'LL BE OVER BEFORE YOU KNOW IT.
VZZZ

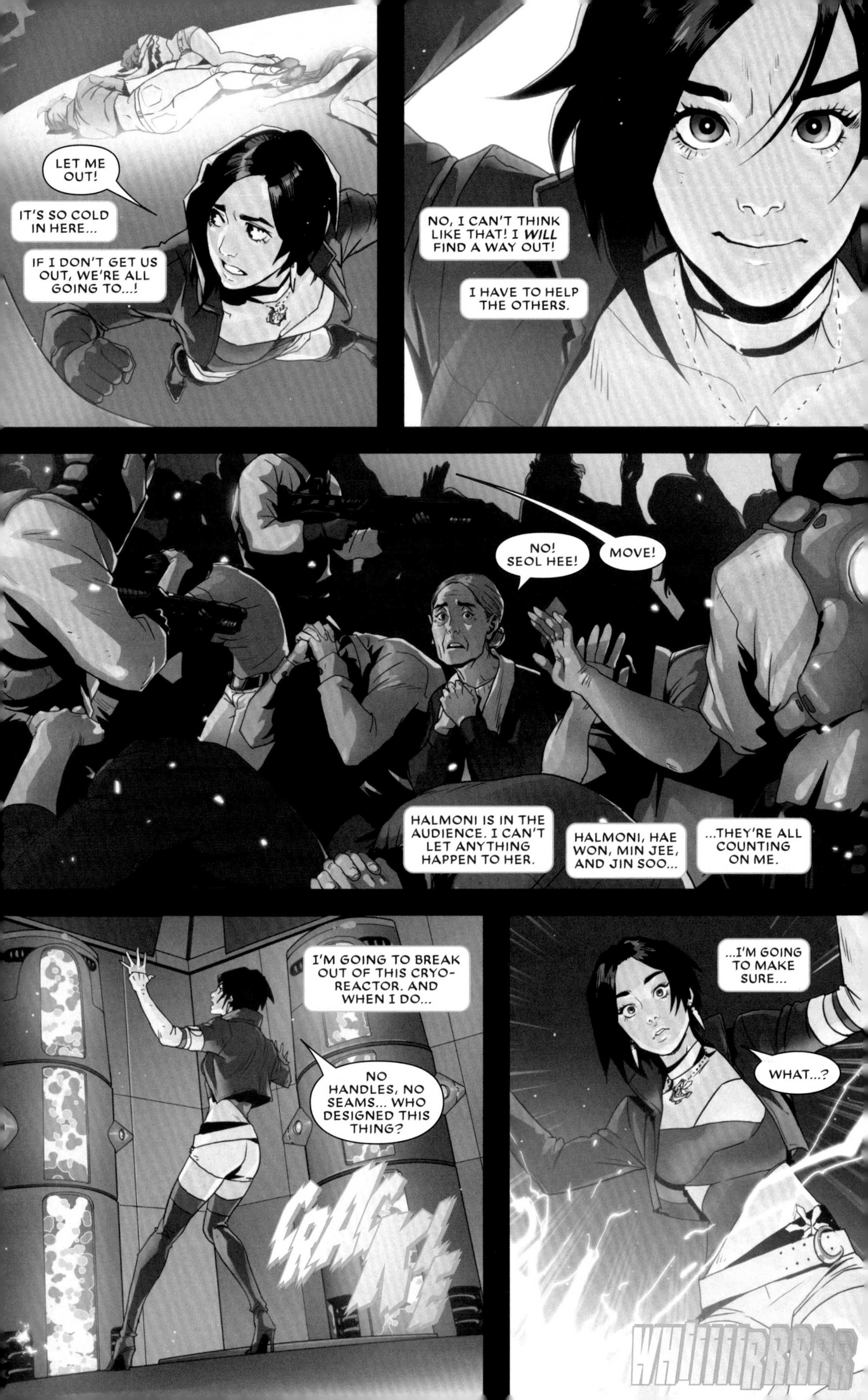
LET ME OUT!
IT'S SO COLD IN HERE...
IF I DON'T GET US OUT, WE'RE ALL GOING TO...!
NO, I CAN'T THINK LIKE THAT! I *WILL* FIND A WAY OUT!
I HAVE TO HELP THE OTHERS.
NO! SEOL HEE!
MOVE!
HALMONI IS IN THE AUDIENCE. I CAN'T LET ANYTHING HAPPEN TO HER.
HALMONI, HAE WON, MIN JEE, AND JIN SOO...
...THEY'RE ALL COUNTING ON ME.
I'M GOING TO BREAK OUT OF THIS CRYO-REACTOR. AND WHEN I DO...
NO HANDLES, NO SEAMS... WHO DESIGNED THIS THING?
CRACK-LE
...I'M GOING TO MAKE SURE...
WHAT...?
WHIIIIIRRRRR

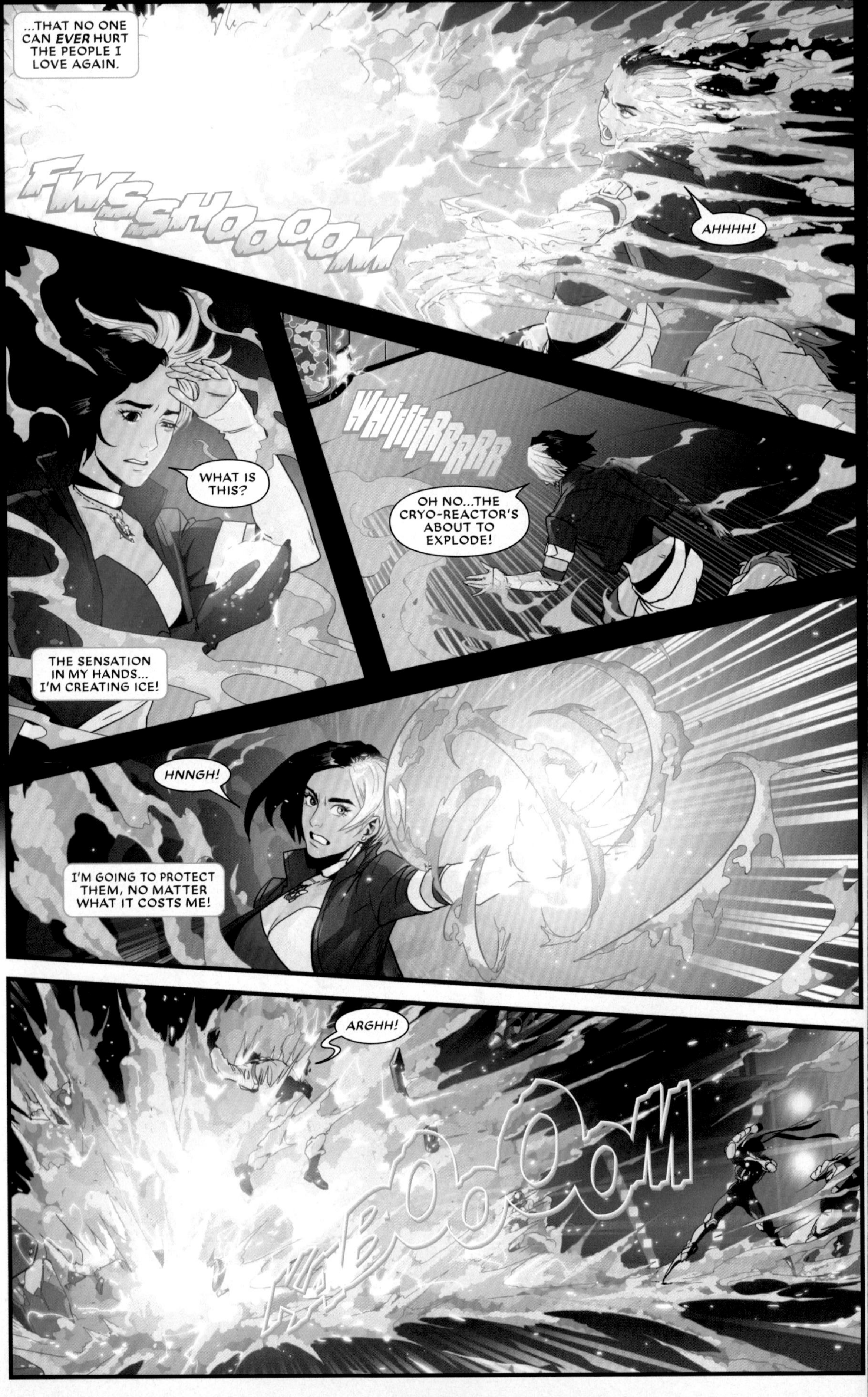
...THAT NO ONE CAN EVER HURT THE PEOPLE I LOVE AGAIN.
FWSSHOOOOOM
AHHHH!
WHAT IS THIS?
WHIIIIRRRRR
OH NO...THE CRYO-REACTOR'S ABOUT TO EXPLODE!
THE SENSATION IN MY HANDS... I'M CREATING ICE!
HNNGH!
I'M GOING TO PROTECT THEM, NO MATTER WHAT IT COSTS ME!
ARGHH!
KA-BOOOOOM

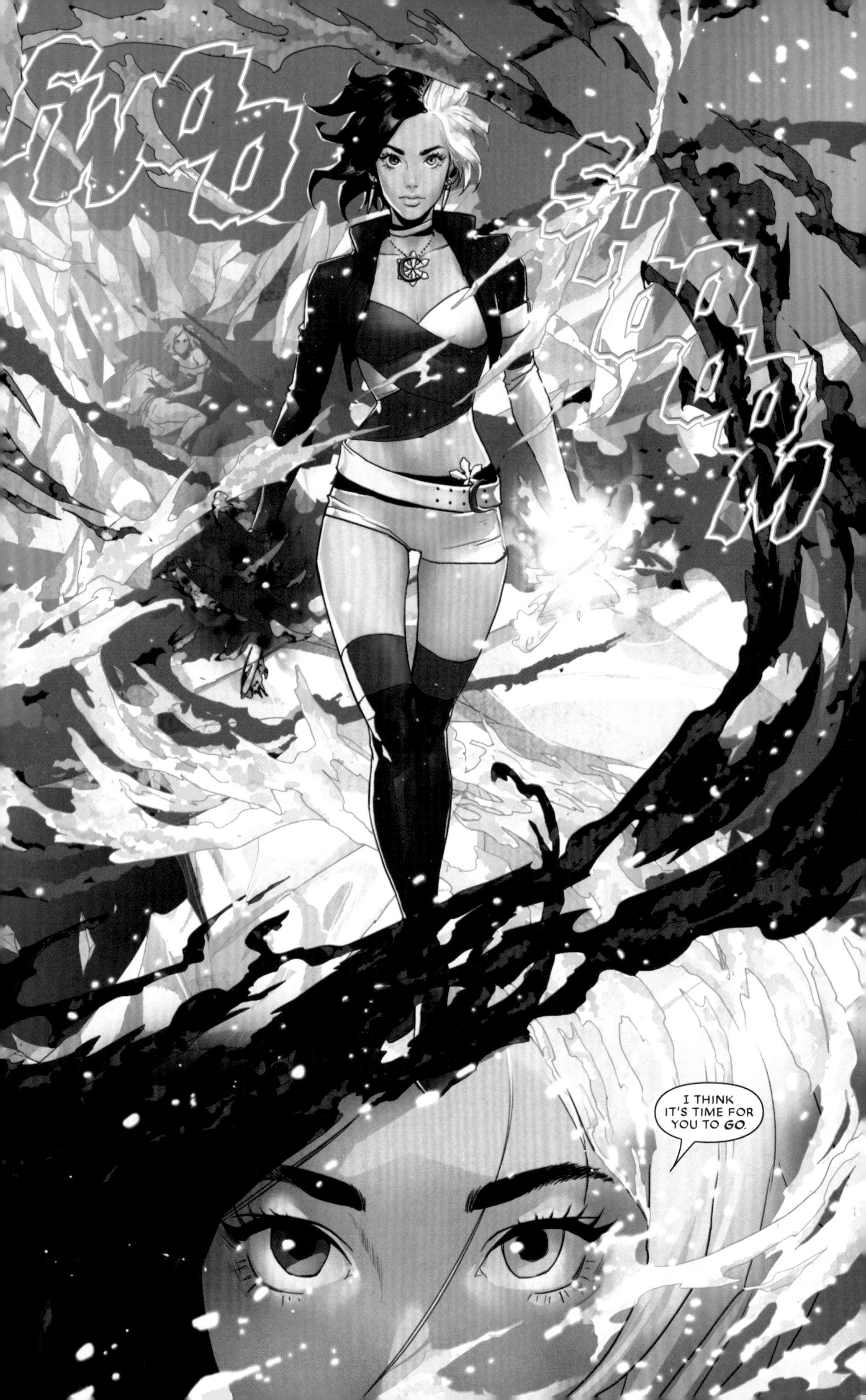
I THINK IT'S TIME FOR YOU TO *GO*.

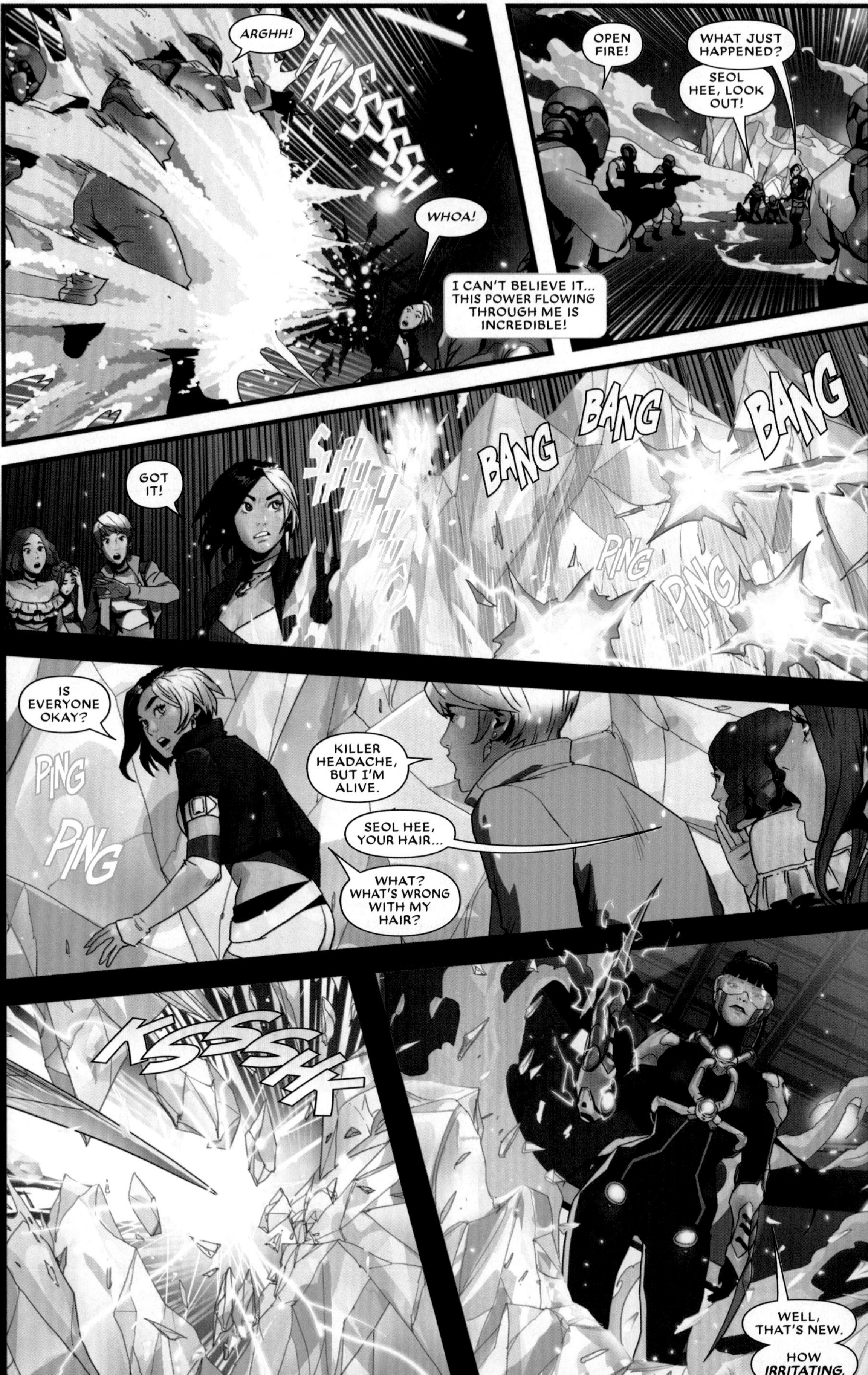
ARGHH!
FWISSSSH
WHOA!
I CAN'T BELIEVE IT... THIS POWER FLOWING THROUGH ME IS INCREDIBLE!
OPEN FIRE!
WHAT JUST HAPPENED?
SEOL HEE, LOOK OUT!
GOT IT!
BANG
BANG
BANG
PING
PING
IS EVERYONE OKAY?
KILLER HEADACHE, BUT I'M ALIVE.
SEOL HEE, YOUR HAIR...
WHAT? WHAT'S WRONG WITH MY HAIR?
PING
PING
KSSSHK
WELL, THAT'S NEW.
HOW *IRRITATING.*

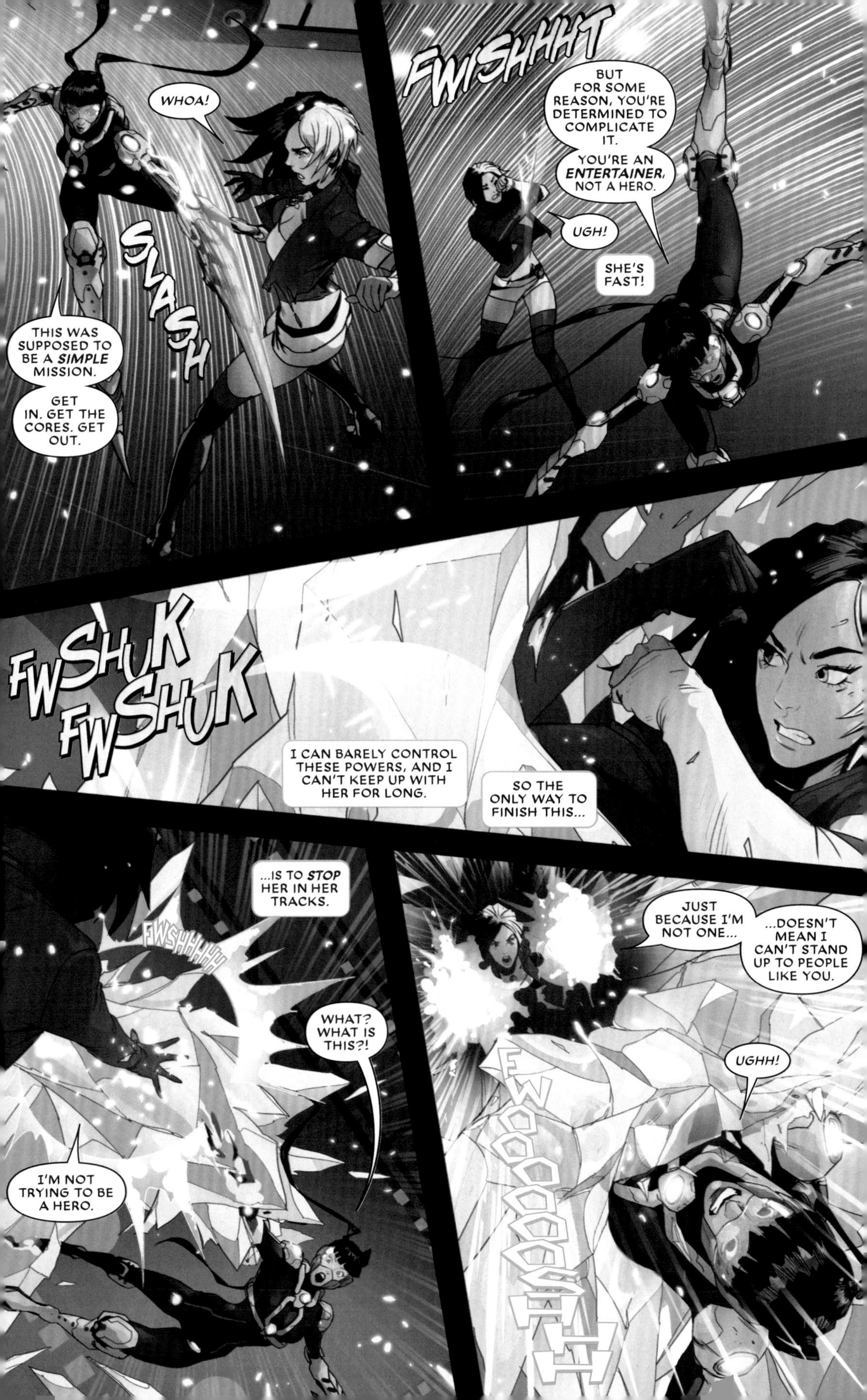
WHOA!
SLASH
THIS WAS SUPPOSED TO BE A SIMPLE MISSION.
GET IN. GET THE CORES. GET OUT.
FWISHHHT
BUT FOR SOME REASON, YOU'RE DETERMINED TO COMPLICATE IT.
YOU'RE AN ENTERTAINER, NOT A HERO.
UGH!
SHE'S FAST!
FWSHUK FWSHUK
I CAN BARELY CONTROL THESE POWERS, AND I CAN'T KEEP UP WITH HER FOR LONG.
SO THE ONLY WAY TO FINISH THIS...
...IS TO STOP HER IN HER TRACKS.
WHAT? WHAT IS THIS?!
I'M NOT TRYING TO BE A HERO.
JUST BECAUSE I'M NOT ONE...
...DOESN'T MEAN I CAN'T STAND UP TO PEOPLE LIKE YOU.
UGHH!
FWOOOOOSHHH

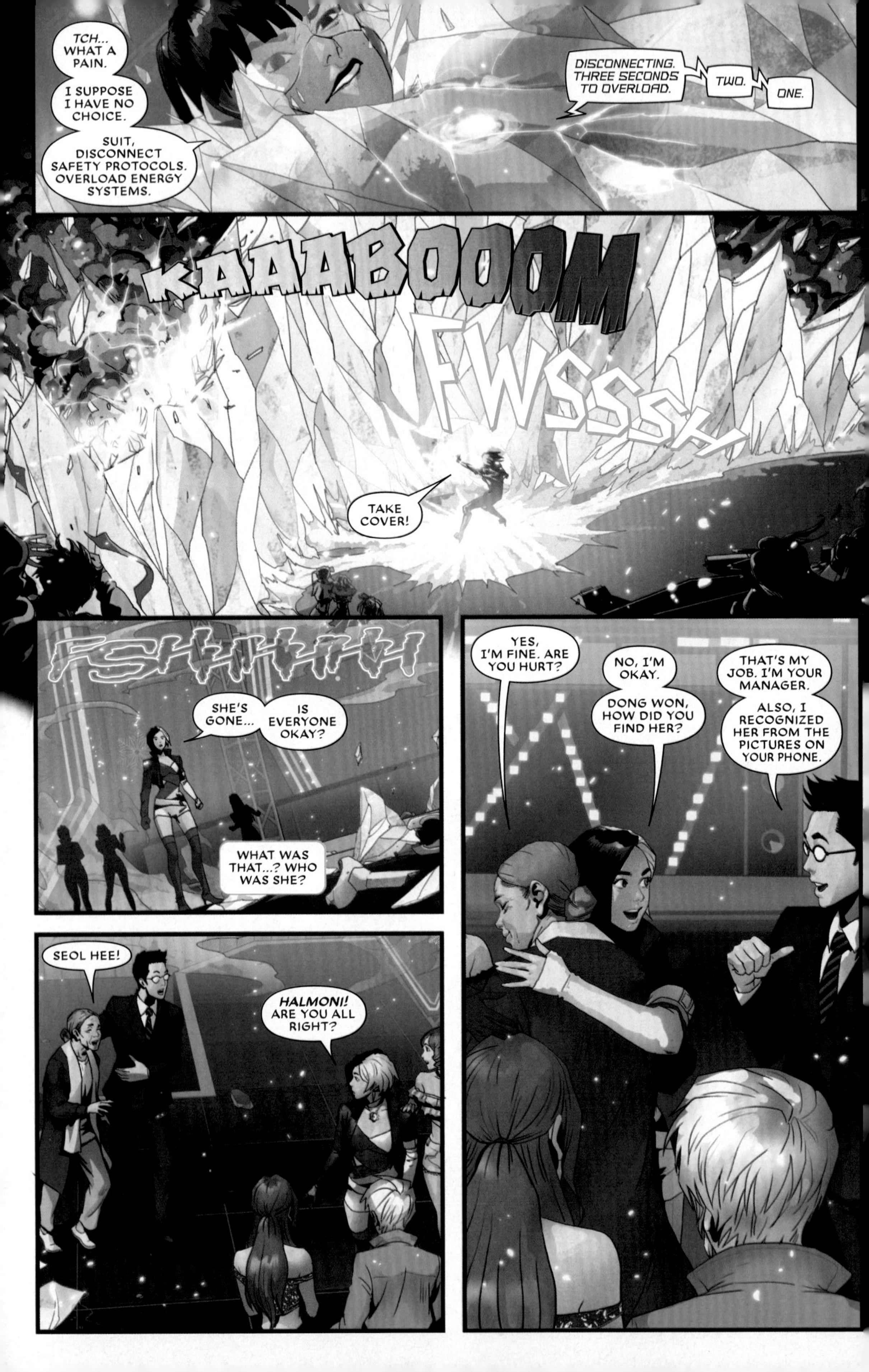
TCH... WHAT A PAIN.
I SUPPOSE I HAVE NO CHOICE.
SUIT, DISCONNECT SAFETY PROTOCOLS. OVERLOAD ENERGY SYSTEMS.
DISCONNECTING. THREE SECONDS TO OVERLOAD.
TWO.
ONE.
KAAABOOOM
FWSSSH
TAKE COVER!
FSHHHHH
SHE'S GONE...
IS EVERYONE OKAY?
WHAT WAS THAT...? WHO WAS SHE?
SEOL HEE!
HALMONI! ARE YOU ALL RIGHT?
YES, I'M FINE. ARE YOU HURT?
NO, I'M OKAY.
DONG WON, HOW DID YOU FIND HER?
THAT'S MY JOB. I'M YOUR MANAGER.
ALSO, I RECOGNIZED HER FROM THE PICTURES ON YOUR PHONE.

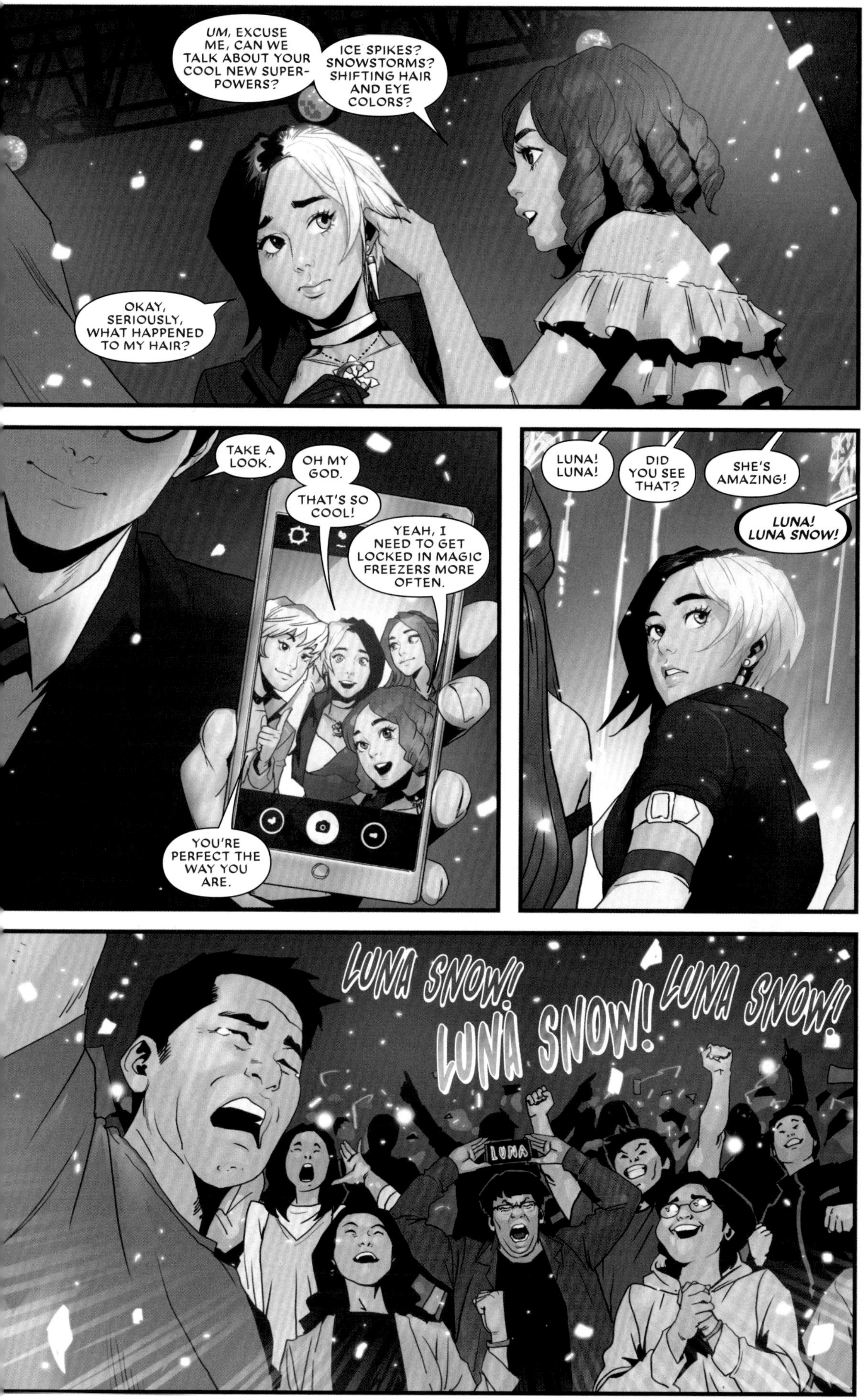

UM, EXCUSE ME, CAN WE TALK ABOUT YOUR COOL NEW SUPER-POWERS?
ICE SPIKES? SNOWSTORMS? SHIFTING HAIR AND EYE COLORS?
OKAY, SERIOUSLY, WHAT HAPPENED TO MY HAIR?
TAKE A LOOK.
OH MY GOD.
THAT'S SO COOL!
YEAH, I NEED TO GET LOCKED IN MAGIC FREEZERS MORE OFTEN.
YOU'RE PERFECT THE WAY YOU ARE.
LUNA! LUNA!
DID YOU SEE THAT?
SHE'S AMAZING!
LUNA! LUNA SNOW!
LUNA SNOW!
LUNA SNOW!
LUNA SNOW!
LUNA

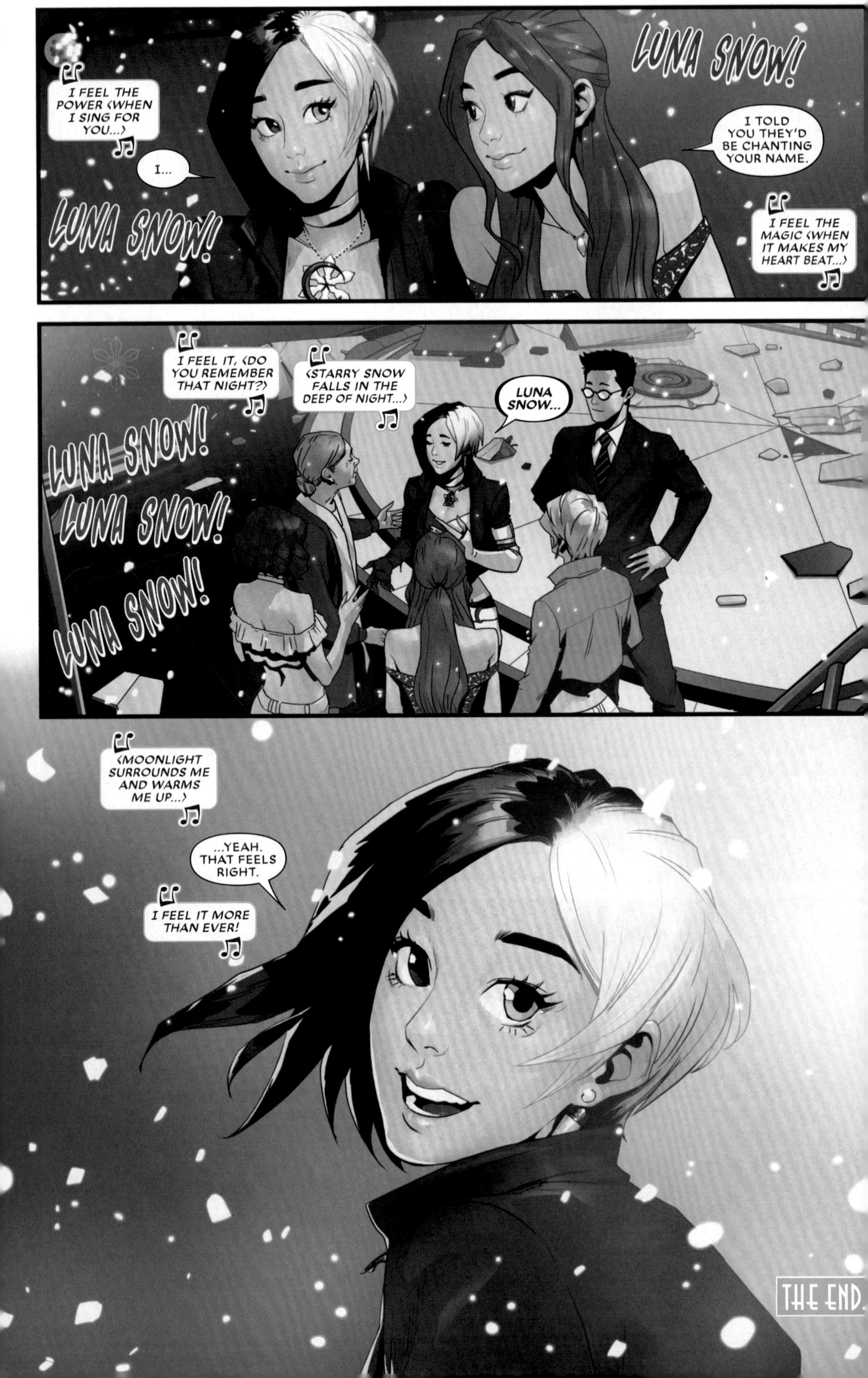
I FEEL THE POWER ‹WHEN I SING FOR YOU...›
I...
LUNA SNOW!
LUNA SNOW!
I TOLD YOU THEY'D BE CHANTING YOUR NAME.
I FEEL THE MAGIC ‹WHEN IT MAKES MY HEART BEAT...›
I FEEL IT, ‹DO YOU REMEMBER THAT NIGHT?›
‹STARRY SNOW FALLS IN THE DEEP OF NIGHT...›
LUNA SNOW...
LUNA SNOW!
LUNA SNOW!
LUNA SNOW!
‹MOONLIGHT SURROUNDS ME AND WARMS ME UP...›
...YEAH. THAT FEELS RIGHT.
I FEEL IT MORE THAN EVER!
THE END

re: LUNA SNOW

Thank you for picking up this comic! Over a year ago, we introduced Marvel's first K-pop super hero, Luna Snow, to the world via our hit mobile game *MARVEL Future Fight*. Her fans have embraced her, and we are grateful for the tremendous support. Since then, she has had two hit singles and two iconic costumes, and now she has her own cool origin story! We are especially ecstatic that the legendary Alyssa Wong is able to explore Luna Snow in this unique tale, expanding on her character and giving her a proper introduction into the Marvel Universe. In celebration, we are hard at work collaborating with the Netmarble Monster team to introduce a brand-new costume that fits her musical lifestyle. Luna Snow is all about balancing her musical career and being a super hero. My favorite part of the costume is the introduction of her custom headphones with her iconic emblems on the outside.

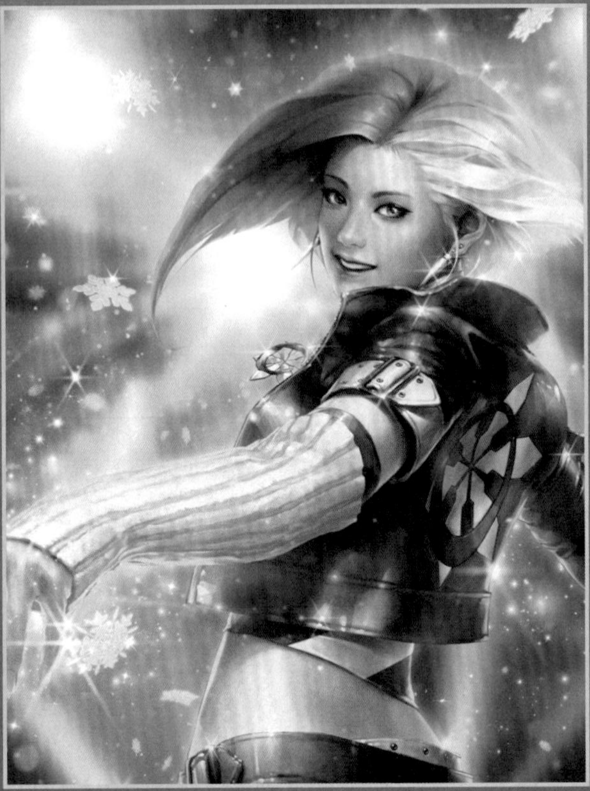

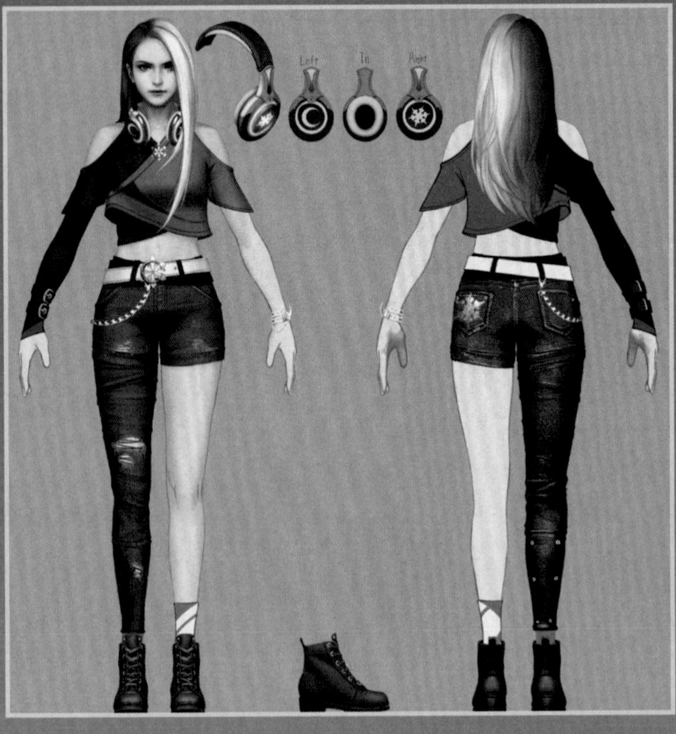
Left
In
Right

Her trendy blouse and jean shorts further her iconic dual-tone colors and designs, which define her look. This time, Luna is also sporting a very cool, long hairstyle and all-new accessories on her belt and wrists. With this brand-new outfit, we are also planning on a special remix version of her original debut song, "Tonight." We hope you like it! Did you know the last panel of this comic is a throwback to Luna's original debut poster (above)? I'm crying with tears of joy. If you haven't played *MARVEL Future Fight*, download it for free and give it a spin!

— Danny Koo
Marvel Games Senior Producer, Asia

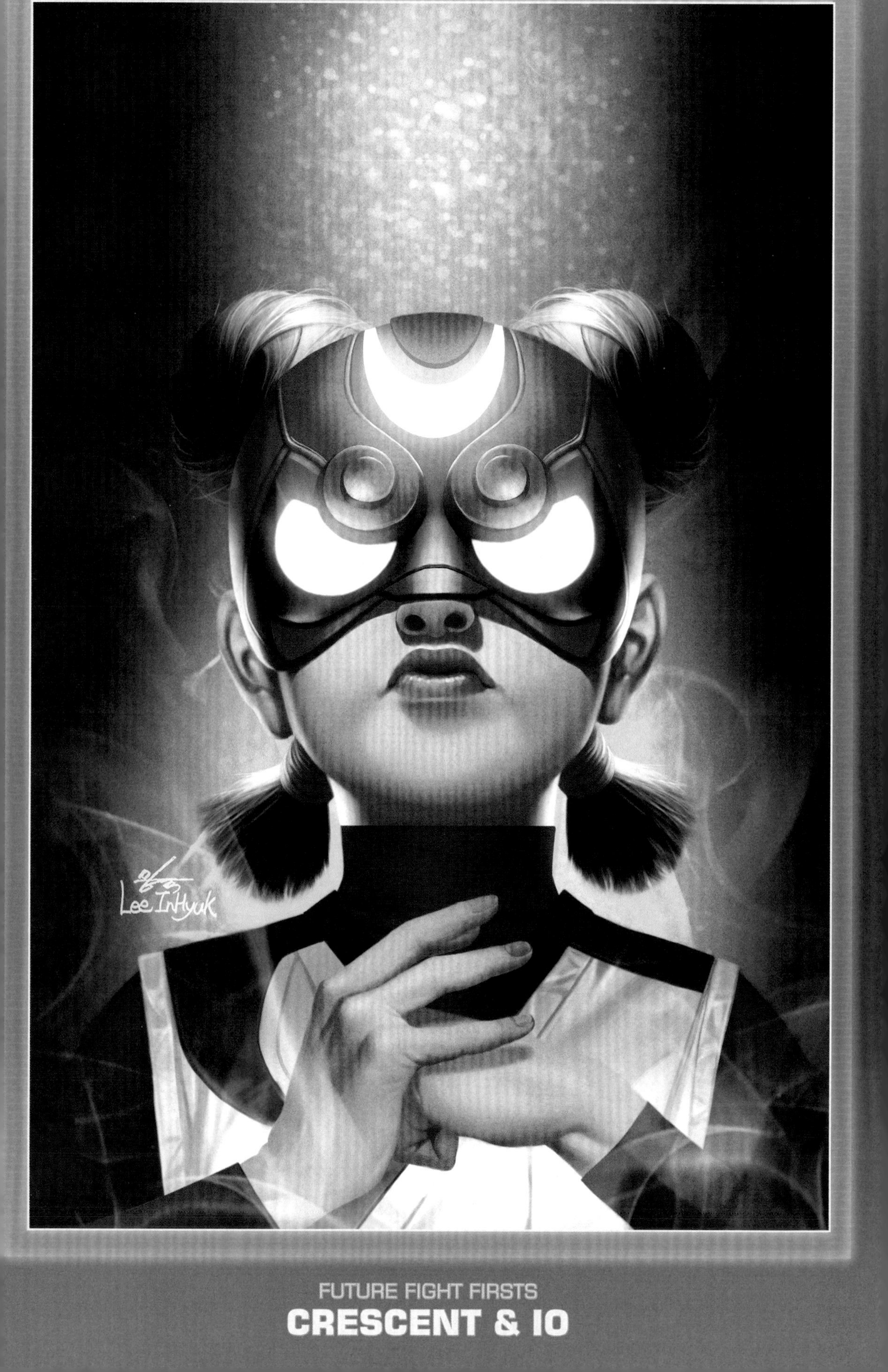
Lee InHyuk

FUTURE FIGHT FIRSTS
CRESCENT & IO

MARVEL

FUTURE FIGHT FIRSTS

Dan Bi is a taekwondo prodigy and the owner of an enchanted mask, which she uses to summon a mystical bear spirit named Io. Together they're the crimefighting duo known as

CRESCENT & IO

With Io by her side, Dan Bi battles global threats as a member of Jimmy Woo's new Agents of Atlas. But how did Crescent and Io become one of the most formidable fighting forces this side of Seoul?

WRITER
ALYSSA WONG

ARTIST
JON LAM

COLORIST
PARIS ALLEYNE

LETTERER
VC's JOE SABINO

COVER ARTIST
INHYUK LEE

LOGO DESIGN
JAY BOWEN

ASSISTANT EDITORS
LINDSEY COHICK & TOM GRONEMAN

EDITOR
MARK PANICCIA

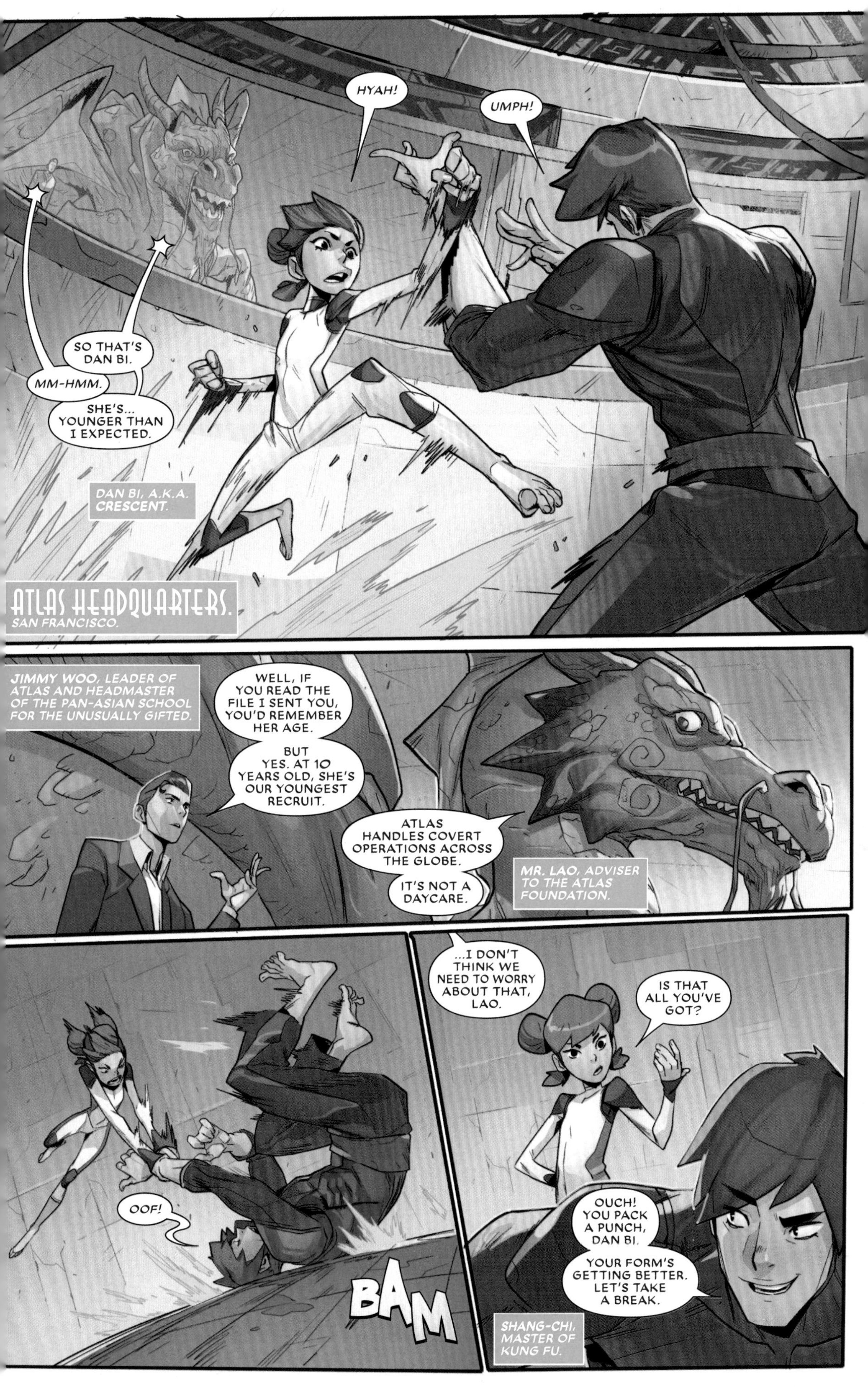
HYAH!
UMPH!
SO THAT'S DAN BI.
MM-HMM.
SHE'S... YOUNGER THAN I EXPECTED.
DAN BI, A.K.A. CRESCENT.
ATLAS HEADQUARTERS.
SAN FRANCISCO.
JIMMY WOO, LEADER OF ATLAS AND HEADMASTER OF THE PAN-ASIAN SCHOOL FOR THE UNUSUALLY GIFTED.
WELL, IF YOU READ THE FILE I SENT YOU, YOU'D REMEMBER HER AGE.
BUT YES. AT 10 YEARS OLD, SHE'S OUR YOUNGEST RECRUIT.
ATLAS HANDLES COVERT OPERATIONS ACROSS THE GLOBE.
IT'S NOT A DAYCARE.
MR. LAO, ADVISER TO THE ATLAS FOUNDATION.
OOF!
BAM
...I DON'T THINK WE NEED TO WORRY ABOUT THAT, LAO.
IS THAT ALL YOU'VE GOT?
OUCH! YOU PACK A PUNCH, DAN BI.
YOUR FORM'S GETTING BETTER. LET'S TAKE A BREAK.
SHANG-CHI, MASTER OF KUNG FU.

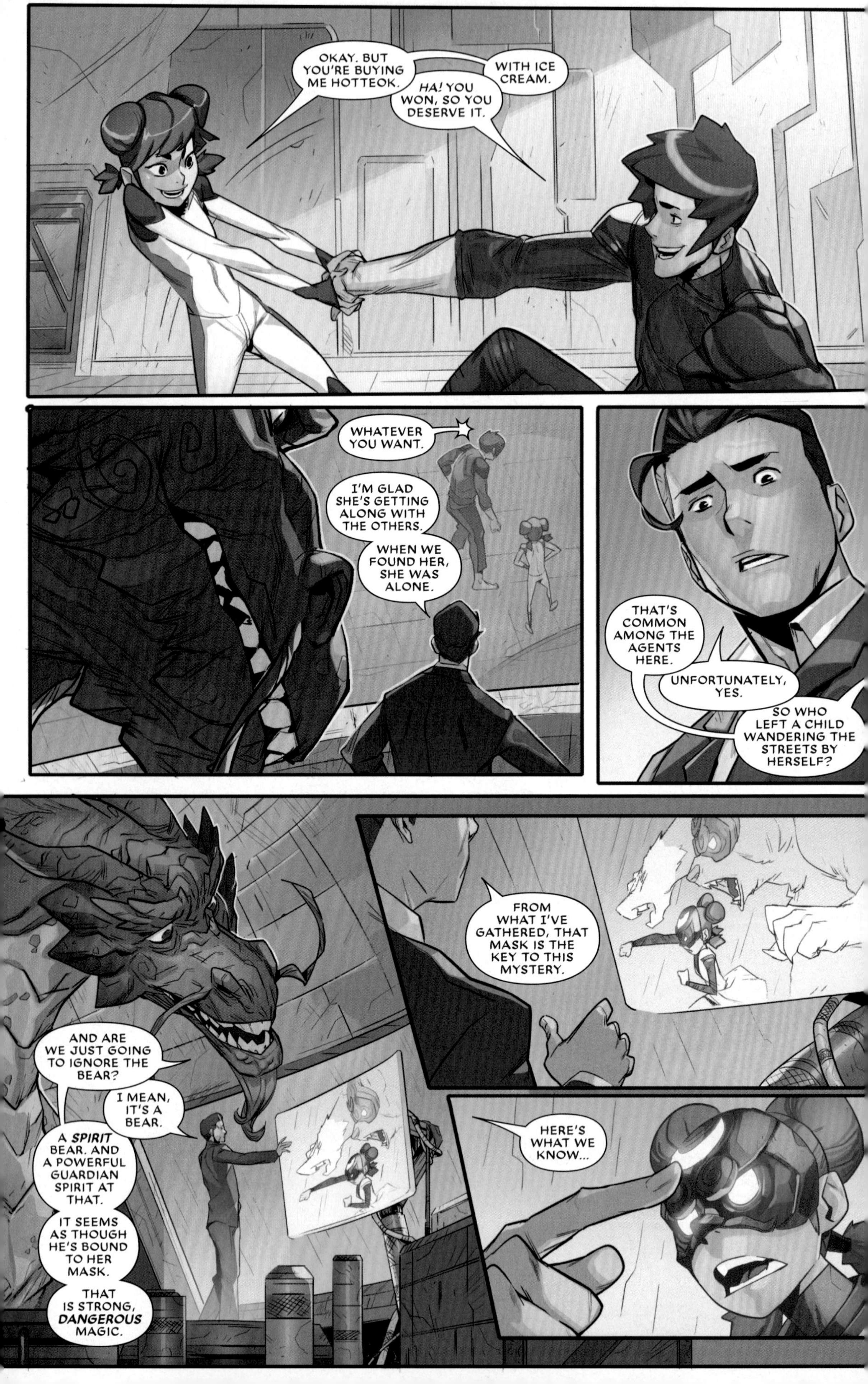
OKAY. BUT YOU'RE BUYING ME HOTTEOK.
WITH ICE CREAM.
HA! YOU WON, SO YOU DESERVE IT.
WHATEVER YOU WANT.
I'M GLAD SHE'S GETTING ALONG WITH THE OTHERS.
WHEN WE FOUND HER, SHE WAS ALONE.
THAT'S COMMON AMONG THE AGENTS HERE.
UNFORTUNATELY, YES.
SO WHO LEFT A CHILD WANDERING THE STREETS BY HERSELF?
FROM WHAT I'VE GATHERED, THAT MASK IS THE KEY TO THIS MYSTERY.
HERE'S WHAT WE KNOW...
AND ARE WE JUST GOING TO IGNORE THE BEAR?
I MEAN, IT'S A BEAR.
A ***SPIRIT*** BEAR. AND A POWERFUL GUARDIAN SPIRIT AT THAT.
IT SEEMS AS THOUGH HE'S BOUND TO HER MASK.
THAT IS STRONG, ***DANGEROUS*** MAGIC.

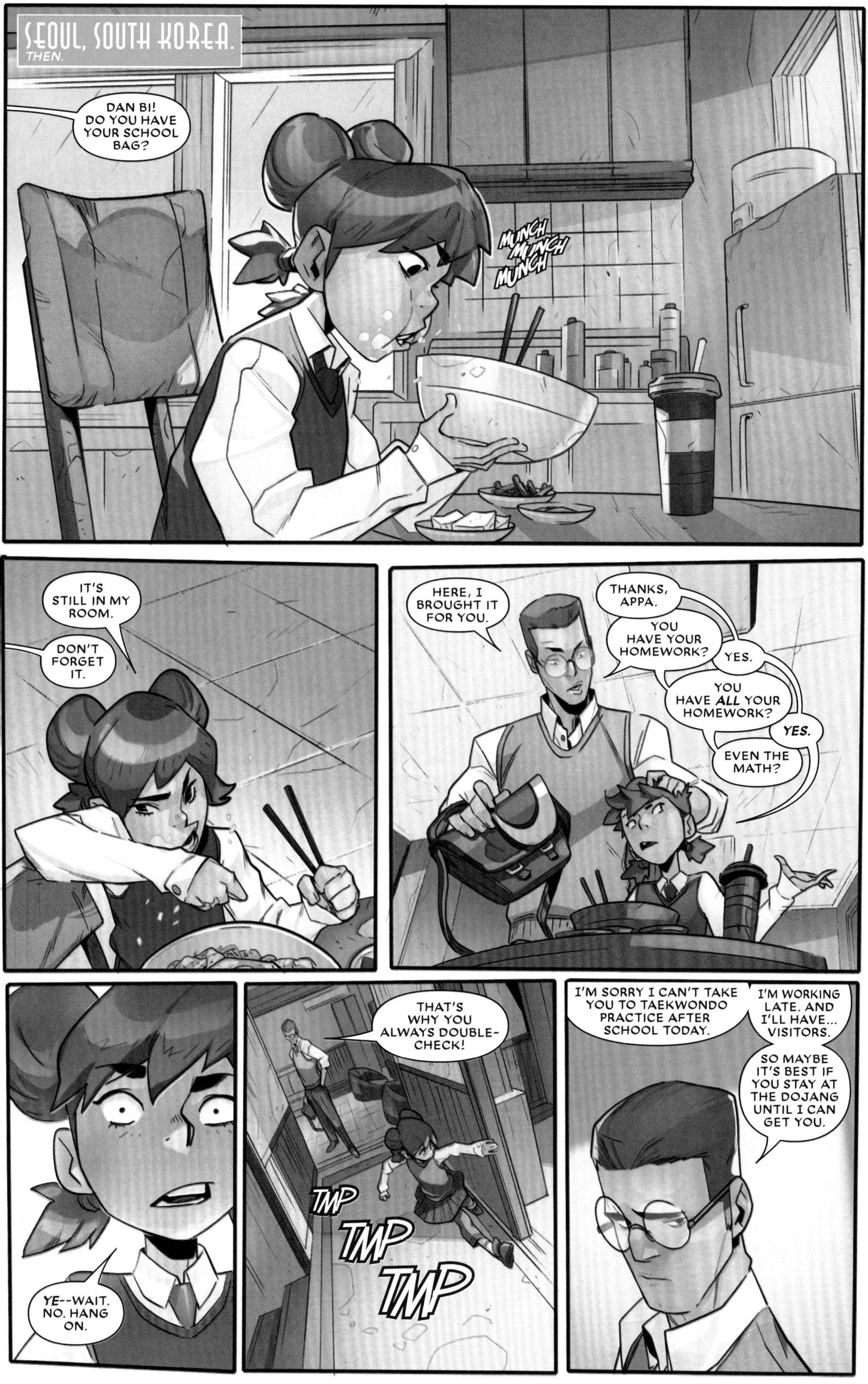
SEOUL, SOUTH KOREA.
THEN.
DAN BI! DO YOU HAVE YOUR SCHOOL BAG?
MUNCH MUNCH MUNCH
IT'S STILL IN MY ROOM.
DON'T FORGET IT.
HERE, I BROUGHT IT FOR YOU.
THANKS, APPA.
YOU HAVE YOUR HOMEWORK?
YES.
YOU HAVE ALL YOUR HOMEWORK?
YES.
EVEN THE MATH?
YE--WAIT. NO. HANG ON.
THAT'S WHY YOU ALWAYS DOUBLE-CHECK!
TMP TMP TMP
I'M SORRY I CAN'T TAKE YOU TO TAEKWONDO PRACTICE AFTER SCHOOL TODAY.
I'M WORKING LATE. AND I'LL HAVE... VISITORS.
SO MAYBE IT'S BEST IF YOU STAY AT THE DOJANG UNTIL I CAN GET YOU.

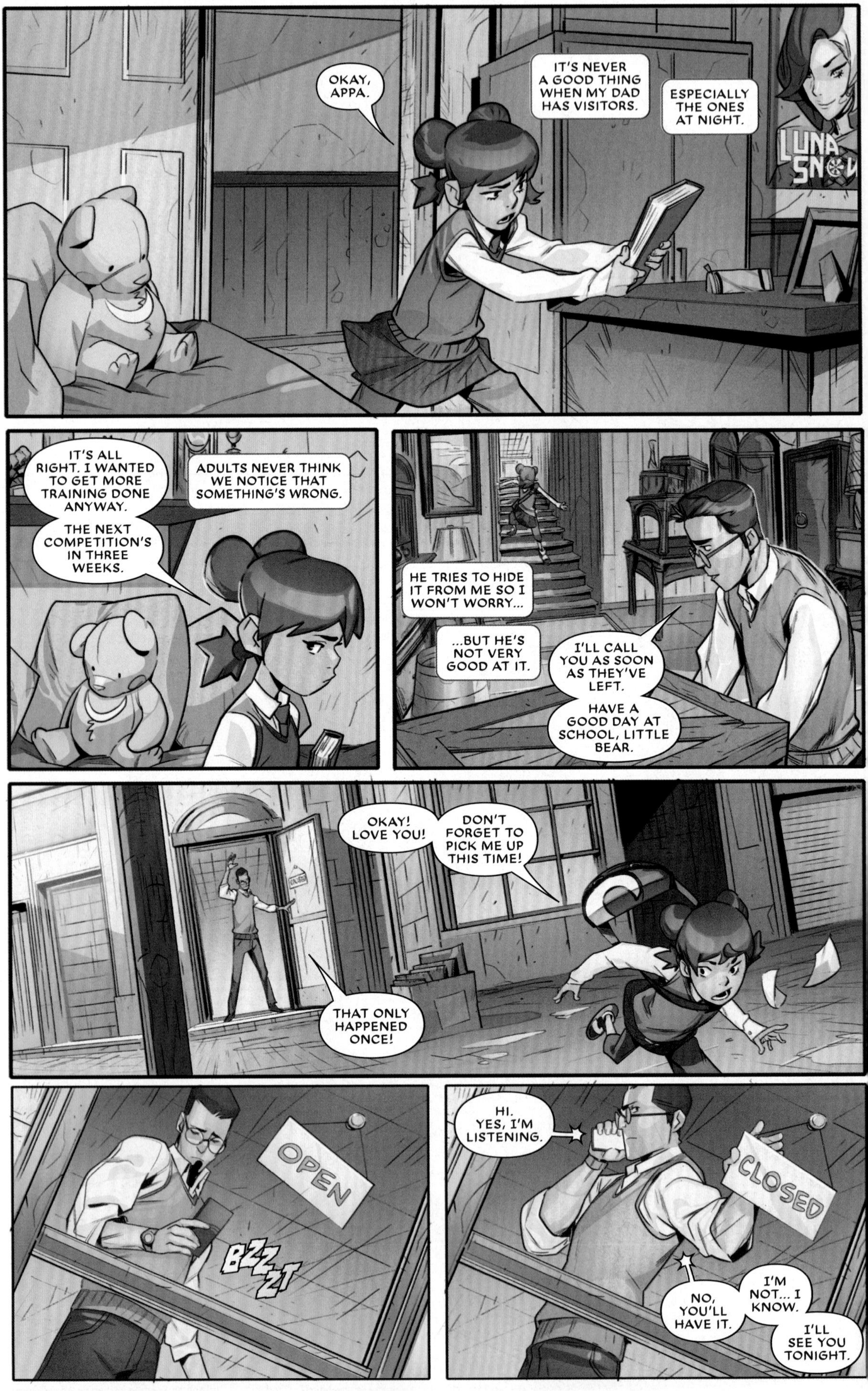

OKAY, APPA.
IT'S NEVER A GOOD THING WHEN MY DAD HAS VISITORS.
ESPECIALLY THE ONES AT NIGHT.
LUNA SNOW
IT'S ALL RIGHT. I WANTED TO GET MORE TRAINING DONE ANYWAY.
THE NEXT COMPETITION'S IN THREE WEEKS.
ADULTS NEVER THINK WE NOTICE THAT SOMETHING'S WRONG.
HE TRIES TO HIDE IT FROM ME SO I WON'T WORRY...
...BUT HE'S NOT VERY GOOD AT IT.
I'LL CALL YOU AS SOON AS THEY'VE LEFT.
HAVE A GOOD DAY AT SCHOOL, LITTLE BEAR.
OKAY! LOVE YOU!
DON'T FORGET TO PICK ME UP THIS TIME!
THAT ONLY HAPPENED ONCE!
OPEN
BZZZT
HI. YES, I'M LISTENING.
CLOSED
NO, YOU'LL HAVE IT.
I'M NOT... I KNOW.
I'LL SEE YOU TONIGHT.

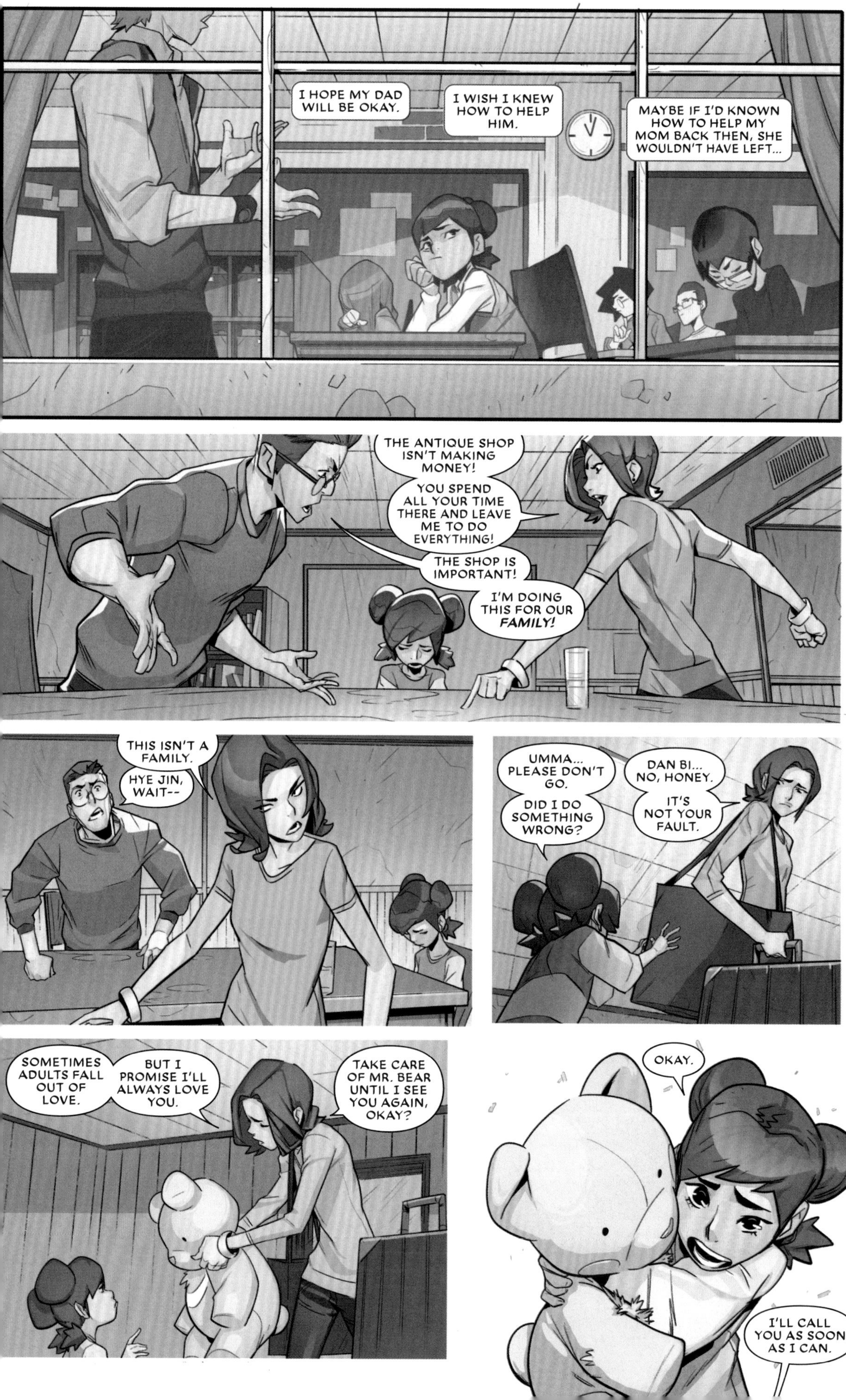
I HOPE MY DAD WILL BE OKAY.
I WISH I KNEW HOW TO HELP HIM.
MAYBE IF I'D KNOWN HOW TO HELP MY MOM BACK THEN, SHE WOULDN'T HAVE LEFT...
THE ANTIQUE SHOP ISN'T MAKING MONEY!
YOU SPEND ALL YOUR TIME THERE AND LEAVE ME TO DO EVERYTHING!
THE SHOP IS IMPORTANT!
I'M DOING THIS FOR OUR *FAMILY!*
THIS ISN'T A FAMILY.
HYE JIN, WAIT--
UMMA... PLEASE DON'T GO.
DID I DO SOMETHING WRONG?
DAN BI... NO, HONEY.
IT'S NOT YOUR FAULT.
SOMETIMES ADULTS FALL OUT OF LOVE.
BUT I PROMISE I'LL ALWAYS LOVE YOU.
TAKE CARE OF MR. BEAR UNTIL I SEE YOU AGAIN, OKAY?
OKAY.
I'LL CALL YOU AS SOON AS I CAN.

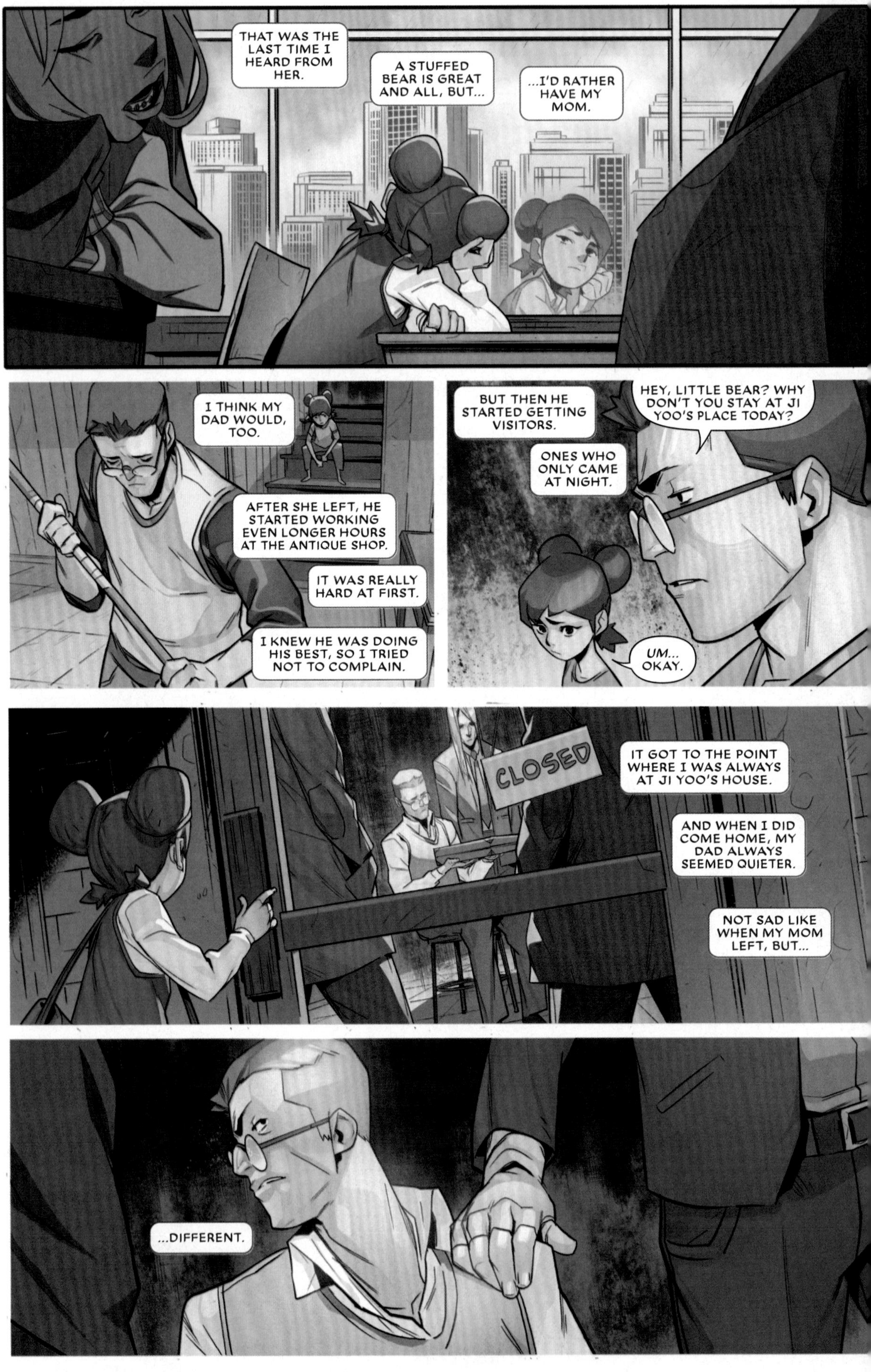
THAT WAS THE LAST TIME I HEARD FROM HER.
A STUFFED BEAR IS GREAT AND ALL, BUT...
...I'D RATHER HAVE MY MOM.
I THINK MY DAD WOULD, TOO.
AFTER SHE LEFT, HE STARTED WORKING EVEN LONGER HOURS AT THE ANTIQUE SHOP.
IT WAS REALLY HARD AT FIRST.
I KNEW HE WAS DOING HIS BEST, SO I TRIED NOT TO COMPLAIN.
BUT THEN HE STARTED GETTING VISITORS.
HEY, LITTLE BEAR? WHY DON'T YOU STAY AT JI YOO'S PLACE TODAY?
ONES WHO ONLY CAME AT NIGHT.
UM... OKAY.
CLOSED
IT GOT TO THE POINT WHERE I WAS ALWAYS AT JI YOO'S HOUSE.
AND WHEN I DID COME HOME, MY DAD ALWAYS SEEMED QUIETER.
NOT SAD LIKE WHEN MY MOM LEFT, BUT...
...DIFFERENT.

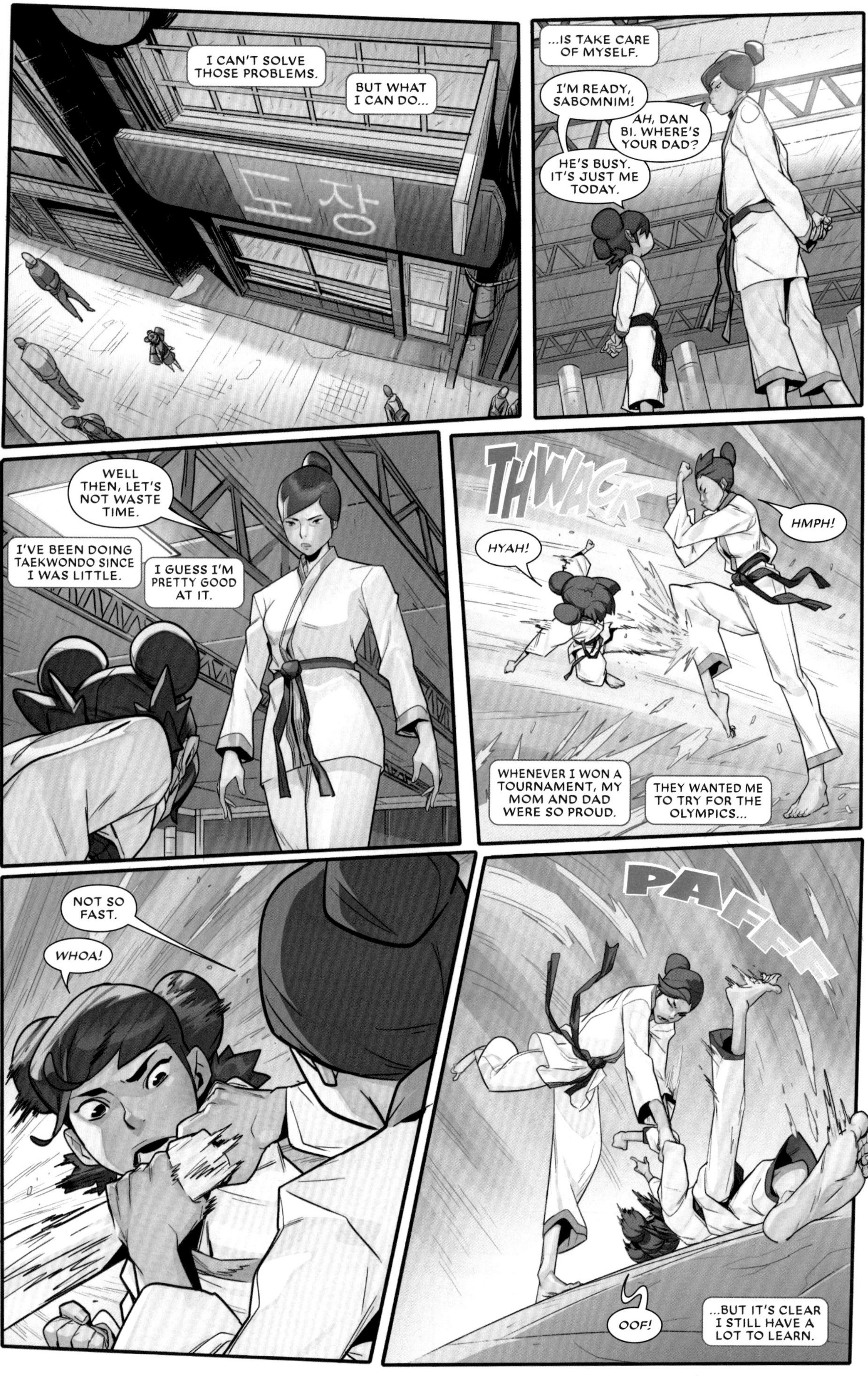

I CAN'T SOLVE THOSE PROBLEMS.
BUT WHAT I CAN DO...
도장
...IS TAKE CARE OF MYSELF.
I'M READY, SABOMNIM!
AH, DAN BI. WHERE'S YOUR DAD?
HE'S BUSY. IT'S JUST ME TODAY.
WELL THEN, LET'S NOT WASTE TIME.
I'VE BEEN DOING TAEKWONDO SINCE I WAS LITTLE.
I GUESS I'M PRETTY GOOD AT IT.
THWACK
HYAH!
HMPH!
WHENEVER I WON A TOURNAMENT, MY MOM AND DAD WERE SO PROUD.
THEY WANTED ME TO TRY FOR THE OLYMPICS...
NOT SO FAST.
WHOA!
PAFFF
OOF!
...BUT IT'S CLEAR I STILL HAVE A LOT TO LEARN.

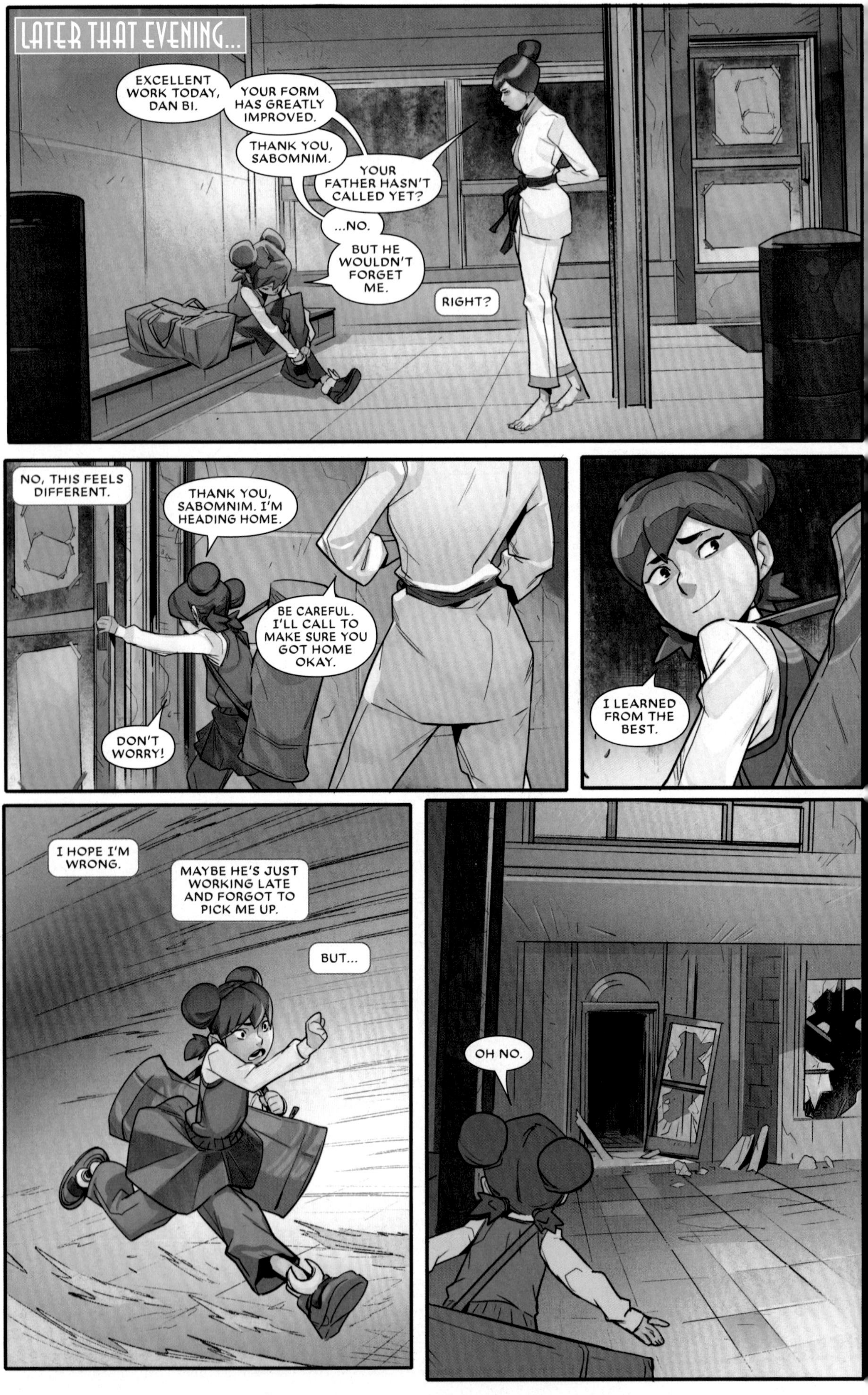
LATER THAT EVENING...
EXCELLENT WORK TODAY, DAN BI.
YOUR FORM HAS GREATLY IMPROVED.
THANK YOU, SABOMNIM.
YOUR FATHER HASN'T CALLED YET?
...NO.
BUT HE WOULDN'T FORGET ME.
RIGHT?
NO, THIS FEELS DIFFERENT.
THANK YOU, SABOMNIM. I'M HEADING HOME.
BE CAREFUL. I'LL CALL TO MAKE SURE YOU GOT HOME OKAY.
DON'T WORRY!
I LEARNED FROM THE BEST.
I HOPE I'M WRONG.
MAYBE HE'S JUST WORKING LATE AND FORGOT TO PICK ME UP.
BUT...
OH NO.

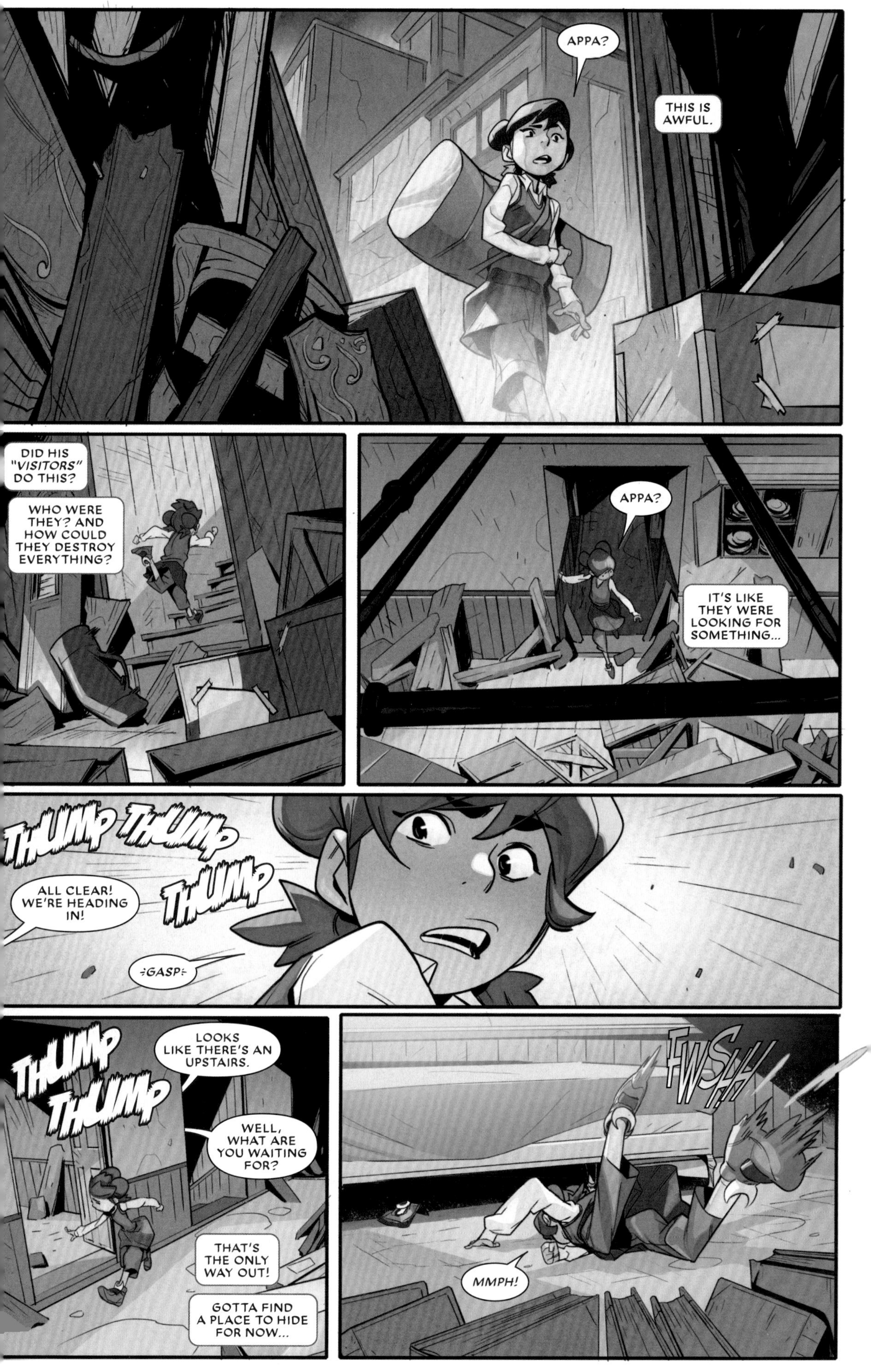
APPA?
THIS IS AWFUL.
DID HIS "VISITORS" DO THIS?
WHO WERE THEY? AND HOW COULD THEY DESTROY EVERYTHING?
APPA?
IT'S LIKE THEY WERE LOOKING FOR SOMETHING...
THUMP THUMP THUMP
ALL CLEAR! WE'RE HEADING IN!
GASP
THUMP THUMP
LOOKS LIKE THERE'S AN UPSTAIRS.
WELL, WHAT ARE YOU WAITING FOR?
THAT'S THE ONLY WAY OUT!
GOTTA FIND A PLACE TO HIDE FOR NOW...
FWSHH
MMPH!

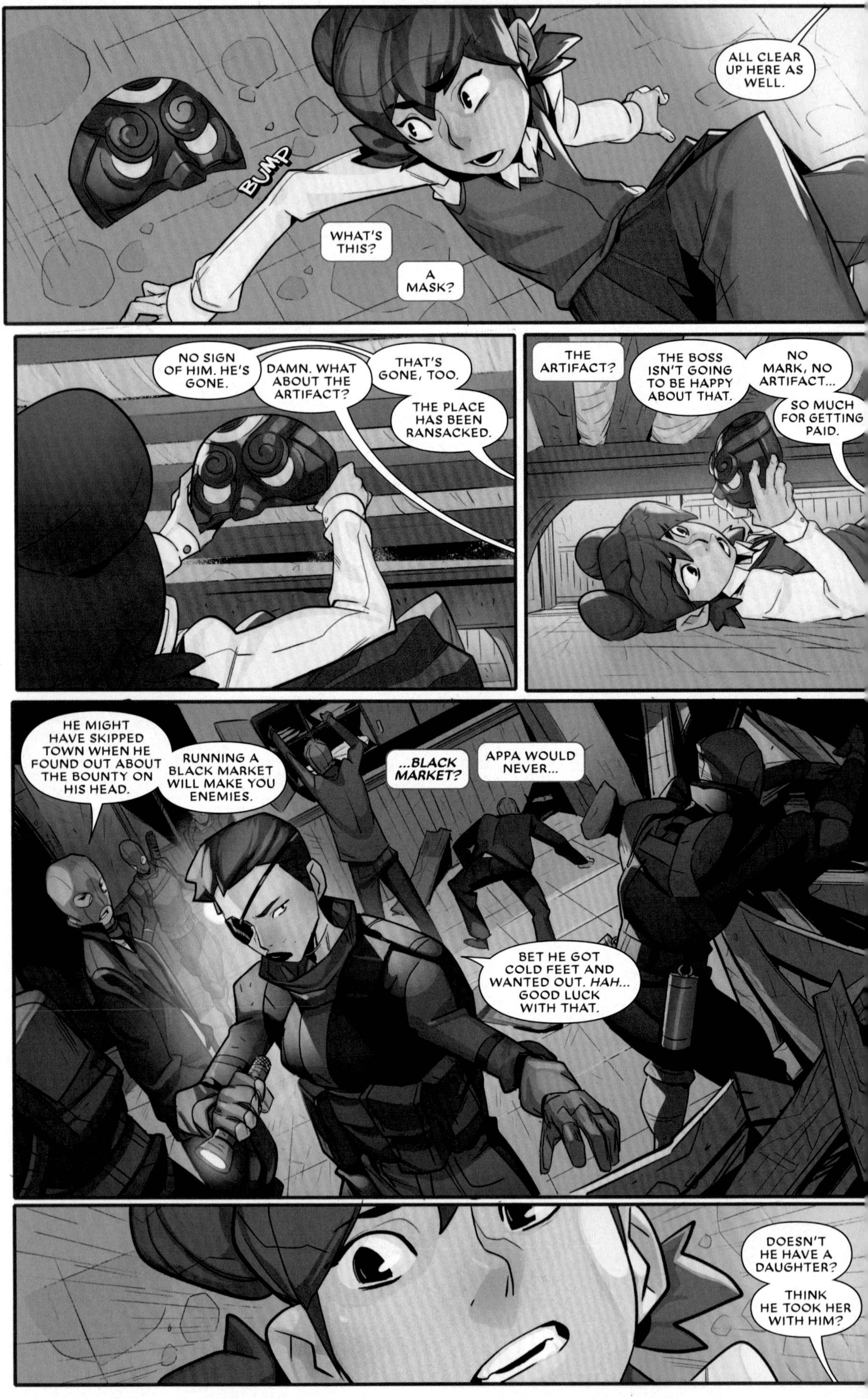
ALL CLEAR UP HERE AS WELL.
BUMP
WHAT'S THIS?
A MASK?
NO SIGN OF HIM. HE'S GONE.
DAMN. WHAT ABOUT THE ARTIFACT?
THAT'S GONE, TOO.
THE PLACE HAS BEEN RANSACKED.
THE ARTIFACT?
THE BOSS ISN'T GOING TO BE HAPPY ABOUT THAT.
NO MARK, NO ARTIFACT...
SO MUCH FOR GETTING PAID.
HE MIGHT HAVE SKIPPED TOWN WHEN HE FOUND OUT ABOUT THE BOUNTY ON HIS HEAD.
RUNNING A BLACK MARKET WILL MAKE YOU ENEMIES.
...*BLACK MARKET?*
APPA WOULD NEVER...
BET HE GOT COLD FEET AND WANTED OUT. *HAH...* GOOD LUCK WITH THAT.
DOESN'T HE HAVE A DAUGHTER?
THINK HE TOOK HER WITH HIM?

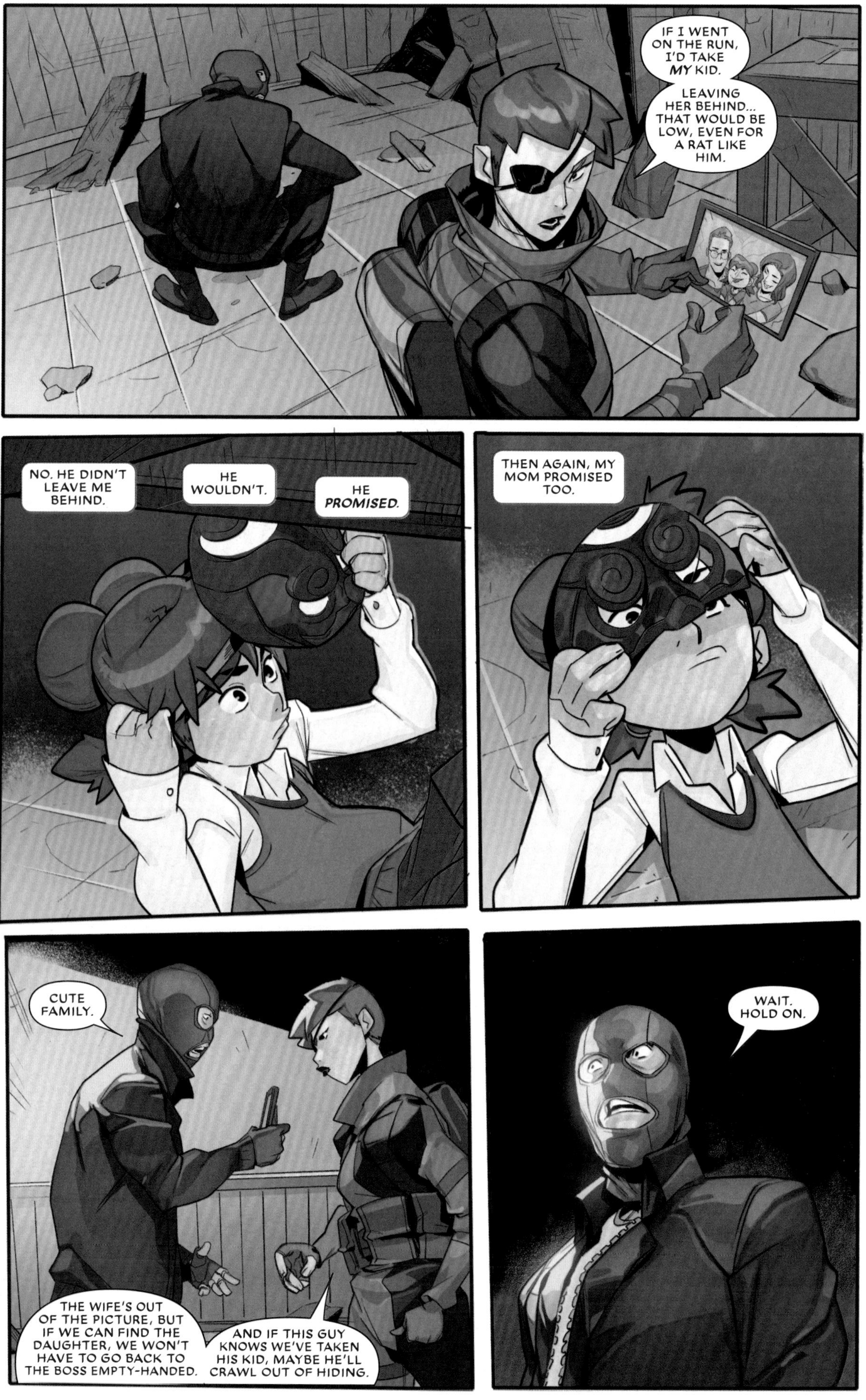
IF I WENT ON THE RUN, I'D TAKE MY KID.
LEAVING HER BEHIND... THAT WOULD BE LOW, EVEN FOR A RAT LIKE HIM.
NO. HE DIDN'T LEAVE ME BEHIND.
HE WOULDN'T.
HE PROMISED.
THEN AGAIN, MY MOM PROMISED TOO.
CUTE FAMILY.
THE WIFE'S OUT OF THE PICTURE, BUT IF WE CAN FIND THE DAUGHTER, WE WON'T HAVE TO GO BACK TO THE BOSS EMPTY-HANDED.
AND IF THIS GUY KNOWS WE'VE TAKEN HIS KID, MAYBE HE'LL CRAWL OUT OF HIDING.
WAIT. HOLD ON.

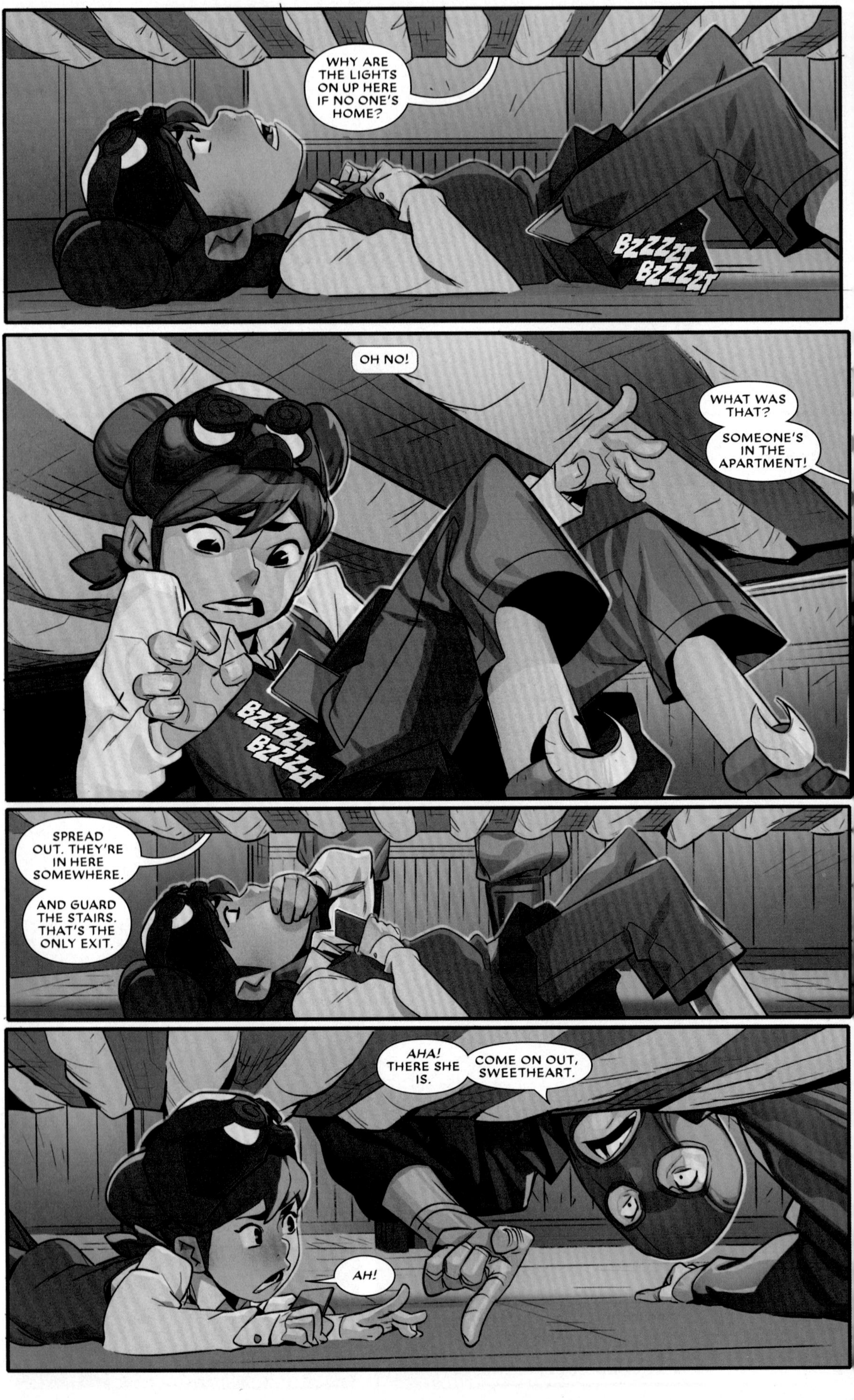
WHY ARE THE LIGHTS ON UP HERE IF NO ONE'S HOME?
BZZZZT BZZZZT
OH NO!
WHAT WAS THAT?
SOMEONE'S IN THE APARTMENT!
BZZZZT BZZZZT
SPREAD OUT. THEY'RE IN HERE SOMEWHERE.
AND GUARD THE STAIRS. THAT'S THE ONLY EXIT.
AHA! THERE SHE IS.
COME ON OUT, SWEETHEART.
AH!

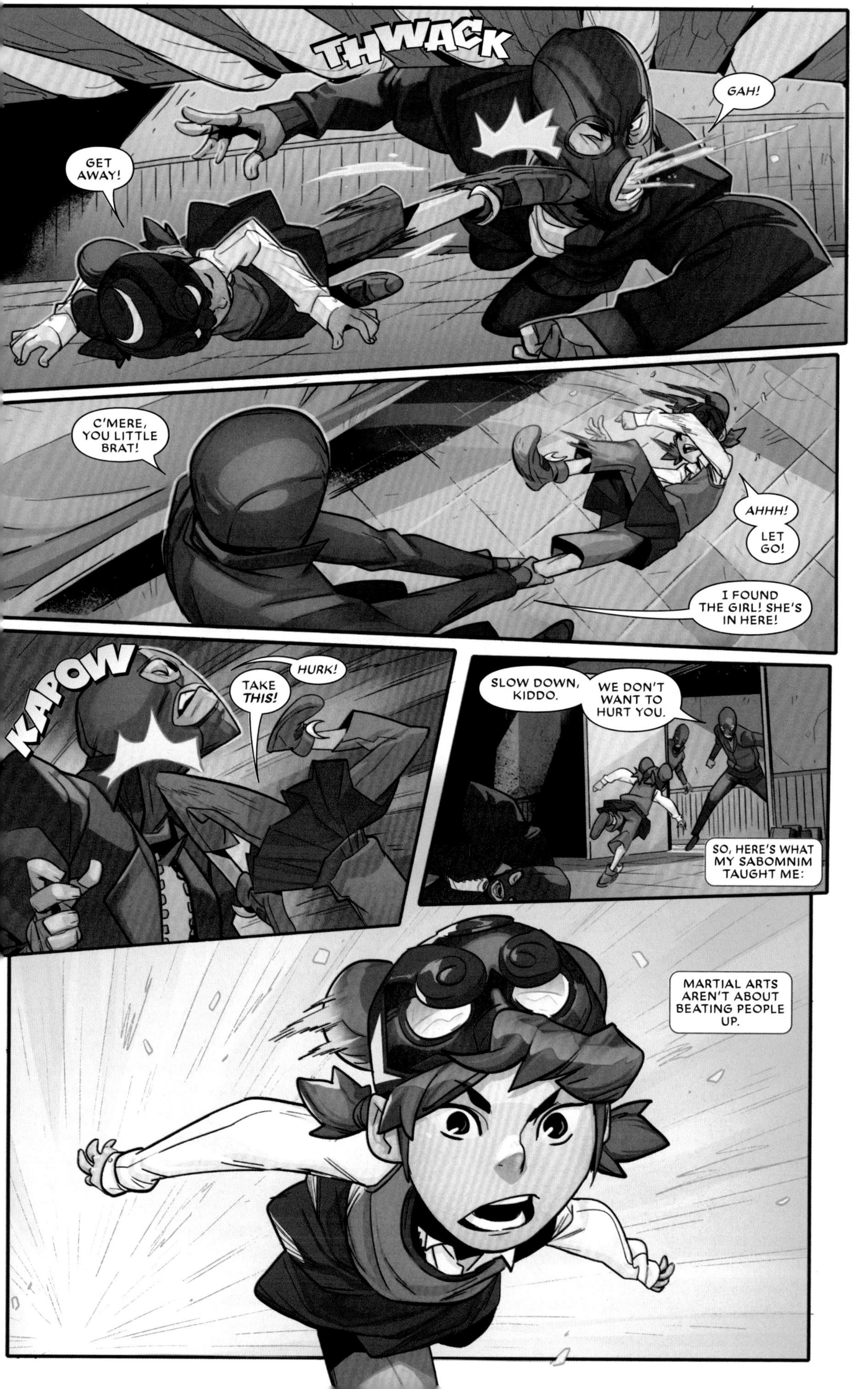
THWACK
GAH!
GET AWAY!
C'MERE, YOU LITTLE BRAT!
AHHH!
LET GO!
I FOUND THE GIRL! SHE'S IN HERE!
KAPOW
TAKE *THIS!*
HURK!
SLOW DOWN, KIDDO.
WE DON'T WANT TO HURT YOU.
SO, HERE'S WHAT MY SABOMNIM TAUGHT ME:
MARTIAL ARTS AREN'T ABOUT BEATING PEOPLE UP.

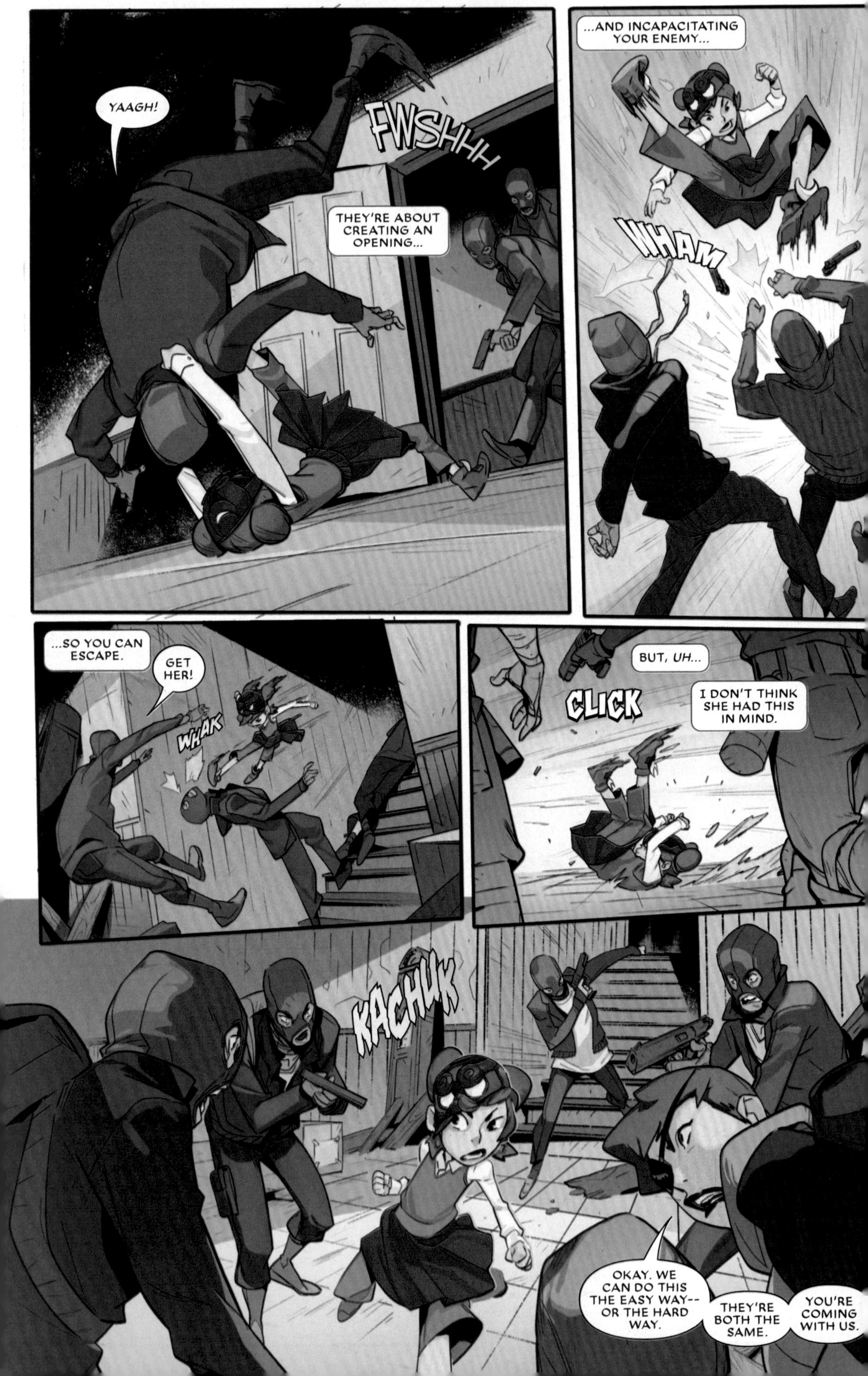
YAAGH!
FWSHHH
THEY'RE ABOUT CREATING AN OPENING...
...AND INCAPACITATING YOUR ENEMY...
WHAM
...SO YOU CAN ESCAPE.
GET HER!
WHAK
BUT, UH...
CLICK
I DON'T THINK SHE HAD THIS IN MIND.
KACHUK
OKAY. WE CAN DO THIS THE EASY WAY-- OR THE HARD WAY.
THEY'RE BOTH THE SAME.
YOU'RE COMING WITH US.

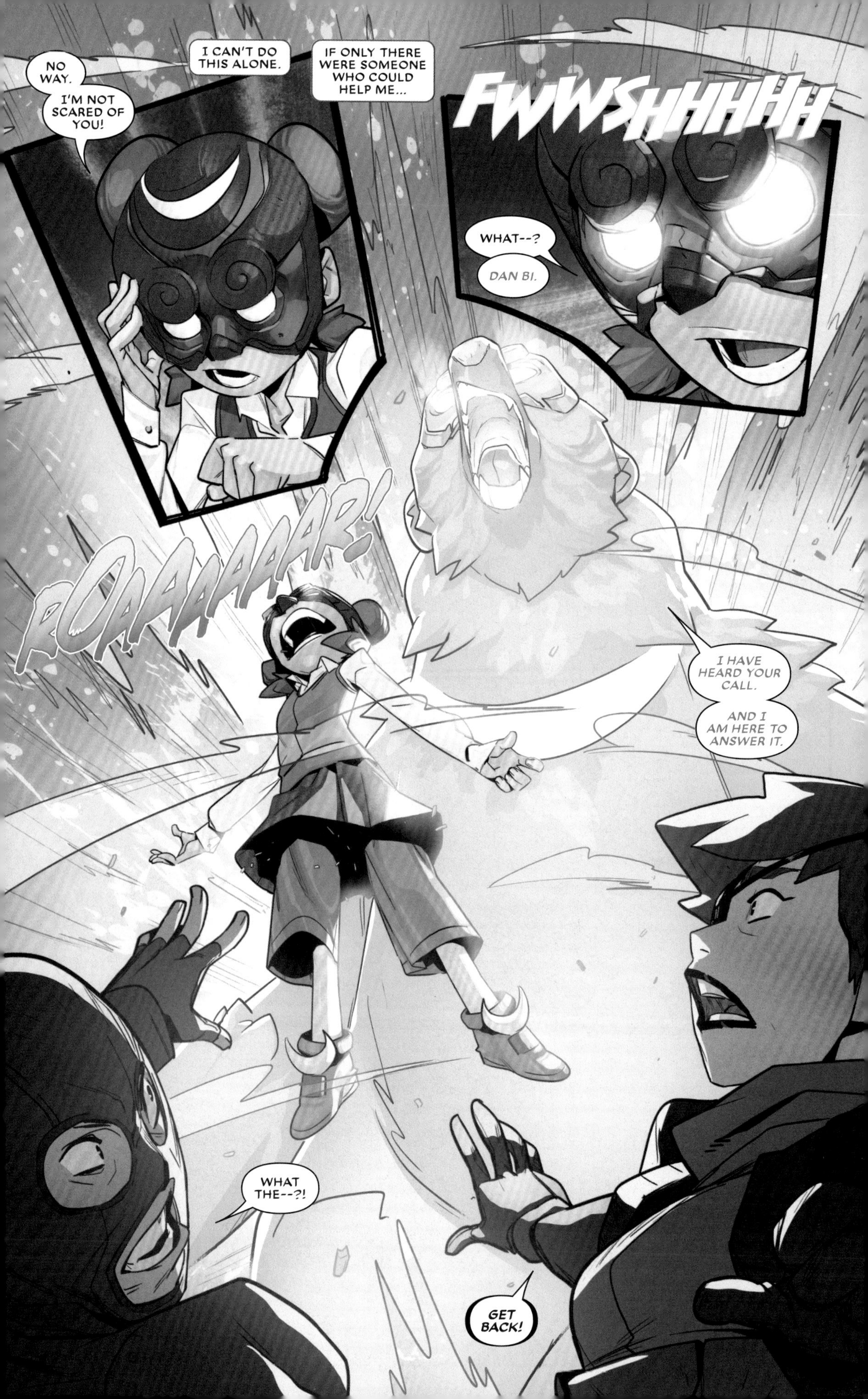

NO WAY.
I'M NOT SCARED OF YOU!
I CAN'T DO THIS ALONE.
IF ONLY THERE WERE SOMEONE WHO COULD HELP ME...
FWWSHHHHH
WHAT--?
DAN BI.
ROAAAAAAR!
I HAVE HEARD YOUR CALL.
AND I AM HERE TO ANSWER IT.
WHAT THE--?!
GET BACK!

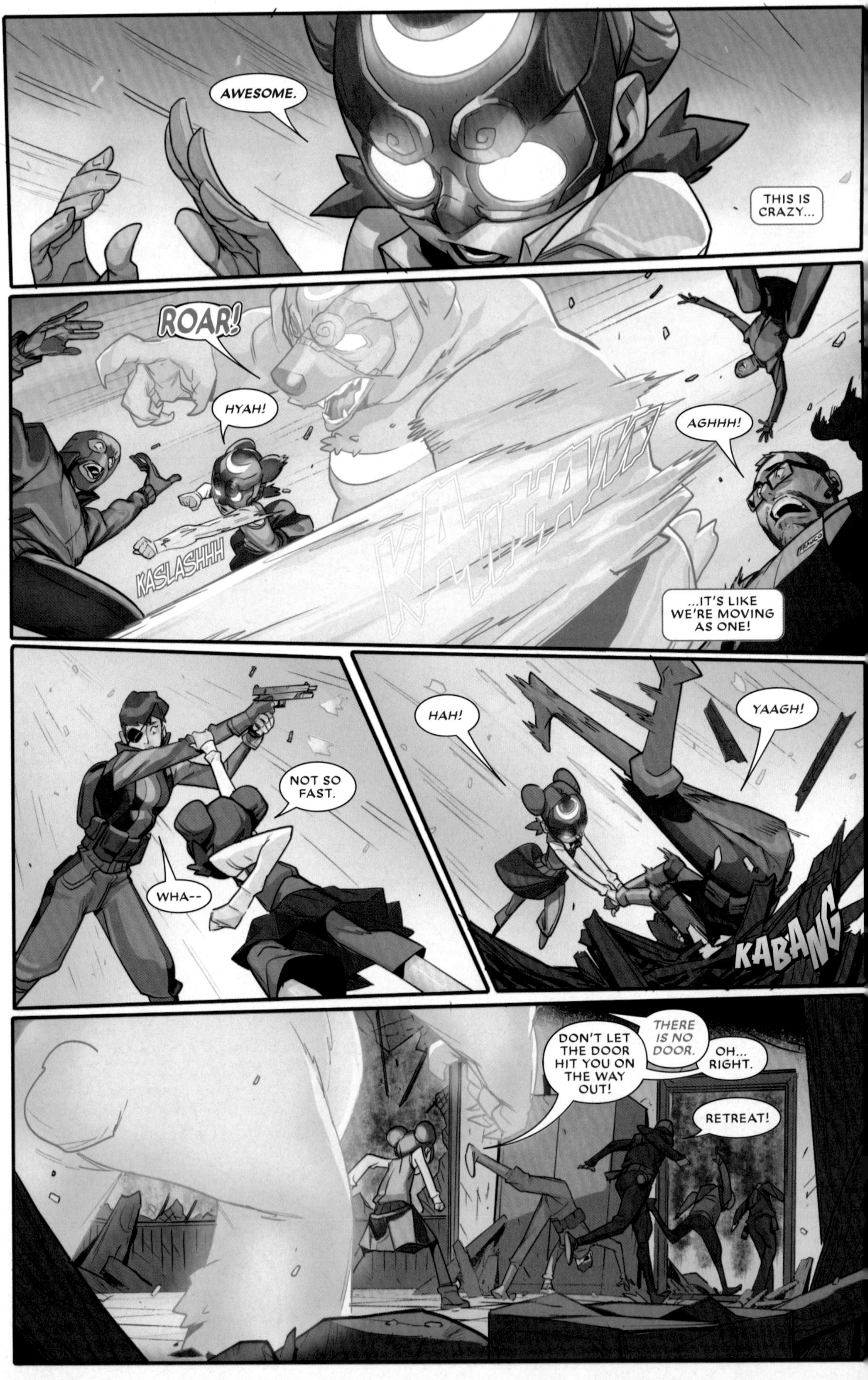
AWESOME.
THIS IS CRAZY...
ROAR!
HYAH!
KASLASHHH
AGHHH!
...IT'S LIKE WE'RE MOVING AS ONE!
NOT SO FAST.
WHA--
HAH!
YAAGH!
KABANG
DON'T LET THE DOOR HIT YOU ON THE WAY OUT!
THERE IS NO DOOR.
OH... RIGHT.
RETREAT!

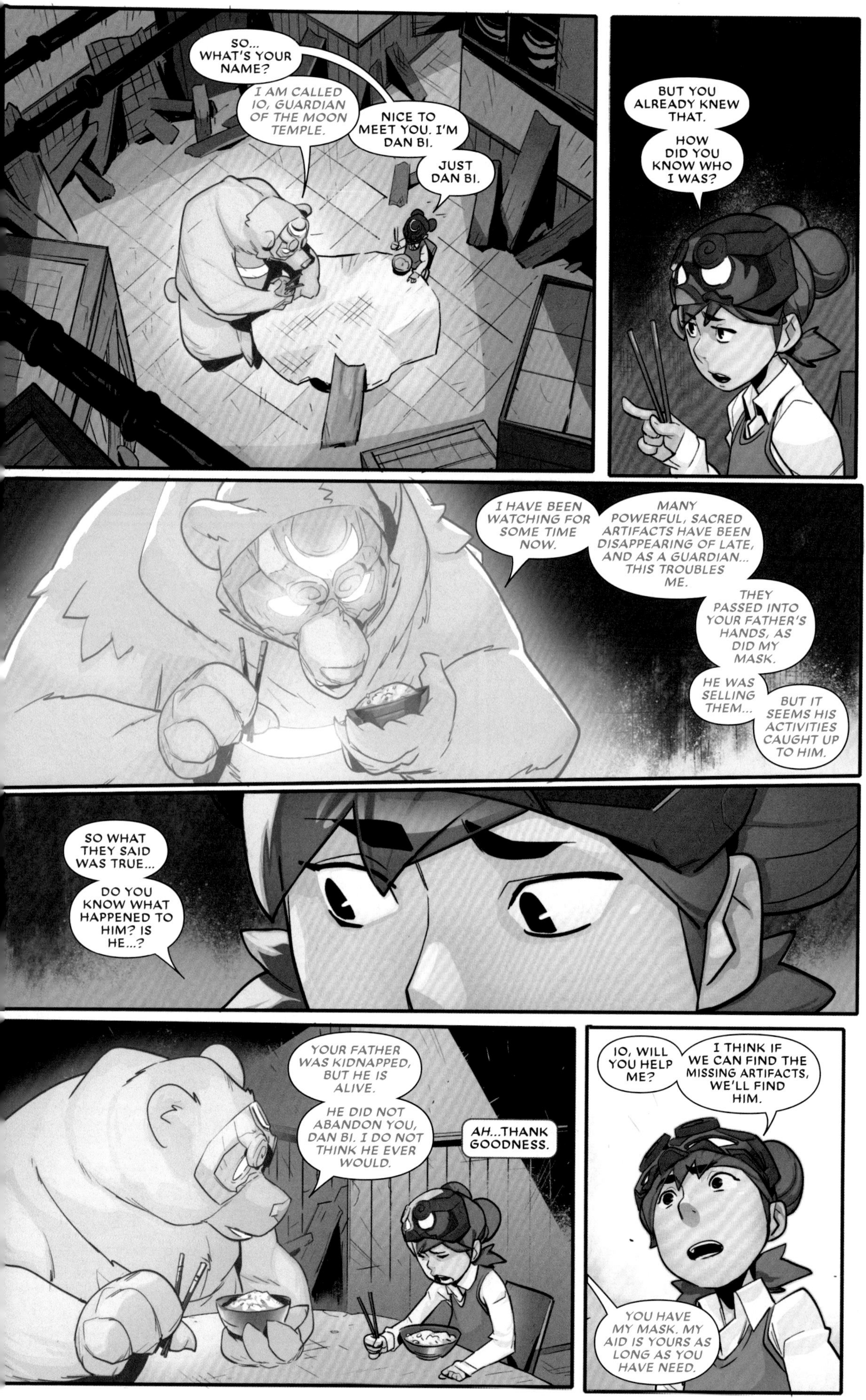
SO... WHAT'S YOUR NAME?
I AM CALLED IO, GUARDIAN OF THE MOON TEMPLE.
NICE TO MEET YOU. I'M DAN BI.
JUST DAN BI.
BUT YOU ALREADY KNEW THAT.
HOW DID YOU KNOW WHO I WAS?
I HAVE BEEN WATCHING FOR SOME TIME NOW.
MANY POWERFUL, SACRED ARTIFACTS HAVE BEEN DISAPPEARING OF LATE, AND AS A GUARDIAN... THIS TROUBLES ME.
THEY PASSED INTO YOUR FATHER'S HANDS, AS DID MY MASK.
HE WAS SELLING THEM...
BUT IT SEEMS HIS ACTIVITIES CAUGHT UP TO HIM.
SO WHAT THEY SAID WAS TRUE...
DO YOU KNOW WHAT HAPPENED TO HIM? IS HE...?
YOUR FATHER WAS KIDNAPPED, BUT HE IS ALIVE.
HE DID NOT ABANDON YOU, DAN BI. I DO NOT THINK HE EVER WOULD.
AH...THANK GOODNESS.
IO, WILL YOU HELP ME?
I THINK IF WE CAN FIND THE MISSING ARTIFACTS, WE'LL FIND HIM.
YOU HAVE MY MASK. MY AID IS YOURS AS LONG AS YOU HAVE NEED.

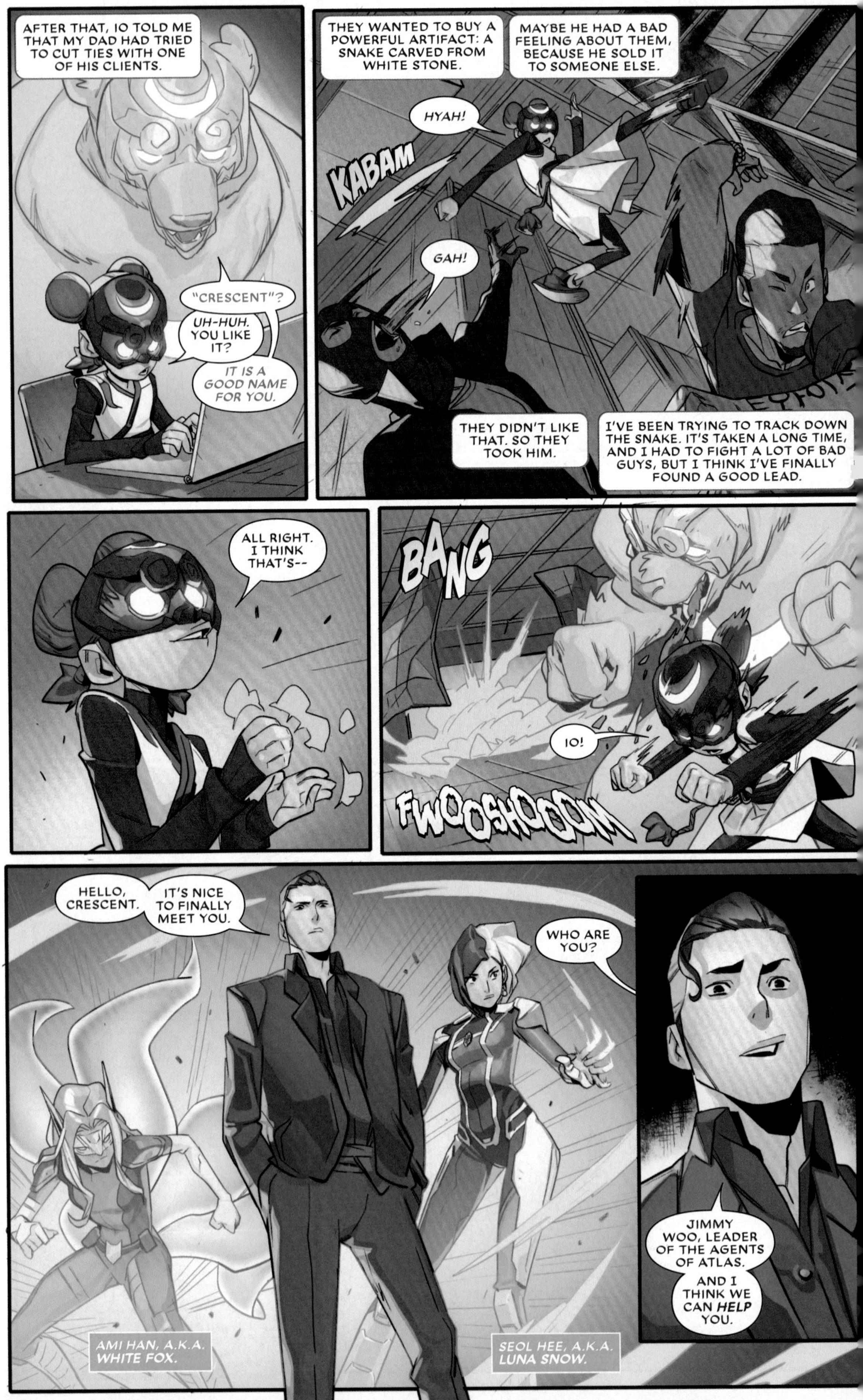
AFTER THAT, IO TOLD ME THAT MY DAD HAD TRIED TO CUT TIES WITH ONE OF HIS CLIENTS.
"CRESCENT"?
UH-HUH. YOU LIKE IT?
IT IS A GOOD NAME FOR YOU.
THEY WANTED TO BUY A POWERFUL ARTIFACT: A SNAKE CARVED FROM WHITE STONE.
MAYBE HE HAD A BAD FEELING ABOUT THEM, BECAUSE HE SOLD IT TO SOMEONE ELSE.
HYAH!
KABAM
GAH!
THEY DIDN'T LIKE THAT. SO THEY TOOK HIM.
I'VE BEEN TRYING TO TRACK DOWN THE SNAKE. IT'S TAKEN A LONG TIME, AND I HAD TO FIGHT A LOT OF BAD GUYS, BUT I THINK I'VE FINALLY FOUND A GOOD LEAD.
ALL RIGHT. I THINK THAT'S--
BANG
IO!
FWOOSHOOOM
HELLO, CRESCENT.
IT'S NICE TO FINALLY MEET YOU.
WHO ARE YOU?
AMI HAN, A.K.A. WHITE FOX.
SEOL HEE, A.K.A. LUNA SNOW.
JIMMY WOO, LEADER OF THE AGENTS OF ATLAS.
AND I THINK WE CAN HELP YOU.

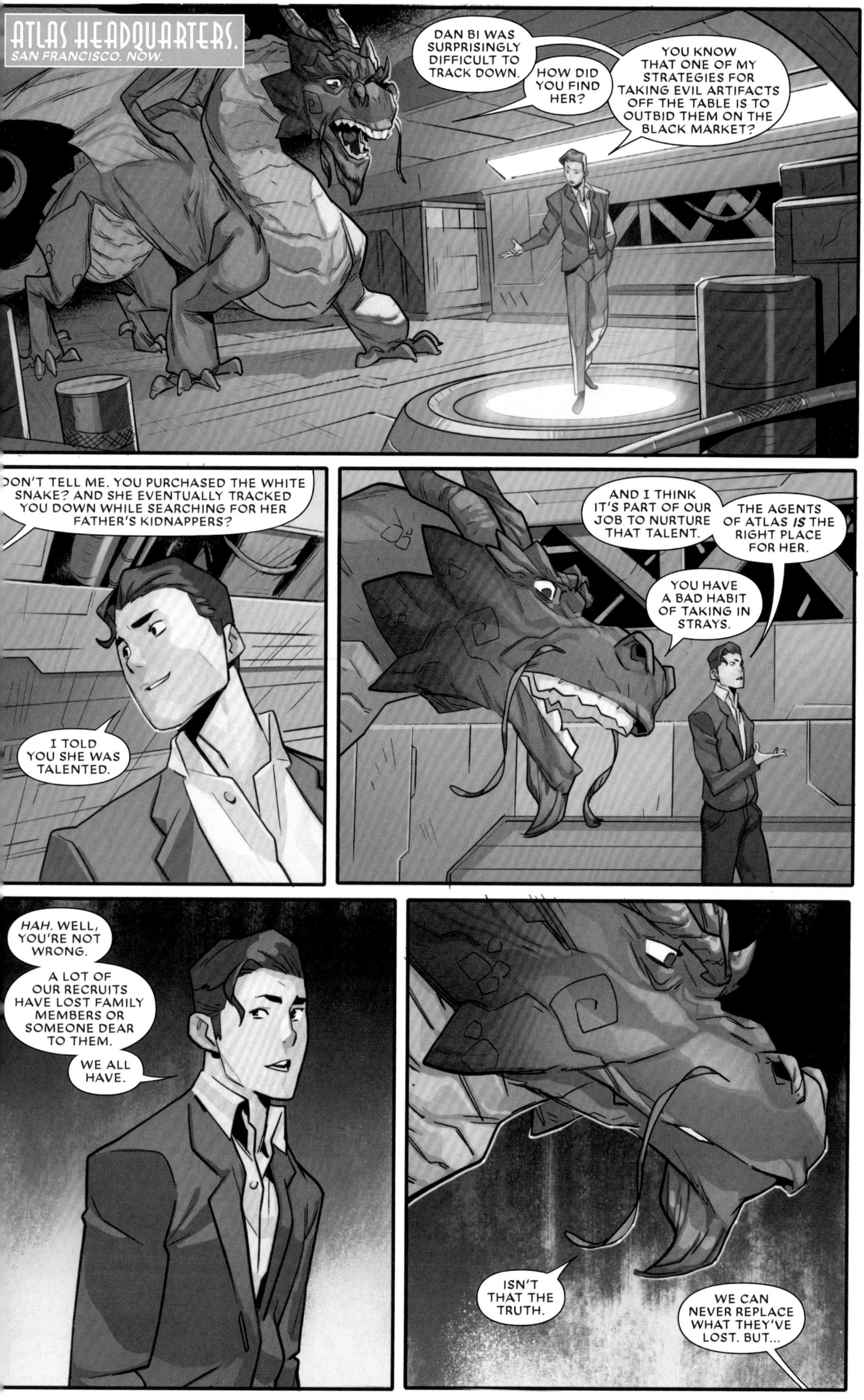
ATLAS HEADQUARTERS.
SAN FRANCISCO. NOW.
DAN BI WAS SURPRISINGLY DIFFICULT TO TRACK DOWN.
HOW DID YOU FIND HER?
YOU KNOW THAT ONE OF MY STRATEGIES FOR TAKING EVIL ARTIFACTS OFF THE TABLE IS TO OUTBID THEM ON THE BLACK MARKET?
DON'T TELL ME. YOU PURCHASED THE WHITE SNAKE? AND SHE EVENTUALLY TRACKED YOU DOWN WHILE SEARCHING FOR HER FATHER'S KIDNAPPERS?
I TOLD YOU SHE WAS TALENTED.
AND I THINK IT'S PART OF OUR JOB TO NURTURE THAT TALENT.
THE AGENTS OF ATLAS *IS* THE RIGHT PLACE FOR HER.
YOU HAVE A BAD HABIT OF TAKING IN STRAYS.
HAH. WELL, YOU'RE NOT WRONG.
A LOT OF OUR RECRUITS HAVE LOST FAMILY MEMBERS OR SOMEONE DEAR TO THEM.
WE ALL HAVE.
ISN'T THAT THE TRUTH.
WE CAN NEVER REPLACE WHAT THEY'VE LOST. BUT...

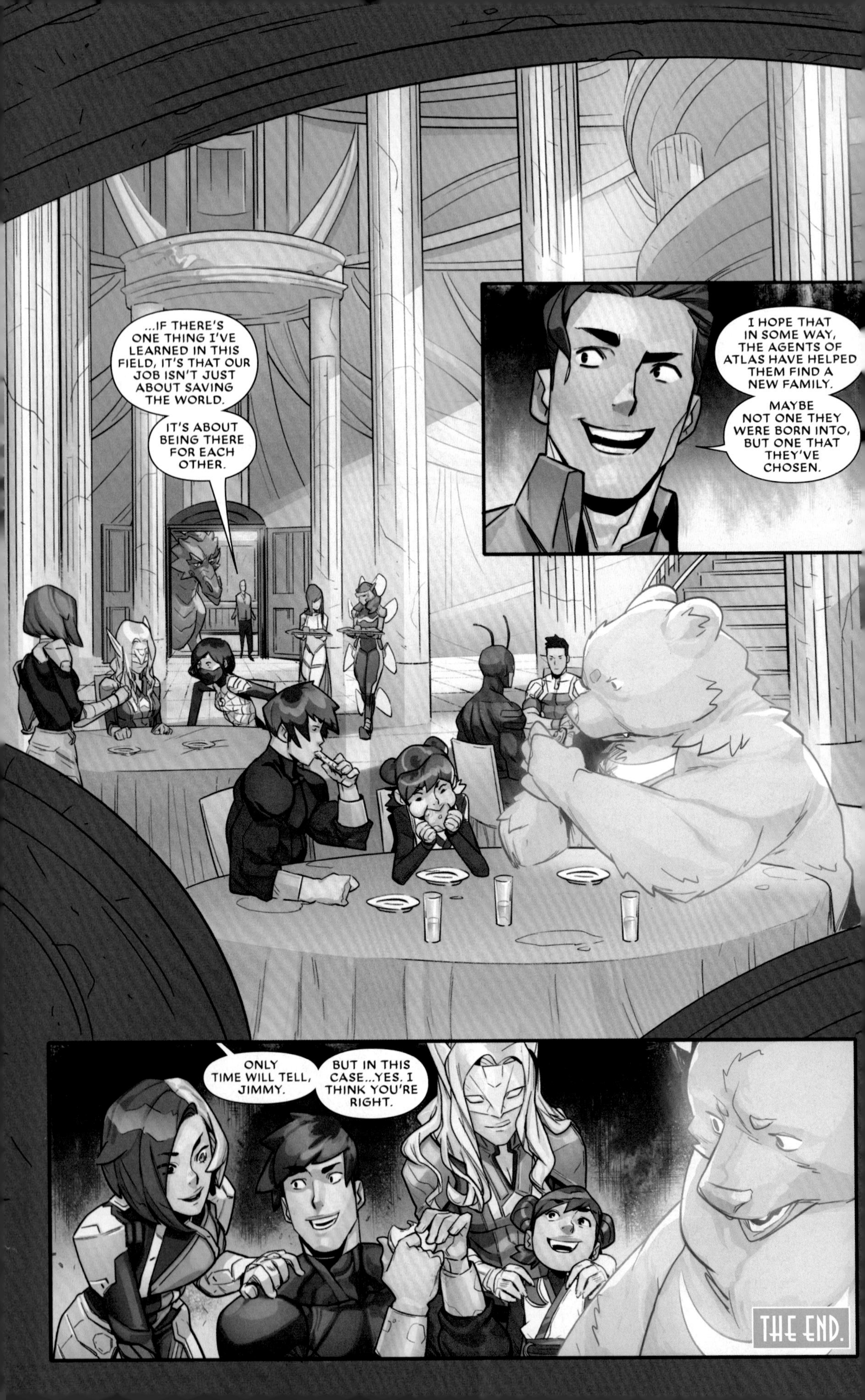
...IF THERE'S ONE THING I'VE LEARNED IN THIS FIELD, IT'S THAT OUR JOB ISN'T JUST ABOUT SAVING THE WORLD.
IT'S ABOUT BEING THERE FOR EACH OTHER.
I HOPE THAT IN SOME WAY, THE AGENTS OF ATLAS HAVE HELPED THEM FIND A NEW FAMILY.
MAYBE NOT ONE THEY WERE BORN INTO, BUT ONE THAT THEY'VE CHOSEN.
ONLY TIME WILL TELL, JIMMY.
BUT IN THIS CASE...YES. I THINK YOU'RE RIGHT.
THE END.

re: CRESCENT & IO

Thank you for picking up this comic! A little under a year ago we debuted Crescent and Io in an all-new original characters update for our hit mobile game *MARVEL Future Fight*. I really love how Alyssa Wong explores Crescent's backstory and shows her heroic side. Why a 10-year-old girl with a mask and a giant protector? The arrival of my newborn daughter and witnessing my young son holding onto his soft toy to feel safe really inspired me to pursue this character design. Crescent and Io were born after an in-depth collaboration with the Netmarble Monster team regarding this theme.

Did you know Crescent's real name is Dan Bi? Dan Bi is Korean for both "welcome rain after a drought" and "a big bear." Dan Bi's original costume is a modernized version of the traditional Korean hanbok, and her accessories can be used for taekwondo action. Her primary colors reflect her origin as well. We designed the half-moon motif for Crescent's mask to match Io's design.

Io's design is inspired by the Asian black bear, also known as the half-moon bear! Did you spot the cute half-moon teddy bear in the comic?

The school costume in this comic is another result of our collaboration with the Netmarble Monster team. We maintained her colors and gave her a cool shoulder-strap school bag with a matching crescent moon design, and of course, this kid always needs a pair of new shoes! We hope you like her new school outfit. You can play as Crescent with this costume in the game. If you haven't played *MARVEL Future Fight*, download it for free and give it a spin!

— Danny Koo
Marvel Games Senior Producer, Asia

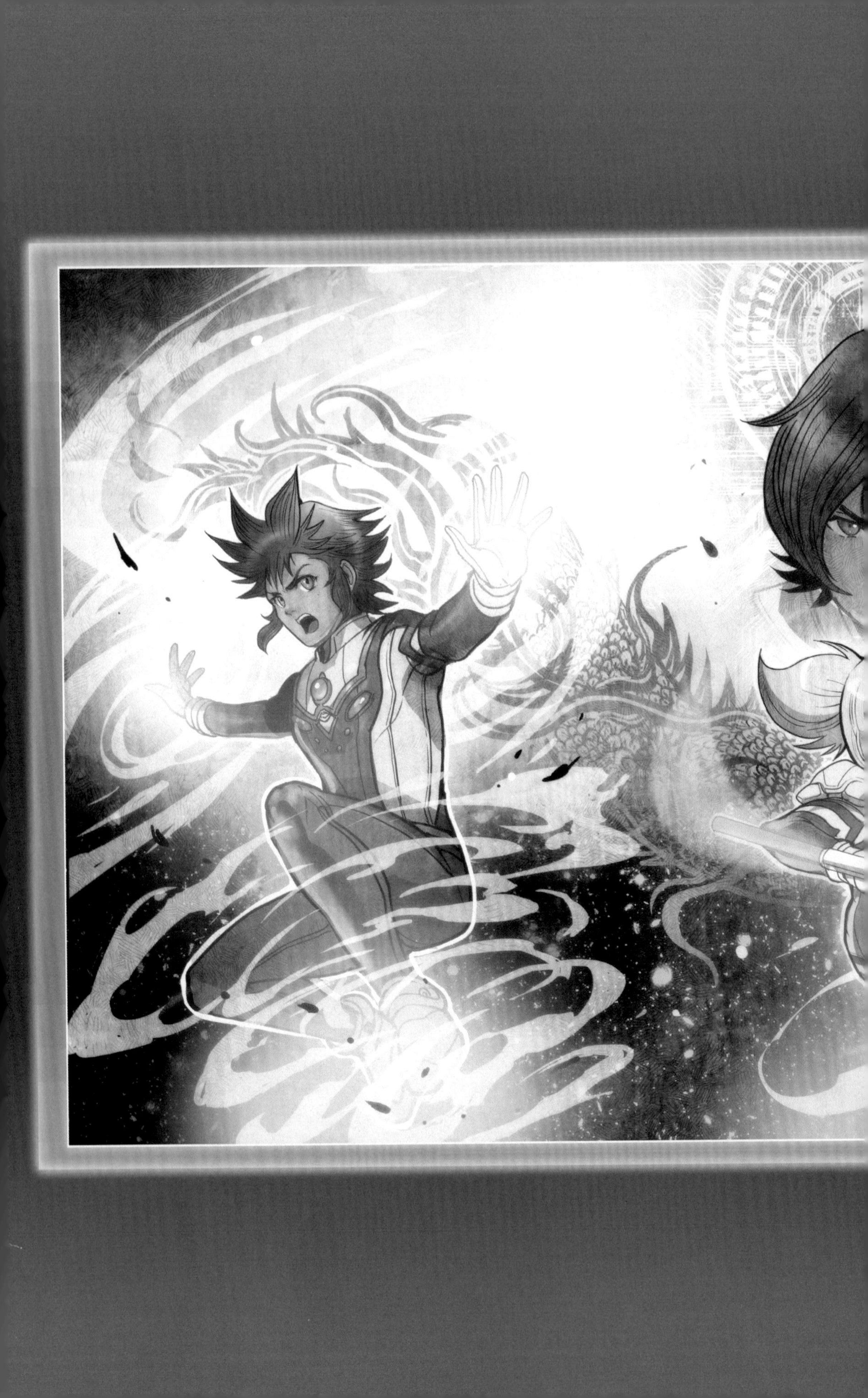

WHITE FOX #1, LUNA SNOW #1 AND CRESCENT & IO #1
CONNECTING VARIANTS BY **SANA TAKEDA**

MARVEL FUTURE FIGHT FIRSTS

Makoto, Chloe, Adi, and Bruno were raised, indoctrinated, and trained by Hydra to defeat the Avengers. After discovering that Hydra were the real villains, everyone but Bruno betrayed the organization and escaped.

Now, Makoto, Chloe, and Adi are learning how to be true heroes...as the

FUTURE AVENGERS

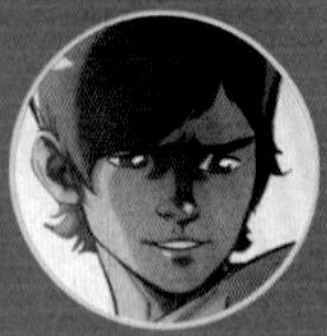

ADI

Alias: CODEC

Skills: Technopathy

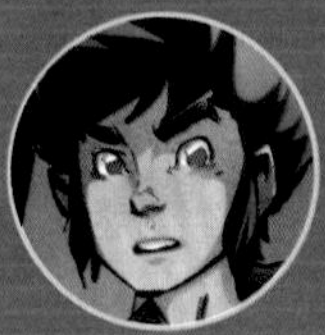

MAKOTO

Alias: HURRICANE

Skills: Wind Powers

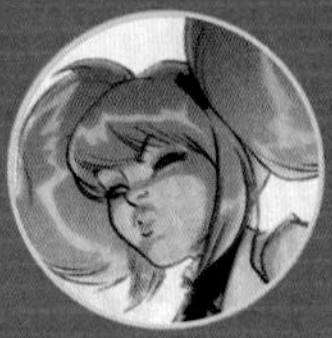

CHLOE

Alias: CHARADE

Skills: Shape-shifting

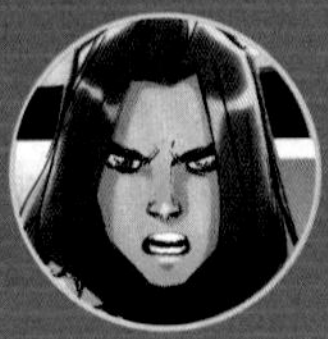

BRUNO

Alias: TWISTER

Skills: Nanotech Cyborg

WRITER **ALYSSA WONG**

PENCILS/BREAKDOWNS **ALÉ GARZA**

INKS/FINISHES **ALÉ GARZA & CORY HAMSCHER**

COLORISTS **DONO SÁNCHEZ-ALMARA WITH PROTOBUNKER**

LETTERER **VC's JOE SABINO**

ASSISTANT EDITORS **LINDSEY COHICK & TOM GRONEMAN**

EDITOR **MARK PANICCIA**

EDITOR IN CHIEF **C.B. CEBULSKI**

CHIEF CREATIVE OFFICER **JOE QUESADA**

PRESIDENT **DAN BUCKLEY**

EXECUTIVE PRODUCER **ALAN FINE**

SPECIAL THANKS TO **SCOTT DOLPH**

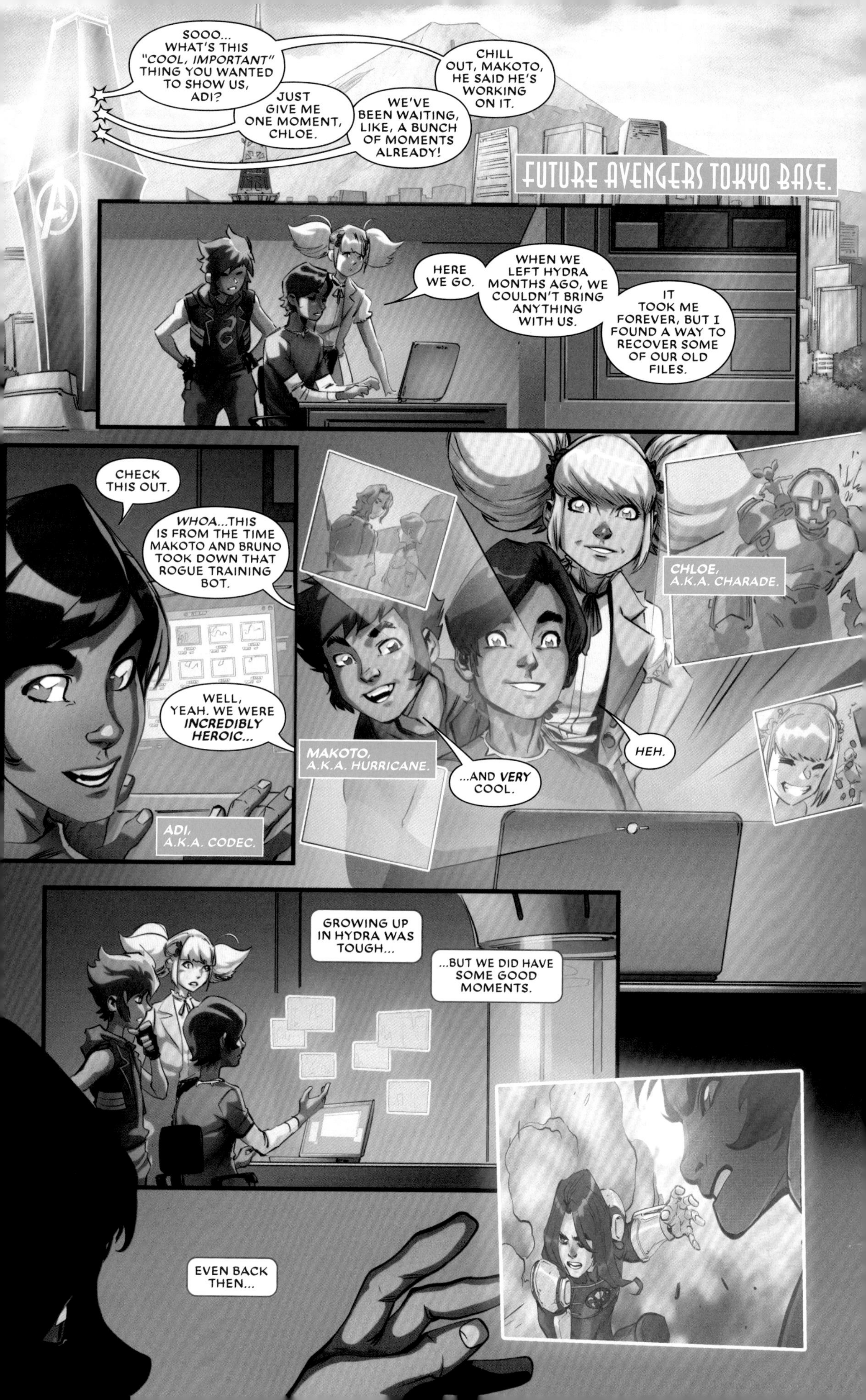

SOOO... WHAT'S THIS "COOL, IMPORTANT" THING YOU WANTED TO SHOW US, ADI?
CHILL OUT, MAKOTO, HE SAID HE'S WORKING ON IT.
JUST GIVE ME ONE MOMENT, CHLOE.
WE'VE BEEN WAITING, LIKE, A BUNCH OF MOMENTS ALREADY!
FUTURE AVENGERS TOKYO BASE.
HERE WE GO.
WHEN WE LEFT HYDRA MONTHS AGO, WE COULDN'T BRING ANYTHING WITH US.
IT TOOK ME FOREVER, BUT I FOUND A WAY TO RECOVER SOME OF OUR OLD FILES.
CHECK THIS OUT.
WHOA...THIS IS FROM THE TIME MAKOTO AND BRUNO TOOK DOWN THAT ROGUE TRAINING BOT.
WELL, YEAH. WE WERE INCREDIBLY HEROIC...
...AND VERY COOL.
HEH.
ADI, A.K.A. CODEC.
MAKOTO, A.K.A. HURRICANE.
CHLOE, A.K.A. CHARADE.
GROWING UP IN HYDRA WAS TOUGH...
...BUT WE DID HAVE SOME GOOD MOMENTS.
EVEN BACK THEN...

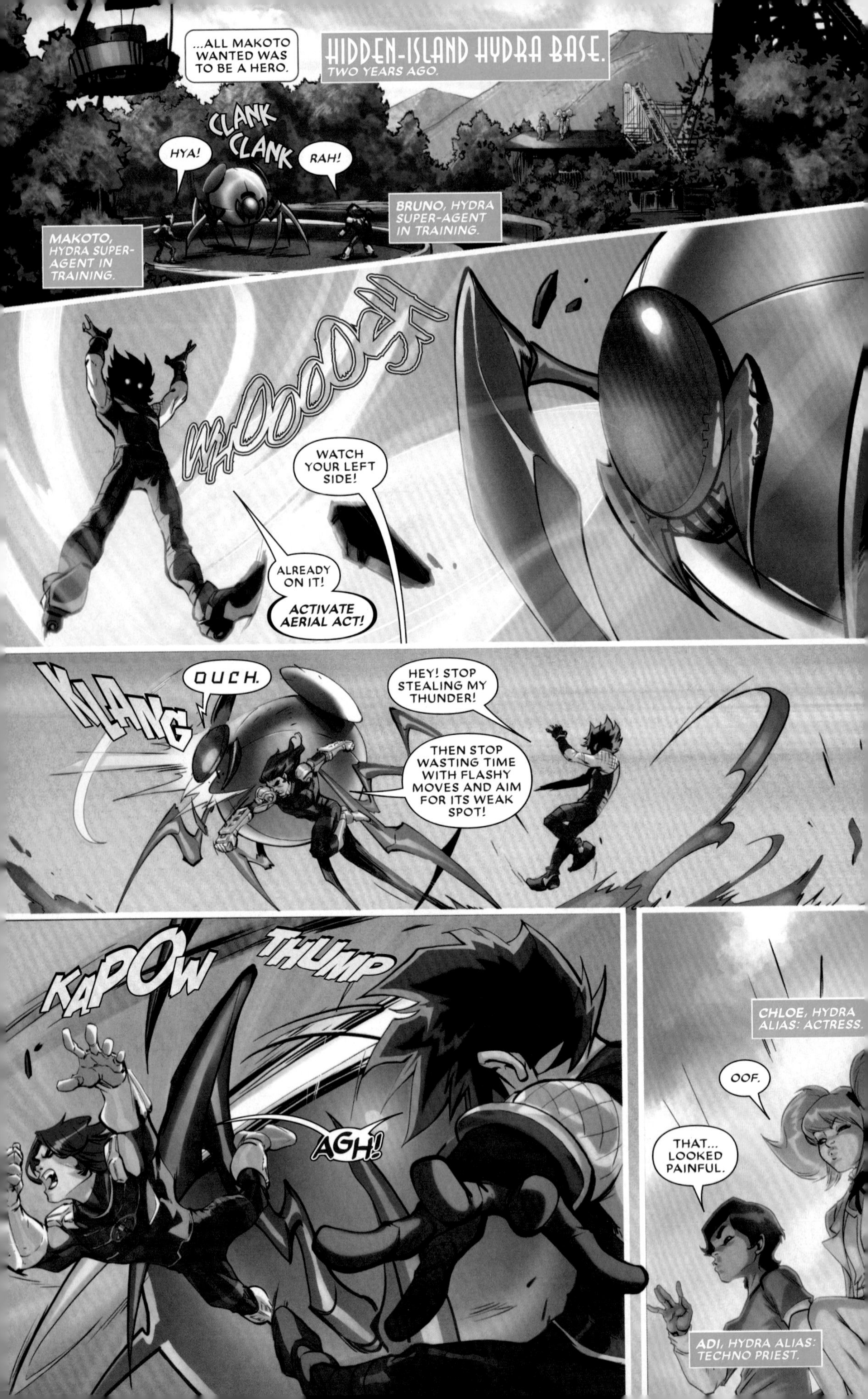
...ALL MAKOTO WANTED WAS TO BE A HERO.
HIDDEN-ISLAND HYDRA BASE.
TWO YEARS AGO.
CLANK CLANK
HYA!
RAH!
MAKOTO, HYDRA SUPER-AGENT IN TRAINING.
BRUNO, HYDRA SUPER-AGENT IN TRAINING.
WHOOOOSH
WATCH YOUR LEFT SIDE!
ALREADY ON IT!
ACTIVATE AERIAL ACT!
KLANG
OUCH.
HEY! STOP STEALING MY THUNDER!
THEN STOP WASTING TIME WITH FLASHY MOVES AND AIM FOR ITS WEAK SPOT!
KAPOW
THUMP
AGH!
CHLOE, HYDRA ALIAS: ACTRESS.
OOF.
THAT... LOOKED PAINFUL.
ADI, HYDRA ALIAS: TECHNO PRIEST.

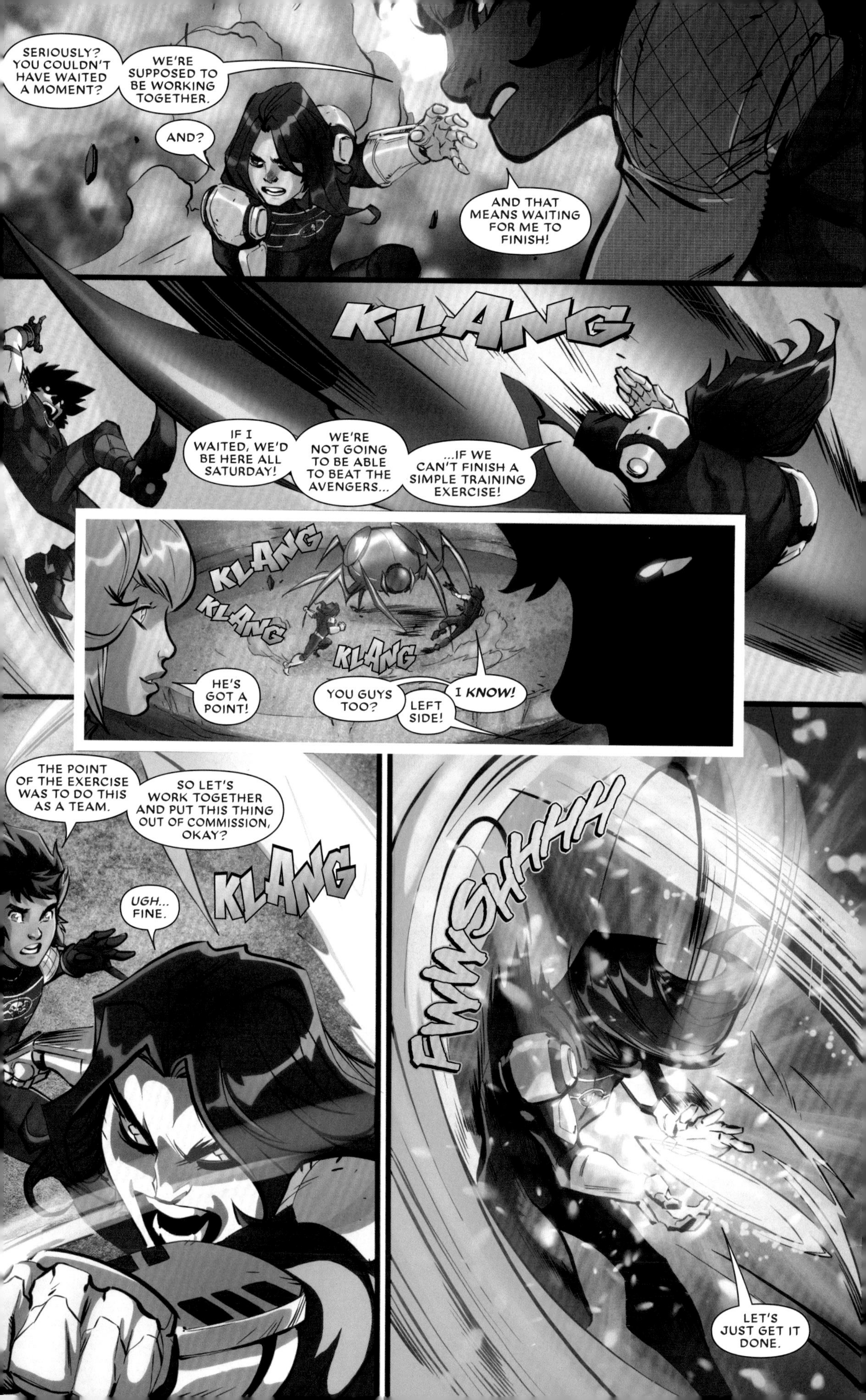
SERIOUSLY? YOU COULDN'T HAVE WAITED A MOMENT?
WE'RE SUPPOSED TO BE WORKING TOGETHER.
AND?
AND THAT MEANS WAITING FOR ME TO FINISH!
KLANG
IF I WAITED, WE'D BE HERE ALL SATURDAY!
WE'RE NOT GOING TO BE ABLE TO BEAT THE AVENGERS...
...IF WE CAN'T FINISH A SIMPLE TRAINING EXERCISE!
KLANG
KLANG
KLANG
HE'S GOT A POINT!
YOU GUYS TOO?
I KNOW!
LEFT SIDE!
THE POINT OF THE EXERCISE WAS TO DO THIS AS A TEAM.
SO LET'S WORK TOGETHER AND PUT THIS THING OUT OF COMMISSION, OKAY?
KLANG
UGH... FINE.
FWWSHHHH
LET'S JUST GET IT DONE.

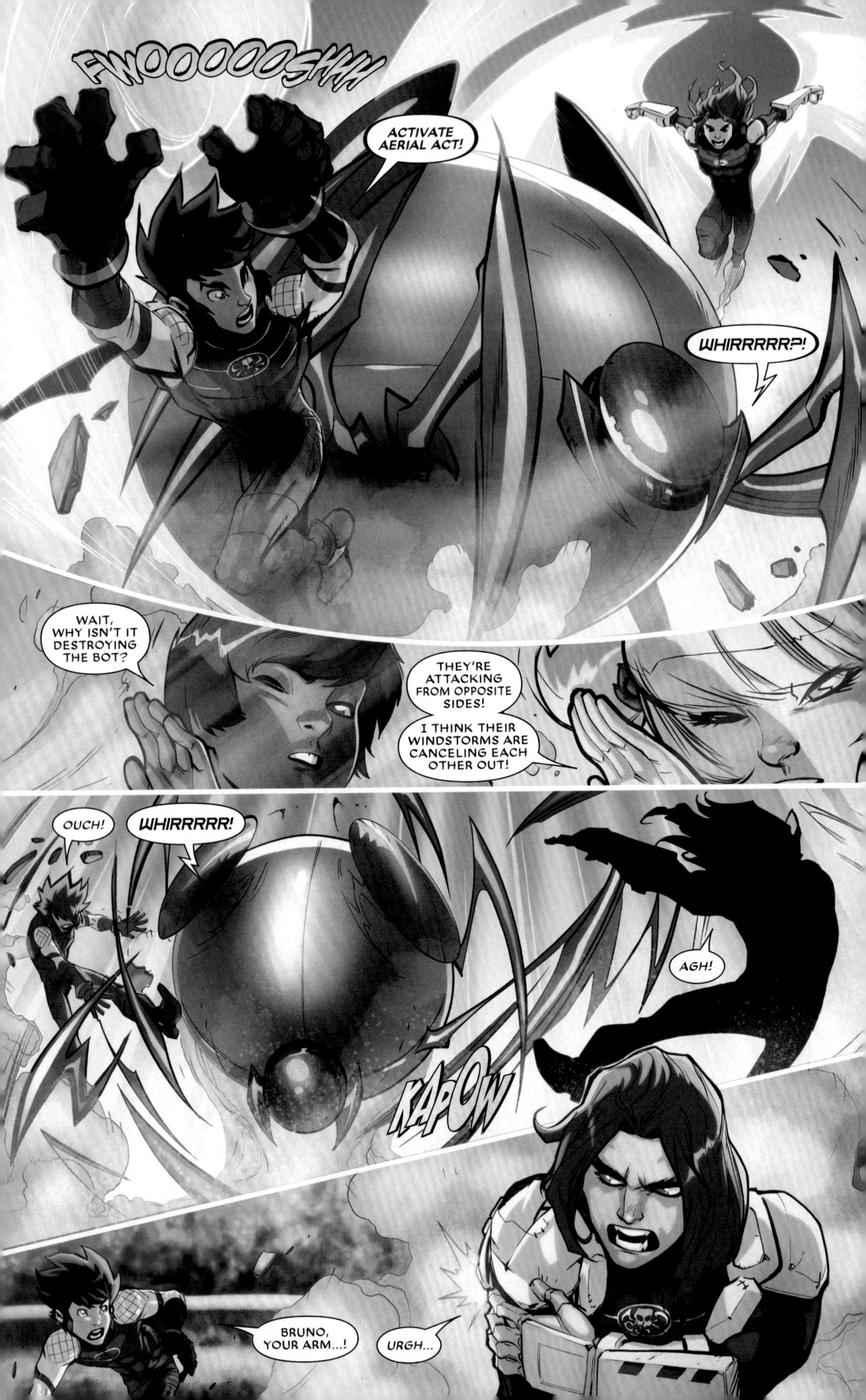
FWOOOOOSHHH
ACTIVATE AERIAL ACT!
WHIRRRRR?!
WAIT, WHY ISN'T IT DESTROYING THE BOT?
THEY'RE ATTACKING FROM OPPOSITE SIDES!
I THINK THEIR WINDSTORMS ARE CANCELING EACH OTHER OUT!
OUCH!
WHIRRRRR!
AGH!
KAPOW
BRUNO, YOUR ARM...!
URGH...

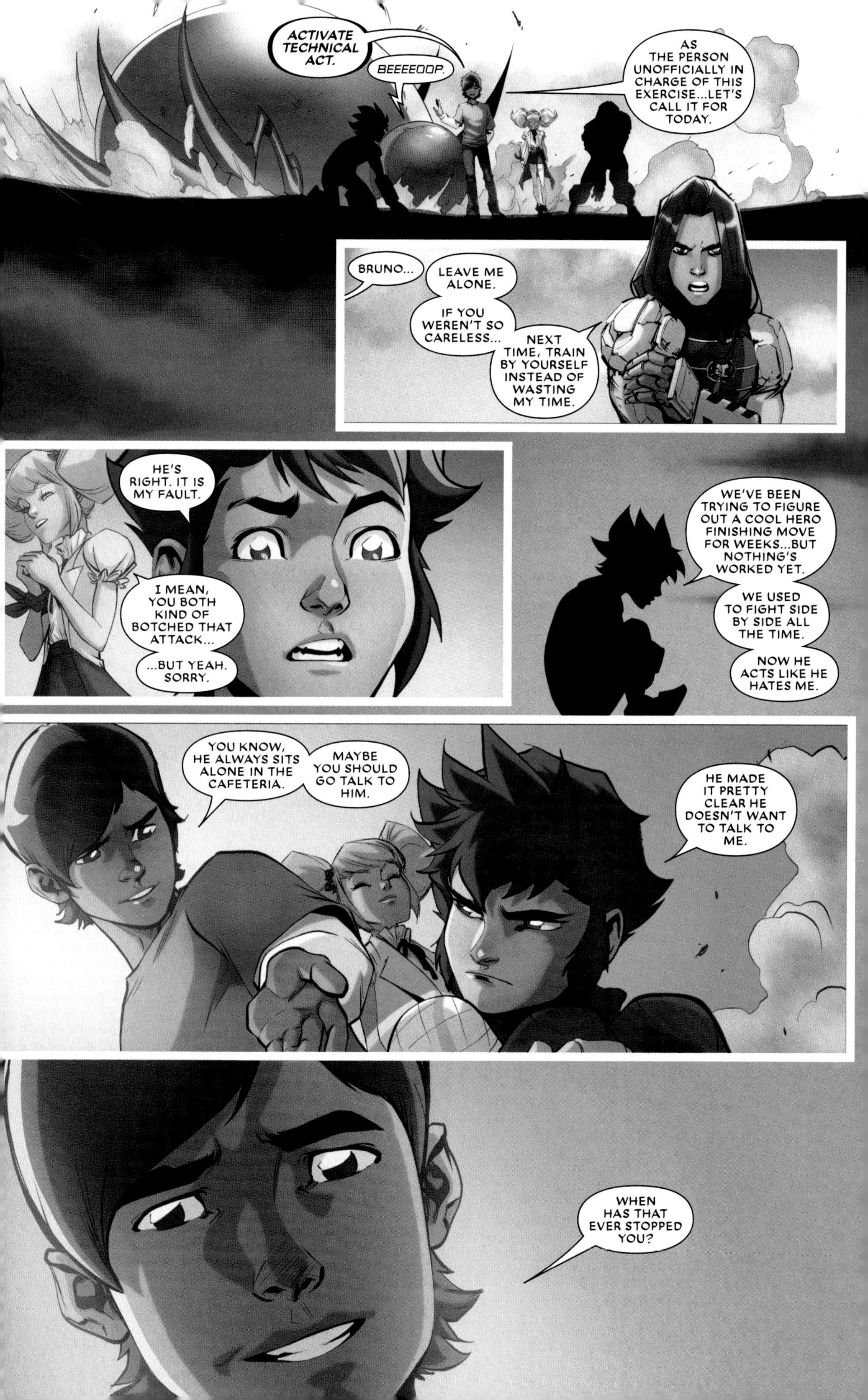
ACTIVATE TECHNICAL ACT.
BEEEEOOP.
AS THE PERSON UNOFFICIALLY IN CHARGE OF THIS EXERCISE...LET'S CALL IT FOR TODAY.
BRUNO...
LEAVE ME ALONE.
IF YOU WEREN'T SO CARELESS...
NEXT TIME, TRAIN BY YOURSELF INSTEAD OF WASTING MY TIME.
HE'S RIGHT. IT IS MY FAULT.
I MEAN, YOU BOTH KIND OF BOTCHED THAT ATTACK...
...BUT YEAH. SORRY.
WE'VE BEEN TRYING TO FIGURE OUT A COOL HERO FINISHING MOVE FOR WEEKS...BUT NOTHING'S WORKED YET.
WE USED TO FIGHT SIDE BY SIDE ALL THE TIME.
NOW HE ACTS LIKE HE HATES ME.
YOU KNOW, HE ALWAYS SITS ALONE IN THE CAFETERIA.
MAYBE YOU SHOULD GO TALK TO HIM.
HE MADE IT PRETTY CLEAR HE DOESN'T WANT TO TALK TO ME.
WHEN HAS THAT EVER STOPPED YOU?

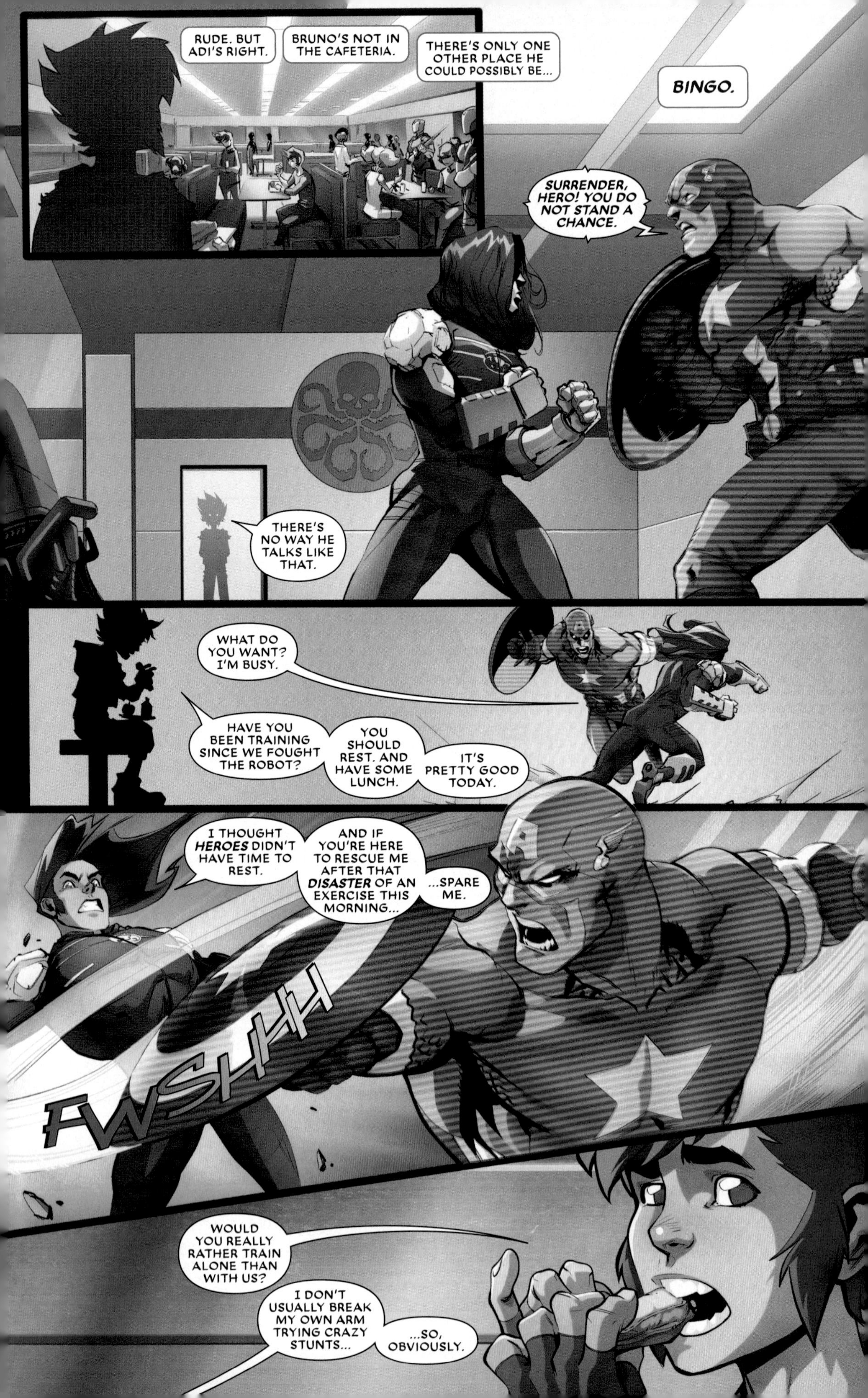
RUDE. BUT ADI'S RIGHT.
BRUNO'S NOT IN THE CAFETERIA.
THERE'S ONLY ONE OTHER PLACE HE COULD POSSIBLY BE...
BINGO.
SURRENDER, HERO! YOU DO NOT STAND A CHANCE.
THERE'S NO WAY HE TALKS LIKE THAT.
WHAT DO YOU WANT? I'M BUSY.
HAVE YOU BEEN TRAINING SINCE WE FOUGHT THE ROBOT?
YOU SHOULD REST. AND HAVE SOME LUNCH.
IT'S PRETTY GOOD TODAY.
I THOUGHT HEROES DIDN'T HAVE TIME TO REST.
AND IF YOU'RE HERE TO RESCUE ME AFTER THAT DISASTER OF AN EXERCISE THIS MORNING...
...SPARE ME.
FWSHHH
WOULD YOU REALLY RATHER TRAIN ALONE THAN WITH US?
I DON'T USUALLY BREAK MY OWN ARM TRYING CRAZY STUNTS...
...SO, OBVIOUSLY.

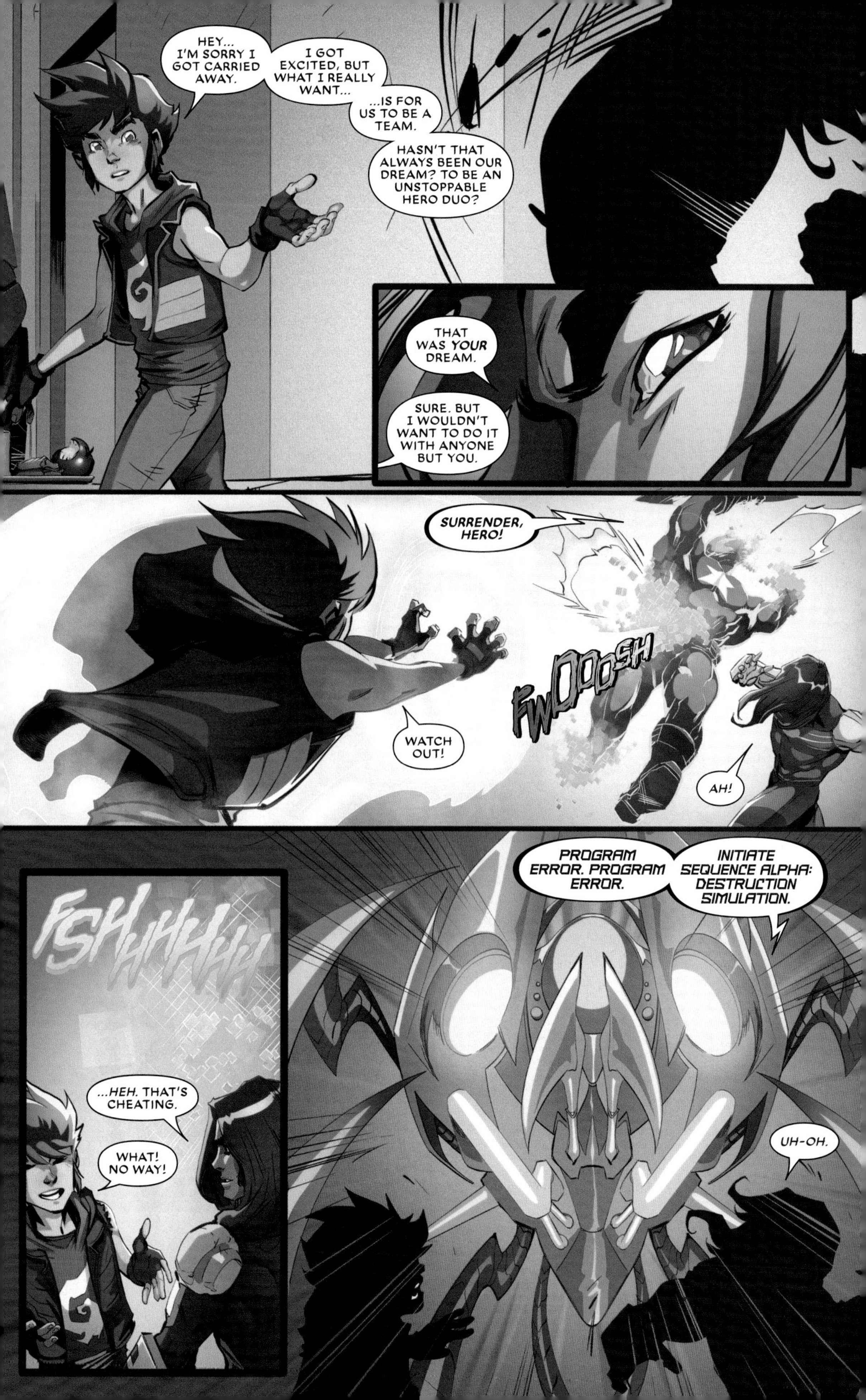
HEY... I'M SORRY I GOT CARRIED AWAY.
I GOT EXCITED, BUT WHAT I REALLY WANT...
...IS FOR US TO BE A TEAM.
HASN'T THAT ALWAYS BEEN OUR DREAM? TO BE AN UNSTOPPABLE HERO DUO?
THAT WAS *YOUR* DREAM.
SURE. BUT I WOULDN'T WANT TO DO IT WITH ANYONE BUT YOU.
SURRENDER, HERO!
FWOOOOSH
WATCH OUT!
AH!
FSHHHHHH
PROGRAM ERROR. PROGRAM ERROR.
INITIATE SEQUENCE ALPHA: DESTRUCTION SIMULATION.
...*HEH.* THAT'S CHEATING.
WHAT! NO WAY!
UH-OH.

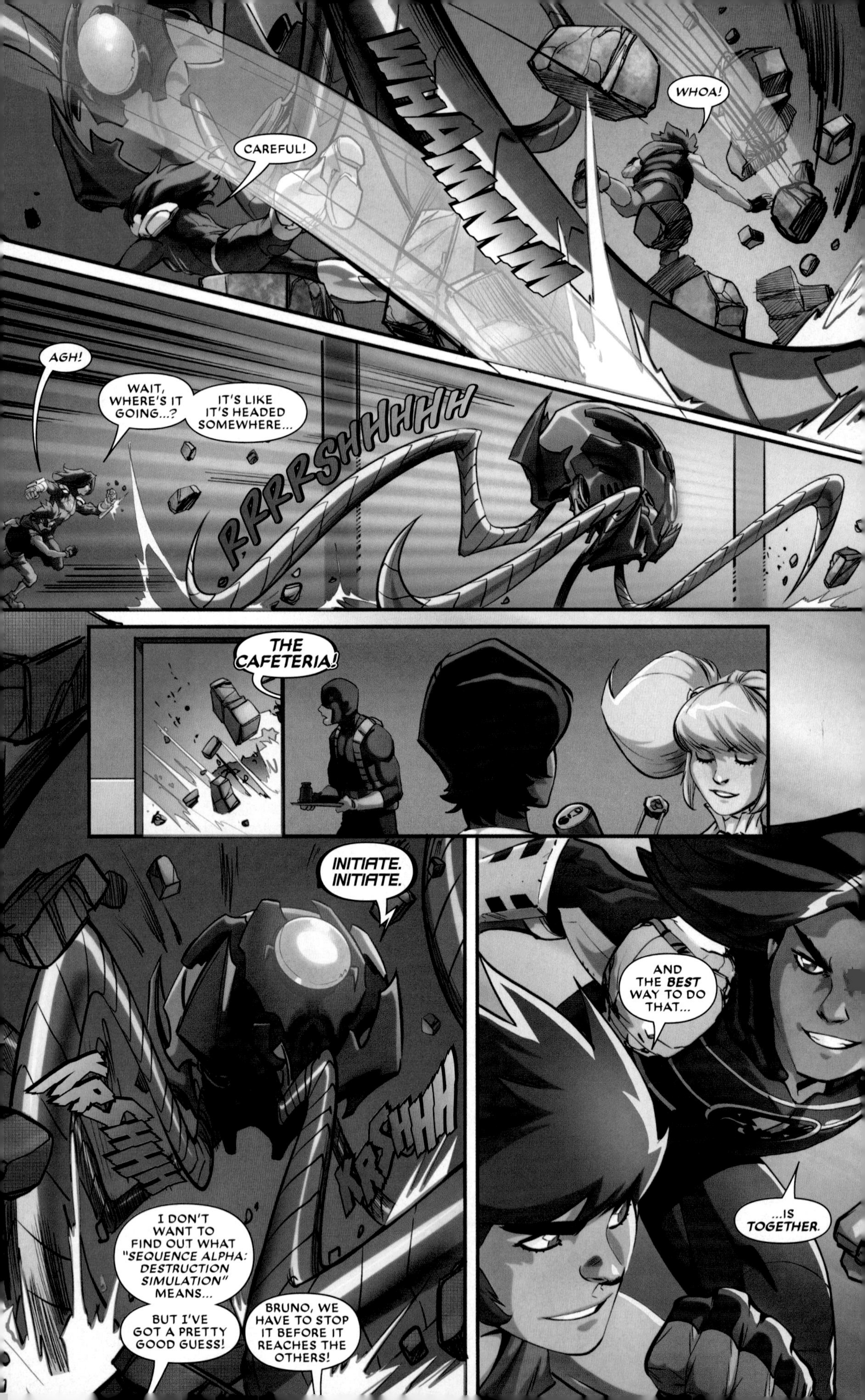
WHAMMMM
CAREFUL!
WHOA!
AGH!
WAIT, WHERE'S IT GOING...?
IT'S LIKE IT'S HEADED SOMEWHERE...
RRRRSHHHHHH
THE CAFETERIA!
INITIATE. INITIATE.
KRSHHH
KRSHHH
I DON'T WANT TO FIND OUT WHAT "SEQUENCE ALPHA: DESTRUCTION SIMULATION" MEANS...
BUT I'VE GOT A PRETTY GOOD GUESS!
BRUNO, WE HAVE TO STOP IT BEFORE IT REACHES THE OTHERS!
AND THE BEST WAY TO DO THAT...
...IS TOGETHER.

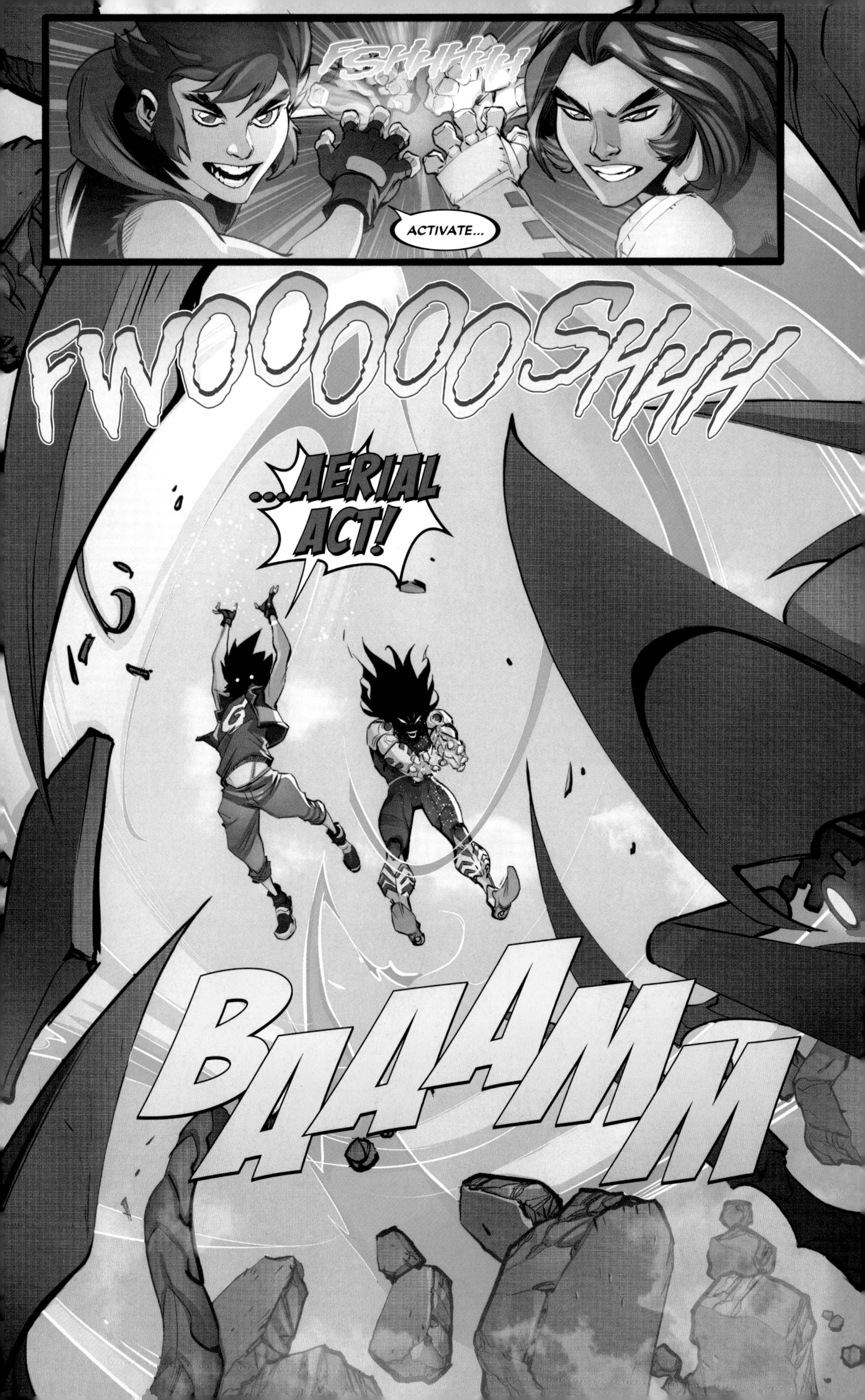
FSHHHHH
ACTIVATE...
FWOOOOOOSHHH
...AERIAL ACT!
BAAAMM

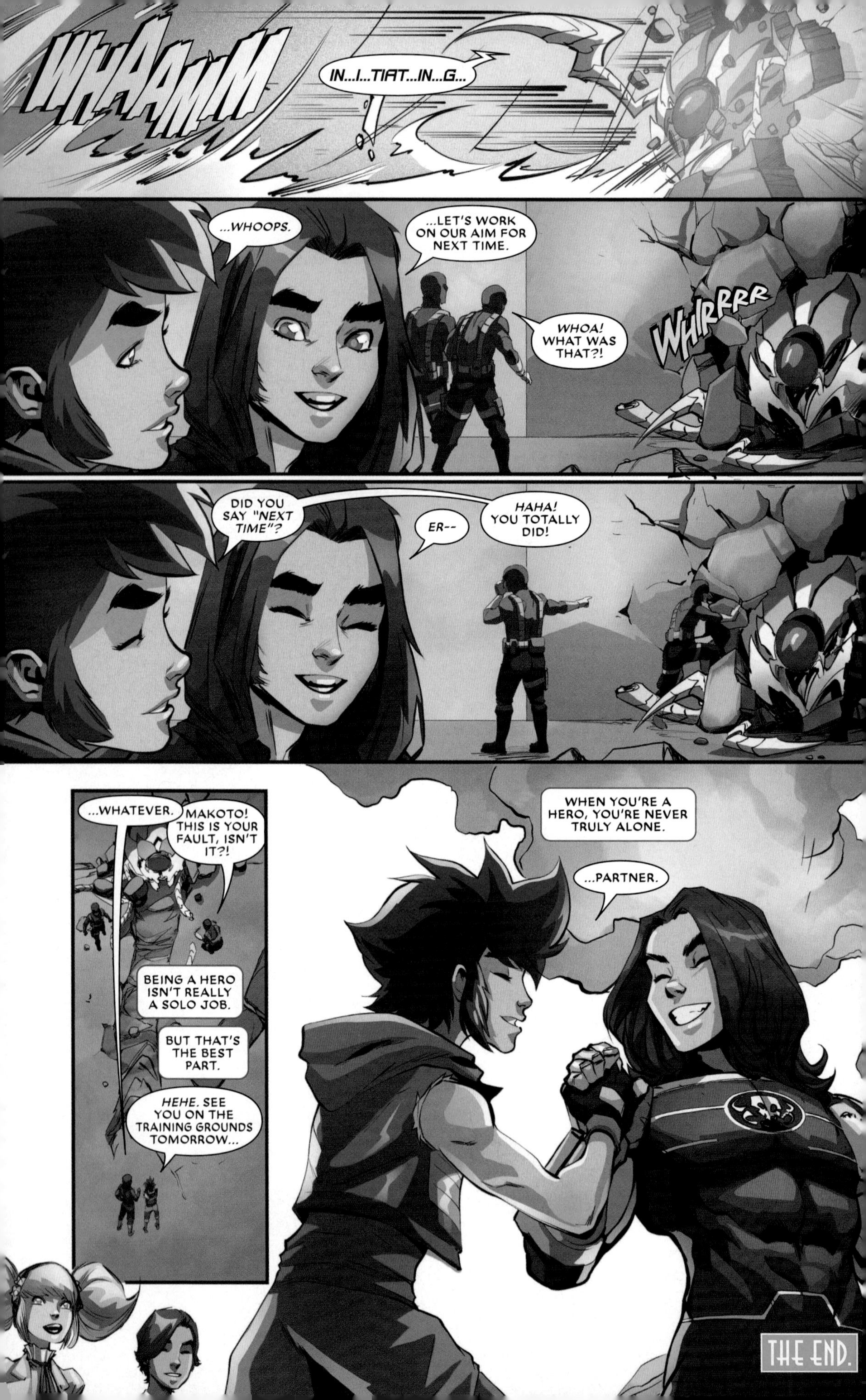
WHAAMM
IN...I...TIAT...IN...G...
...WHOOPS.
...LET'S WORK ON OUR AIM FOR NEXT TIME.
WHOA! WHAT WAS THAT?!
WHIRRRR
DID YOU SAY "NEXT TIME"?
ER--
HAHA! YOU TOTALLY DID!
...WHATEVER.
MAKOTO! THIS IS YOUR FAULT, ISN'T IT?!
BEING A HERO ISN'T REALLY A SOLO JOB.
BUT THAT'S THE BEST PART.
HEHE. SEE YOU ON THE TRAINING GROUNDS TOMORROW...
WHEN YOU'RE A HERO, YOU'RE NEVER TRULY ALONE.
...PARTNER.
THE END.

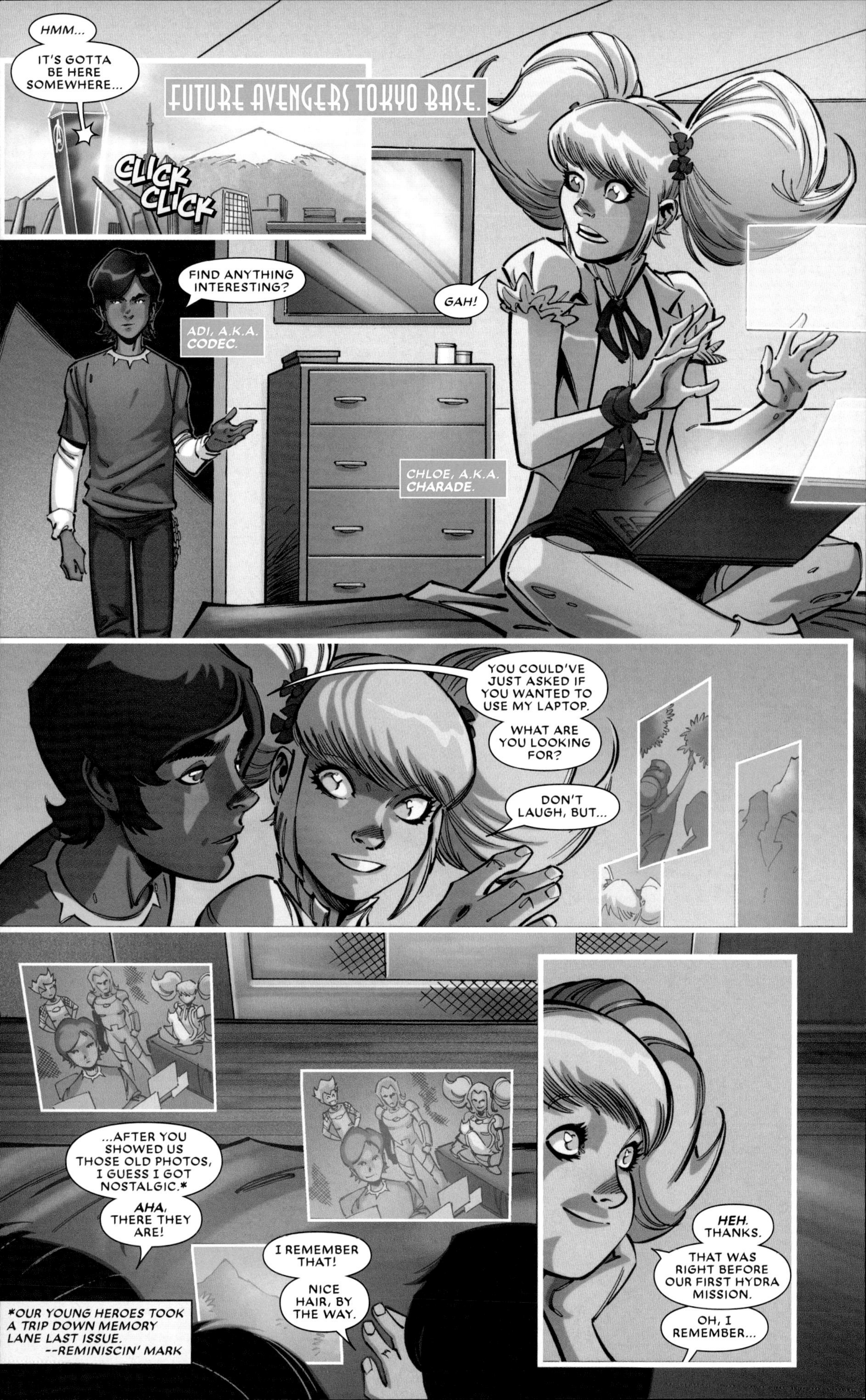

HMM...
IT'S GOTTA BE HERE SOMEWHERE...
FUTURE AVENGERS TOKYO BASE.
CLICK CLICK
FIND ANYTHING INTERESTING?
ADI, A.K.A. CODEC.
GAH!
CHLOE, A.K.A. CHARADE.
YOU COULD'VE JUST ASKED IF YOU WANTED TO USE MY LAPTOP.
WHAT ARE YOU LOOKING FOR?
DON'T LAUGH, BUT...
...AFTER YOU SHOWED US THOSE OLD PHOTOS, I GUESS I GOT NOSTALGIC.*
AHA, THERE THEY ARE!
I REMEMBER THAT!
NICE HAIR, BY THE WAY.
HEH. THANKS.
THAT WAS RIGHT BEFORE OUR FIRST HYDRA MISSION.
OH, I REMEMBER...
*OUR YOUNG HEROES TOOK A TRIP DOWN MEMORY LANE LAST ISSUE. --REMINISCIN' MARK

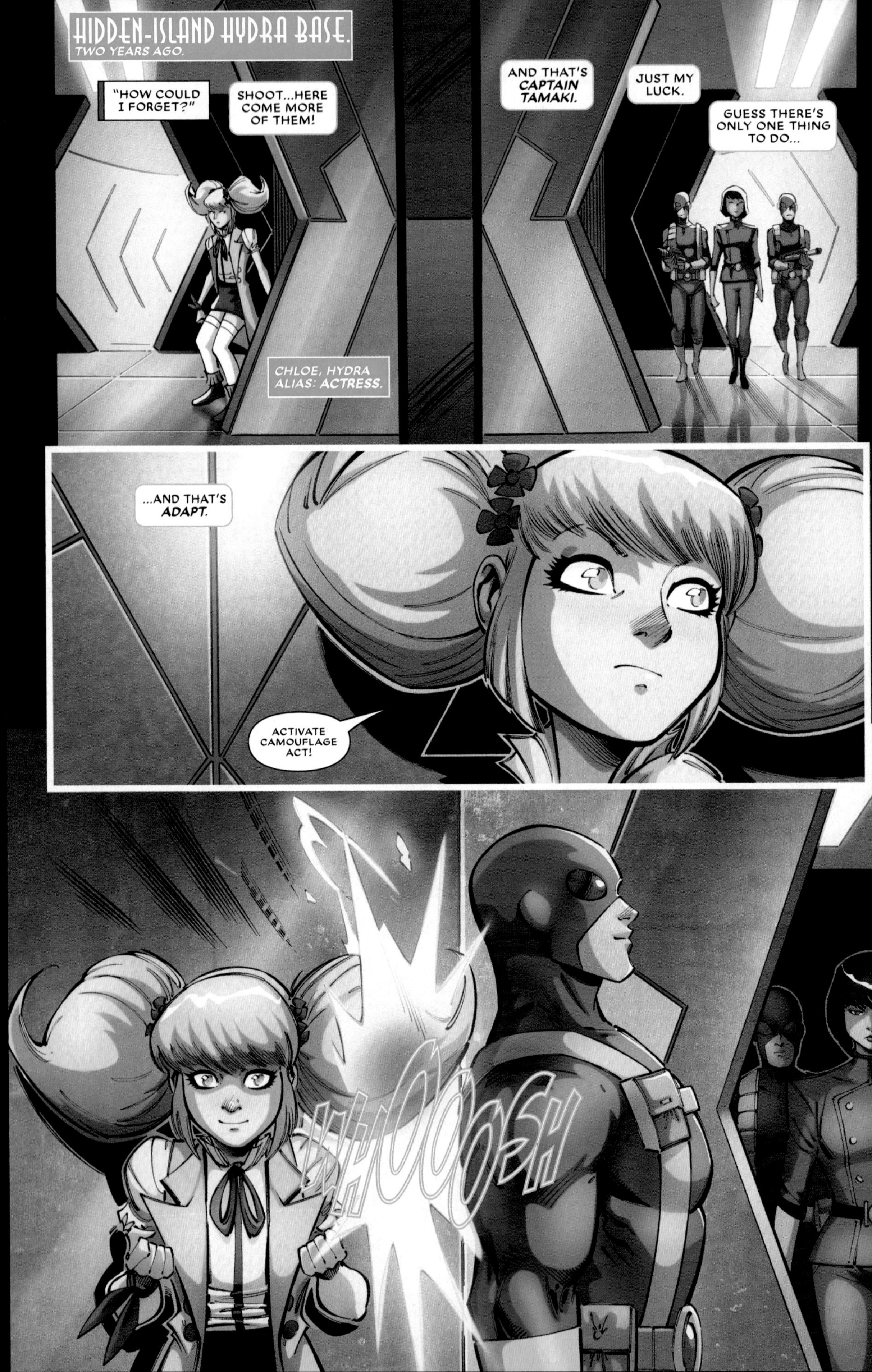
HIDDEN-ISLAND HYDRA BASE.
TWO YEARS AGO.
"HOW COULD I FORGET?"
SHOOT...HERE COME MORE OF THEM!
CHLOE, HYDRA ALIAS: ACTRESS.
AND THAT'S CAPTAIN TAMAKI.
JUST MY LUCK.
GUESS THERE'S ONLY ONE THING TO DO...
...AND THAT'S ADAPT.
ACTIVATE CAMOUFLAGE ACT!
WHOOOOSH

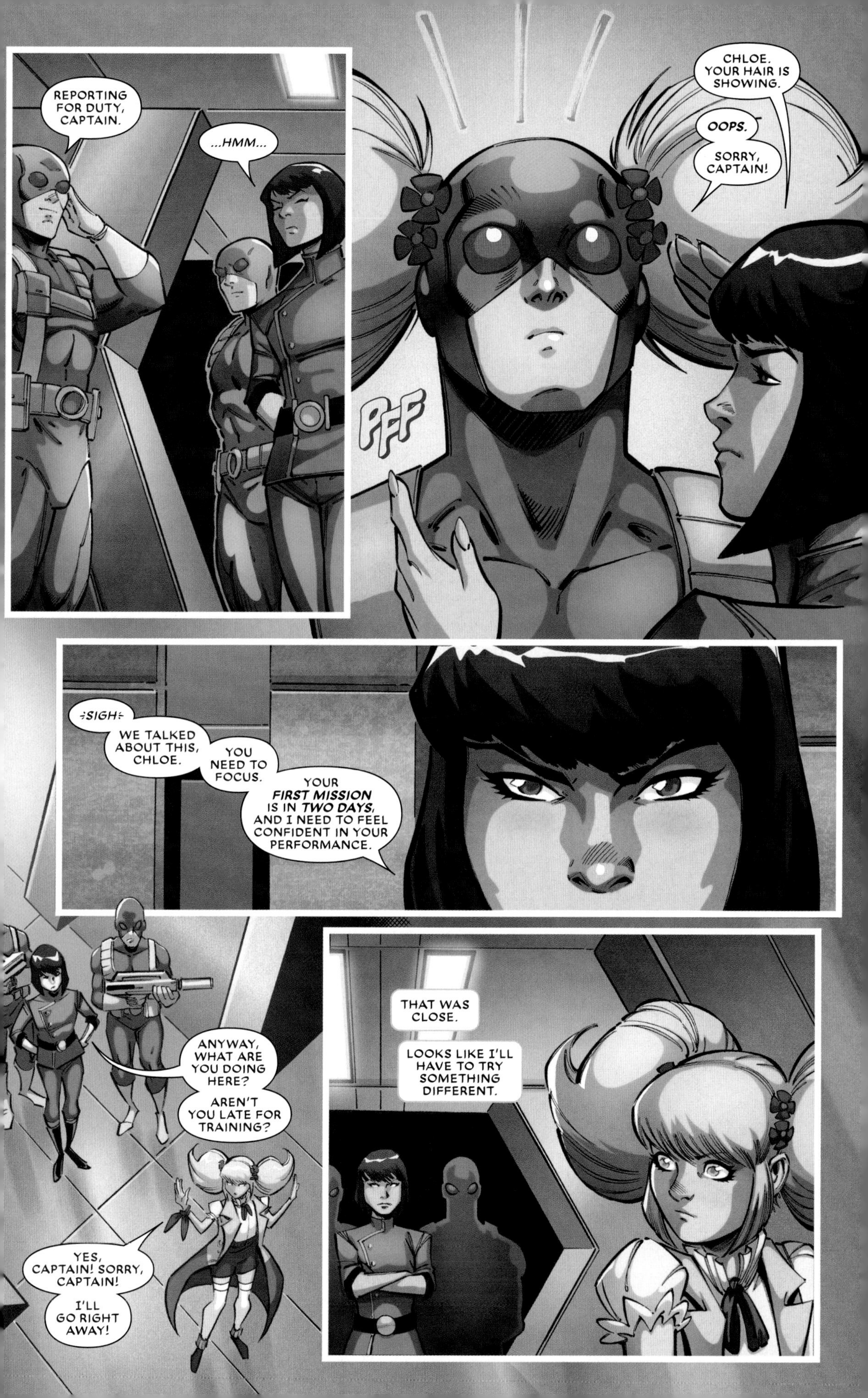

REPORTING FOR DUTY, CAPTAIN.
...HMM...
CHLOE. YOUR HAIR IS SHOWING.
OOPS.
SORRY, CAPTAIN!
PFF
=SIGH=
WE TALKED ABOUT THIS, CHLOE.
YOU NEED TO FOCUS.
YOUR FIRST MISSION IS IN TWO DAYS, AND I NEED TO FEEL CONFIDENT IN YOUR PERFORMANCE.
ANYWAY, WHAT ARE YOU DOING HERE?
AREN'T YOU LATE FOR TRAINING?
YES, CAPTAIN! SORRY, CAPTAIN!
I'LL GO RIGHT AWAY!
THAT WAS CLOSE.
LOOKS LIKE I'LL HAVE TO TRY SOMETHING DIFFERENT.

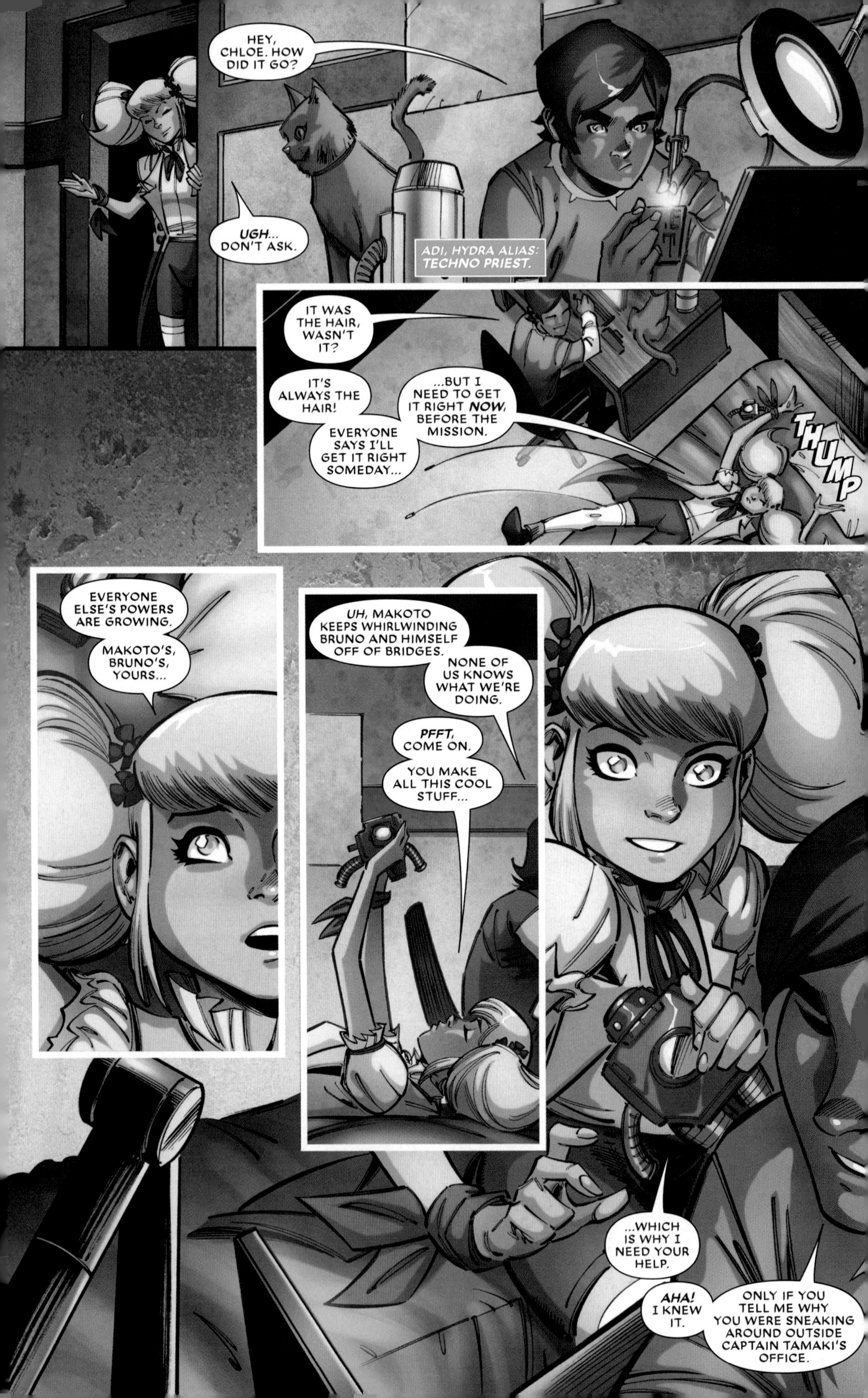
HEY, CHLOE. HOW DID IT GO?
UGH... DON'T ASK.
ADI, HYDRA ALIAS: TECHNO PRIEST.
IT WAS THE HAIR, WASN'T IT?
IT'S ALWAYS THE HAIR!
EVERYONE SAYS I'LL GET IT RIGHT SOMEDAY...
...BUT I NEED TO GET IT RIGHT NOW, BEFORE THE MISSION.
THUMP
EVERYONE ELSE'S POWERS ARE GROWING.
MAKOTO'S, BRUNO'S, YOURS...
UH, MAKOTO KEEPS WHIRLWINDING BRUNO AND HIMSELF OFF OF BRIDGES.
NONE OF US KNOWS WHAT WE'RE DOING.
PFFT, COME ON.
YOU MAKE ALL THIS COOL STUFF...
...WHICH IS WHY I NEED YOUR HELP.
AHA! I KNEW IT.
ONLY IF YOU TELL ME WHY YOU WERE SNEAKING AROUND OUTSIDE CAPTAIN TAMAKI'S OFFICE.

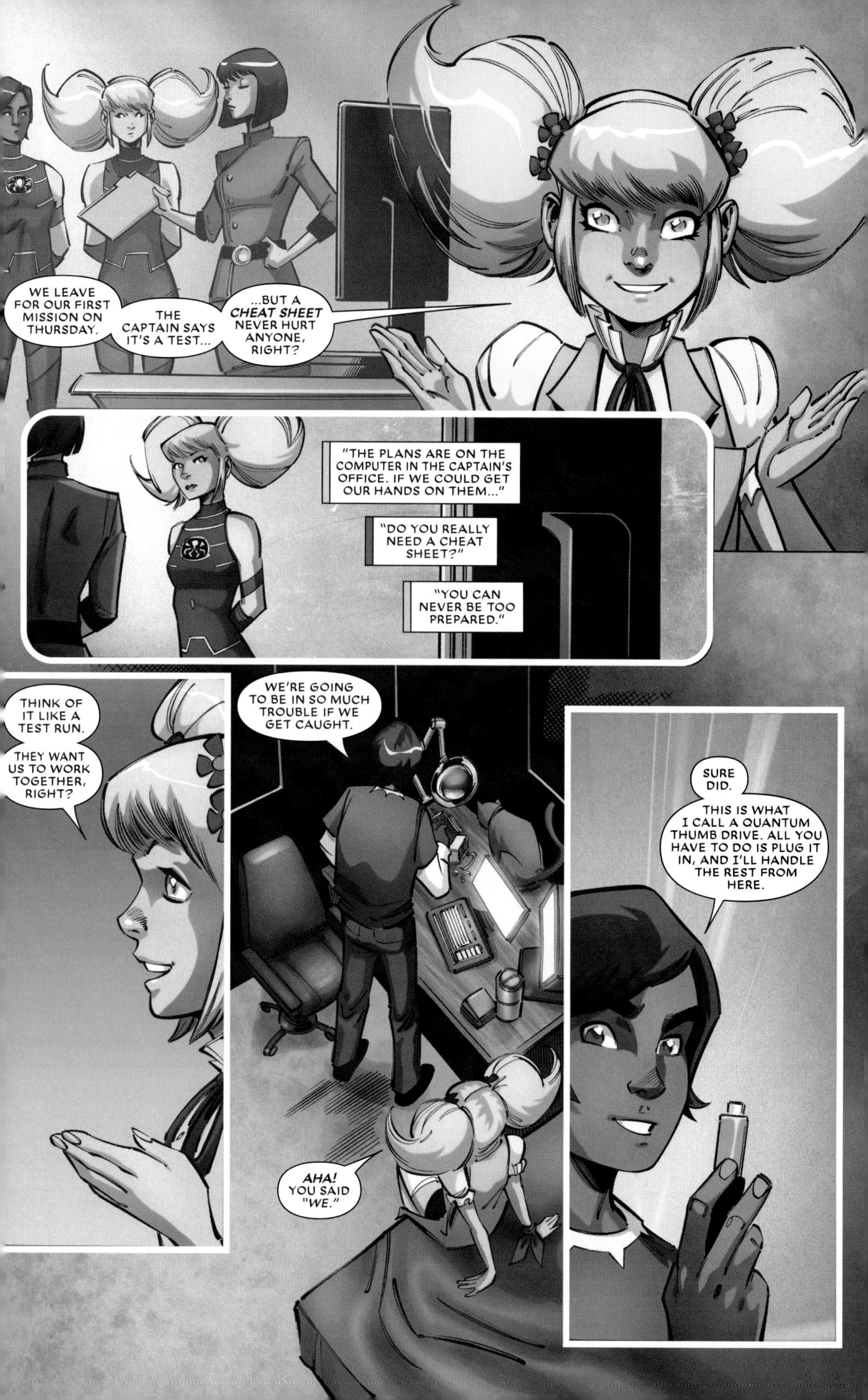

WE LEAVE FOR OUR FIRST MISSION ON THURSDAY.
THE CAPTAIN SAYS IT'S A TEST...
...BUT A *CHEAT SHEET* NEVER HURT ANYONE, RIGHT?
"THE PLANS ARE ON THE COMPUTER IN THE CAPTAIN'S OFFICE. IF WE COULD GET OUR HANDS ON THEM..."
"DO YOU REALLY NEED A CHEAT SHEET?"
"YOU CAN NEVER BE TOO PREPARED."
THINK OF IT LIKE A TEST RUN.
THEY WANT US TO WORK TOGETHER, RIGHT?
WE'RE GOING TO BE IN SO MUCH TROUBLE IF WE GET CAUGHT.
AHA! YOU SAID "*WE*."
SURE DID.
THIS IS WHAT I CALL A QUANTUM THUMB DRIVE. ALL YOU HAVE TO DO IS PLUG IT IN, AND I'LL HANDLE THE REST FROM HERE.

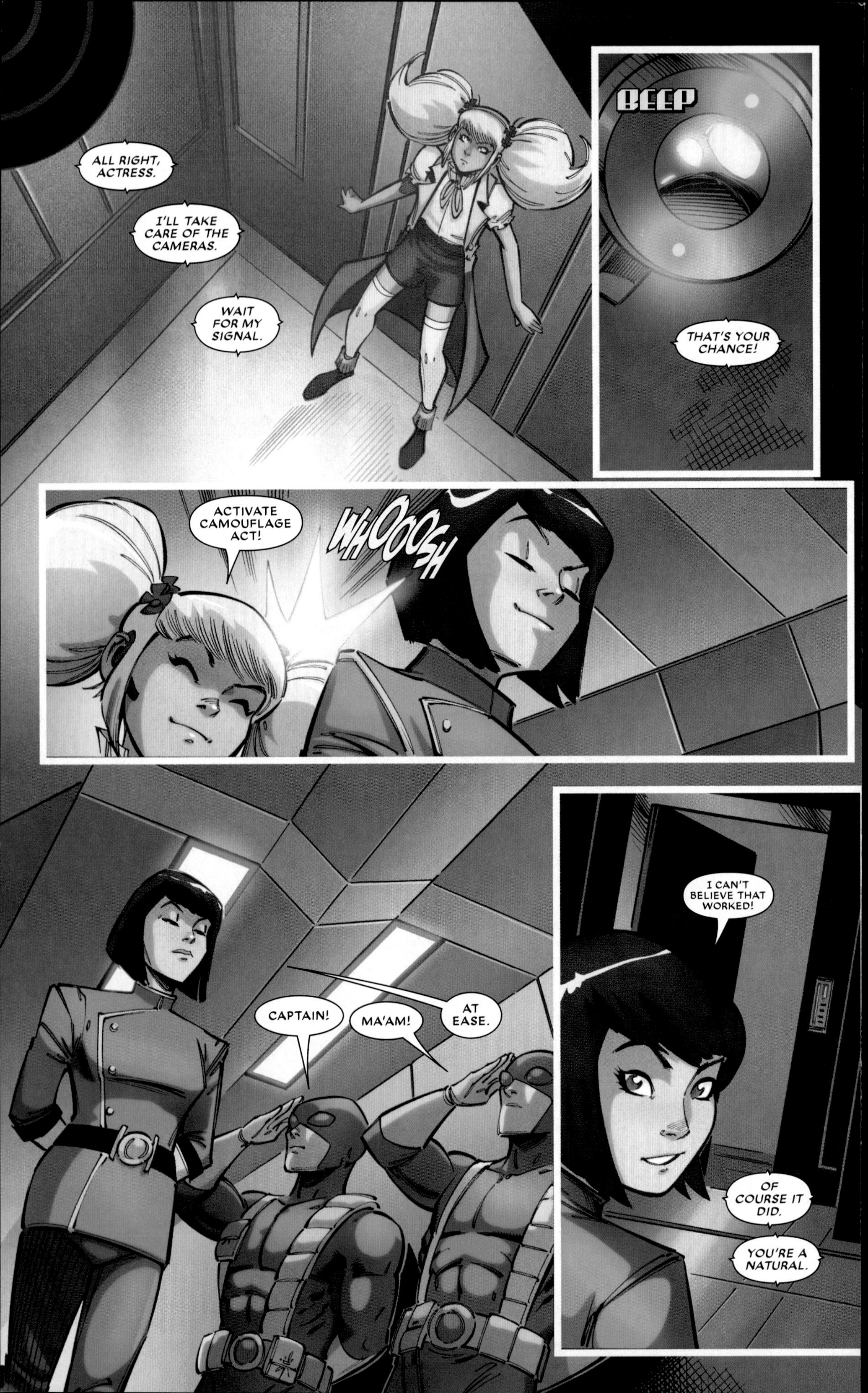
ALL RIGHT, ACTRESS.
I'LL TAKE CARE OF THE CAMERAS.
WAIT FOR MY SIGNAL.
BEEP
THAT'S YOUR CHANCE!
ACTIVATE CAMOUFLAGE ACT!
WHOOOSH
CAPTAIN!
MA'AM!
AT EASE.
I CAN'T BELIEVE THAT WORKED!
OF COURSE IT DID.
YOU'RE A NATURAL.

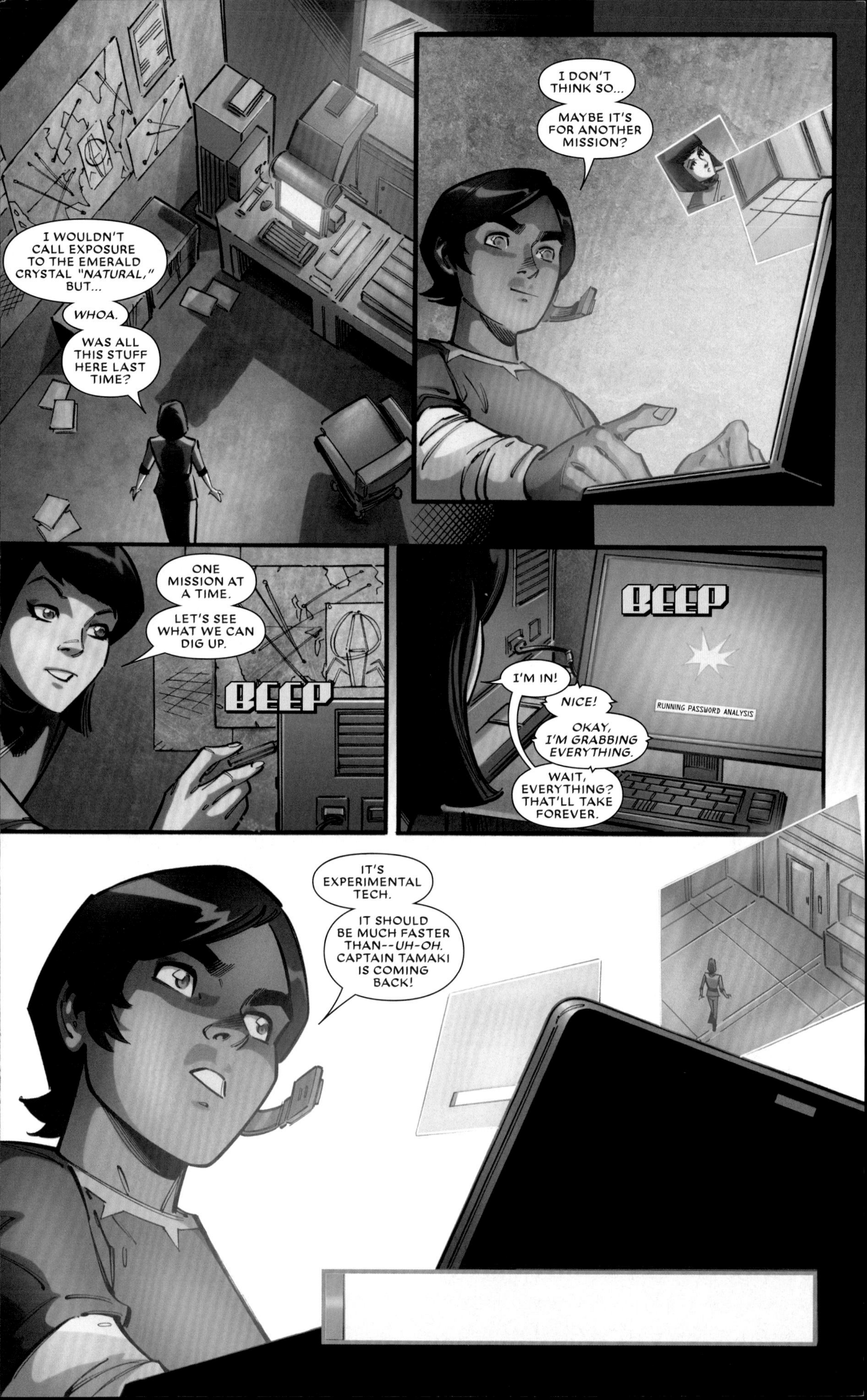
I WOULDN'T CALL EXPOSURE TO THE EMERALD CRYSTAL "NATURAL," BUT...
WHOA.
WAS ALL THIS STUFF HERE LAST TIME?
I DON'T THINK SO...
MAYBE IT'S FOR ANOTHER MISSION?
ONE MISSION AT A TIME.
LET'S SEE WHAT WE CAN DIG UP.
BEEP
BEEP
I'M IN!
NICE!
OKAY, I'M GRABBING EVERYTHING.
RUNNING PASSWORD ANALYSIS
WAIT, EVERYTHING? THAT'LL TAKE FOREVER.
IT'S EXPERIMENTAL TECH.
IT SHOULD BE MUCH FASTER THAN--UH-OH. CAPTAIN TAMAKI IS COMING BACK!

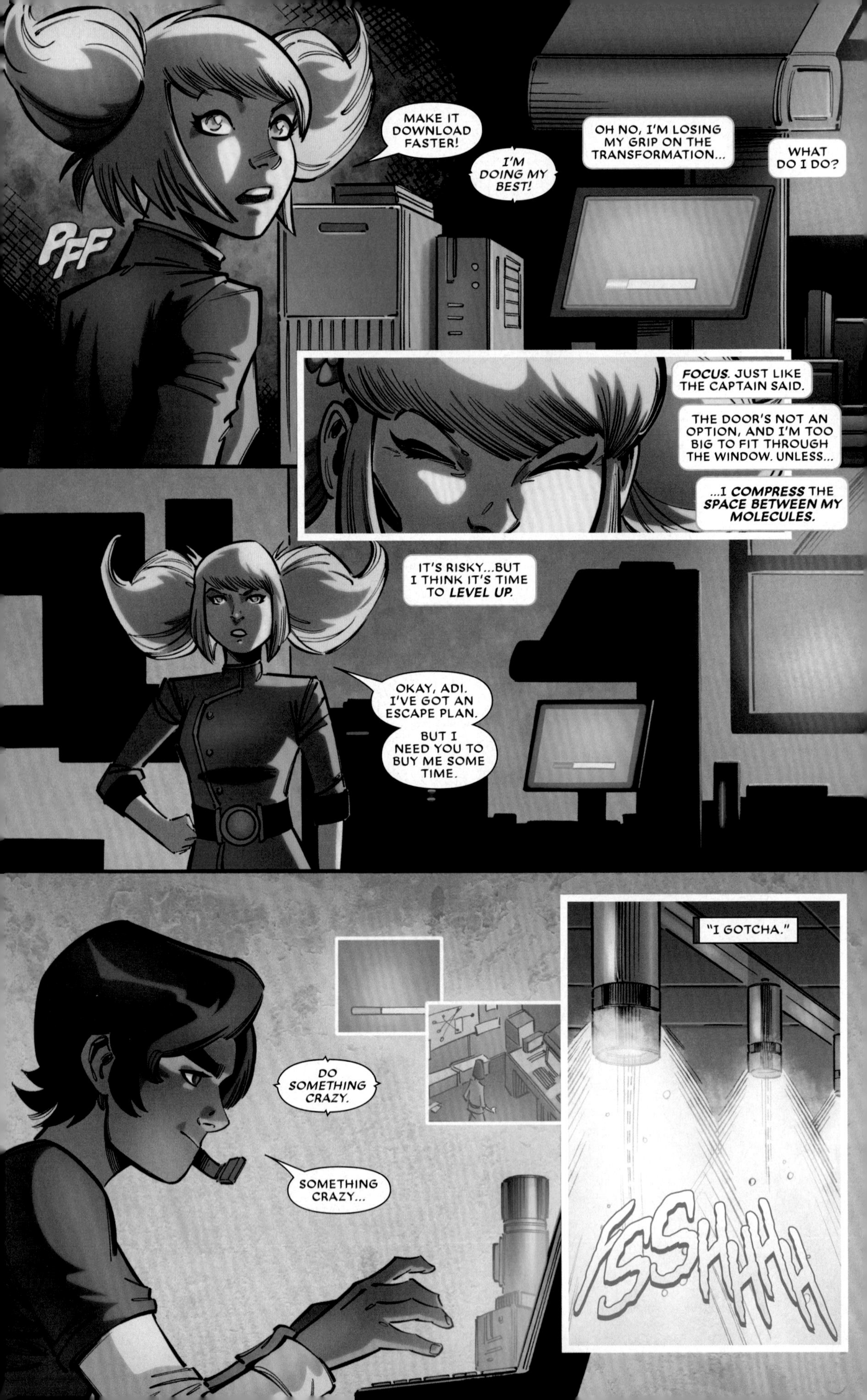
MAKE IT DOWNLOAD FASTER!
I'M DOING MY BEST!
PFF
OH NO, I'M LOSING MY GRIP ON THE TRANSFORMATION...
WHAT DO I DO?
FOCUS. JUST LIKE THE CAPTAIN SAID.
THE DOOR'S NOT AN OPTION, AND I'M TOO BIG TO FIT THROUGH THE WINDOW. UNLESS...
...I COMPRESS THE SPACE BETWEEN MY MOLECULES.
IT'S RISKY...BUT I THINK IT'S TIME TO LEVEL UP.
OKAY, ADI. I'VE GOT AN ESCAPE PLAN.
BUT I NEED YOU TO BUY ME SOME TIME.
DO SOMETHING CRAZY.
SOMETHING CRAZY...
"I GOTCHA."
FSSHHH

WEEEOOWEEOO

FSSSHHHHHH

THAT'S THE FIRE ALARM! EVERYONE, OUT OF THE BUILDING!

DOWNLOAD IN PROGRESS. 65%

EVACUATE THE TRAINING ROOM! MOVE IT!

BUT WE'RE IN THE MIDDLE OF SPARRING.

I WAS ABOUT TO WIN, TOO!

IT'S NOW OR NEVER!

ACTIVATE CAMOUFLAGE ACT!

EWOOSH

DOWNLOAD COMPLETE.

PHEW, JUST IN TIME!

WEEOOOO

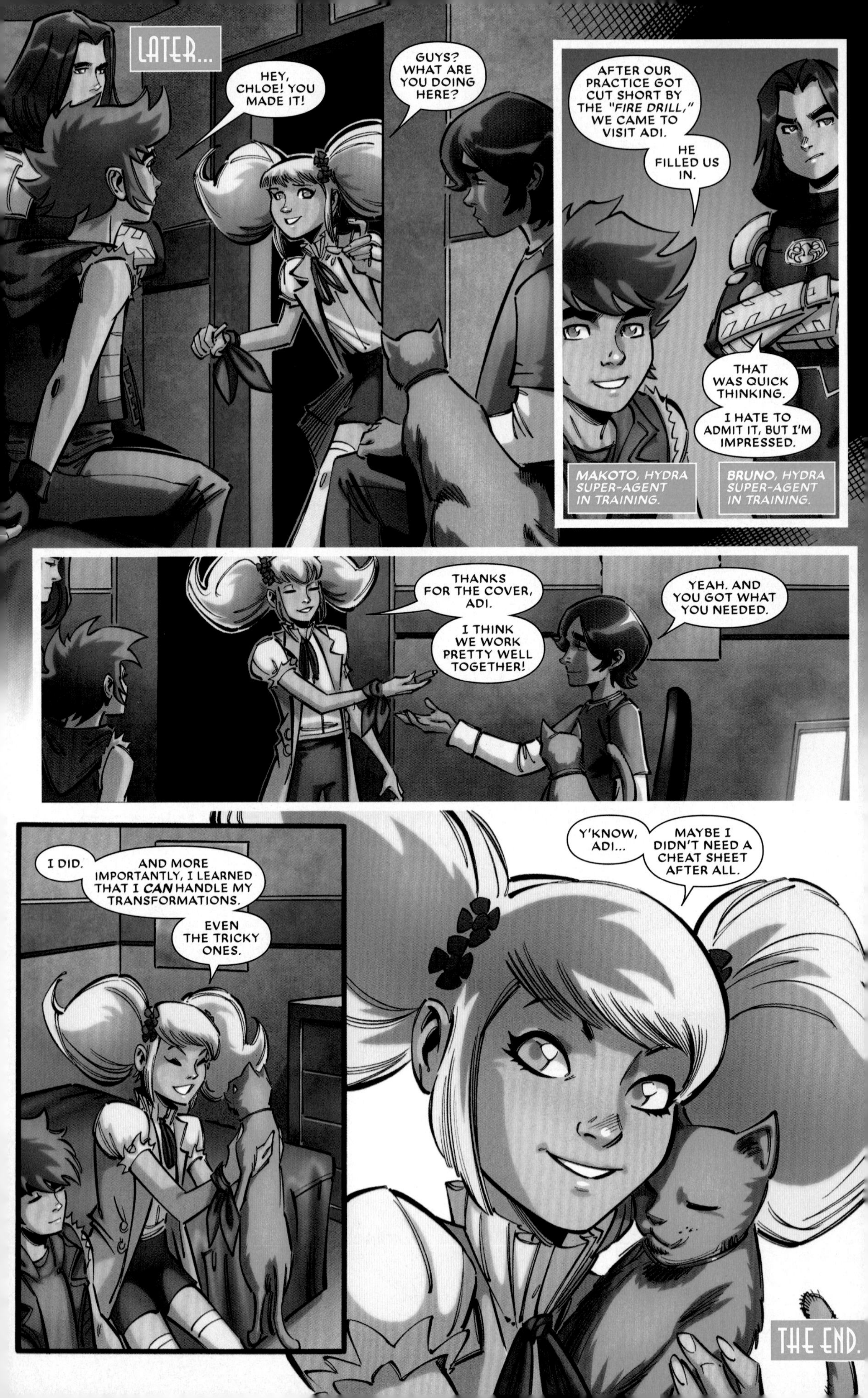
LATER...
HEY, CHLOE! YOU MADE IT!
GUYS? WHAT ARE YOU DOING HERE?
AFTER OUR PRACTICE GOT CUT SHORT BY THE "FIRE DRILL," WE CAME TO VISIT ADI.
HE FILLED US IN.
THAT WAS QUICK THINKING.
I HATE TO ADMIT IT, BUT I'M IMPRESSED.
MAKOTO, HYDRA SUPER-AGENT IN TRAINING.
BRUNO, HYDRA SUPER-AGENT IN TRAINING.
THANKS FOR THE COVER, ADI.
I THINK WE WORK PRETTY WELL TOGETHER!
YEAH. AND YOU GOT WHAT YOU NEEDED.
I DID.
AND MORE IMPORTANTLY, I LEARNED THAT I CAN HANDLE MY TRANSFORMATIONS.
EVEN THE TRICKY ONES.
Y'KNOW, ADI...
MAYBE I DIDN'T NEED A CHEAT SHEET AFTER ALL.
THE END.

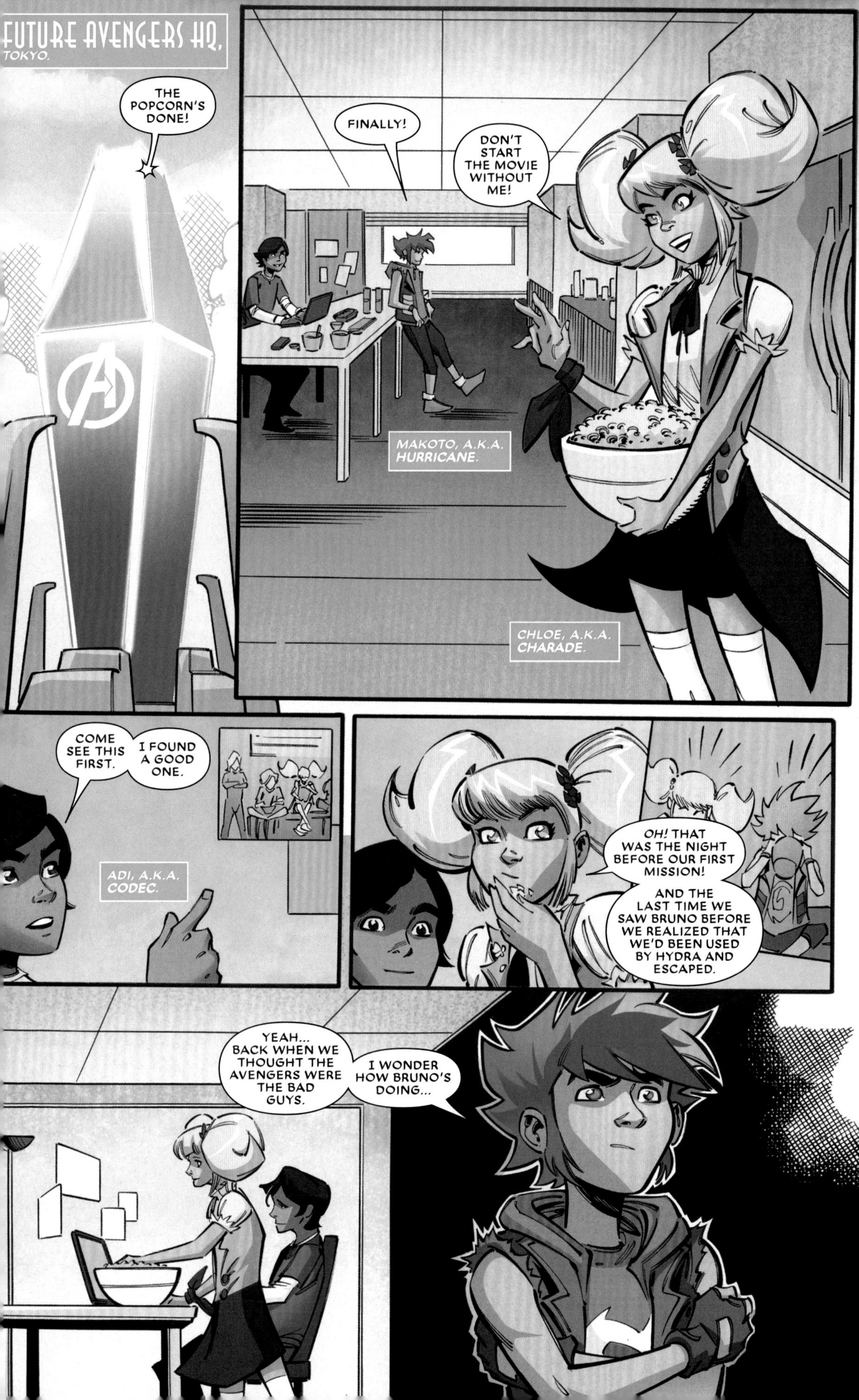
FUTURE AVENGERS HQ,
TOKYO.
THE POPCORN'S DONE!
FINALLY!
DON'T START THE MOVIE WITHOUT ME!
MAKOTO, A.K.A. HURRICANE.
CHLOE, A.K.A. CHARADE.
COME SEE THIS FIRST.
I FOUND A GOOD ONE.
ADI, A.K.A. CODEC.
OH! THAT WAS THE NIGHT BEFORE OUR FIRST MISSION!
AND THE LAST TIME WE SAW BRUNO BEFORE WE REALIZED THAT WE'D BEEN USED BY HYDRA AND ESCAPED.
YEAH... BACK WHEN WE THOUGHT THE AVENGERS WERE THE BAD GUYS.
I WONDER HOW BRUNO'S DOING...

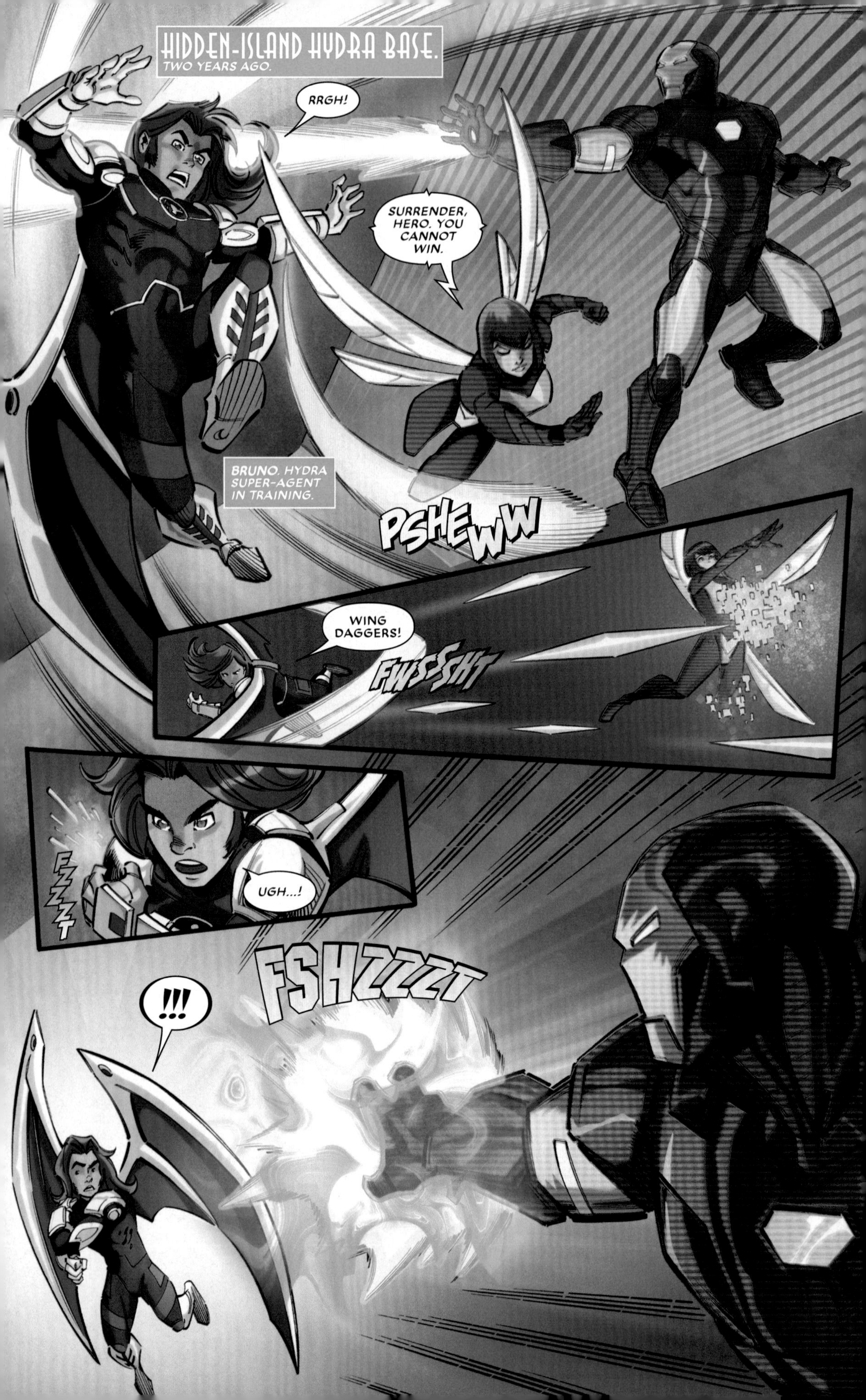
HIDDEN-ISLAND HYDRA BASE.
TWO YEARS AGO.
RRGH!
SURRENDER, HERO. YOU CANNOT WIN.
BRUNO. HYDRA SUPER-AGENT IN TRAINING.
PSHEWW
WING DAGGERS!
FWSSSHT
FZZZT
UGH...!
FSHZZZZT
!!!

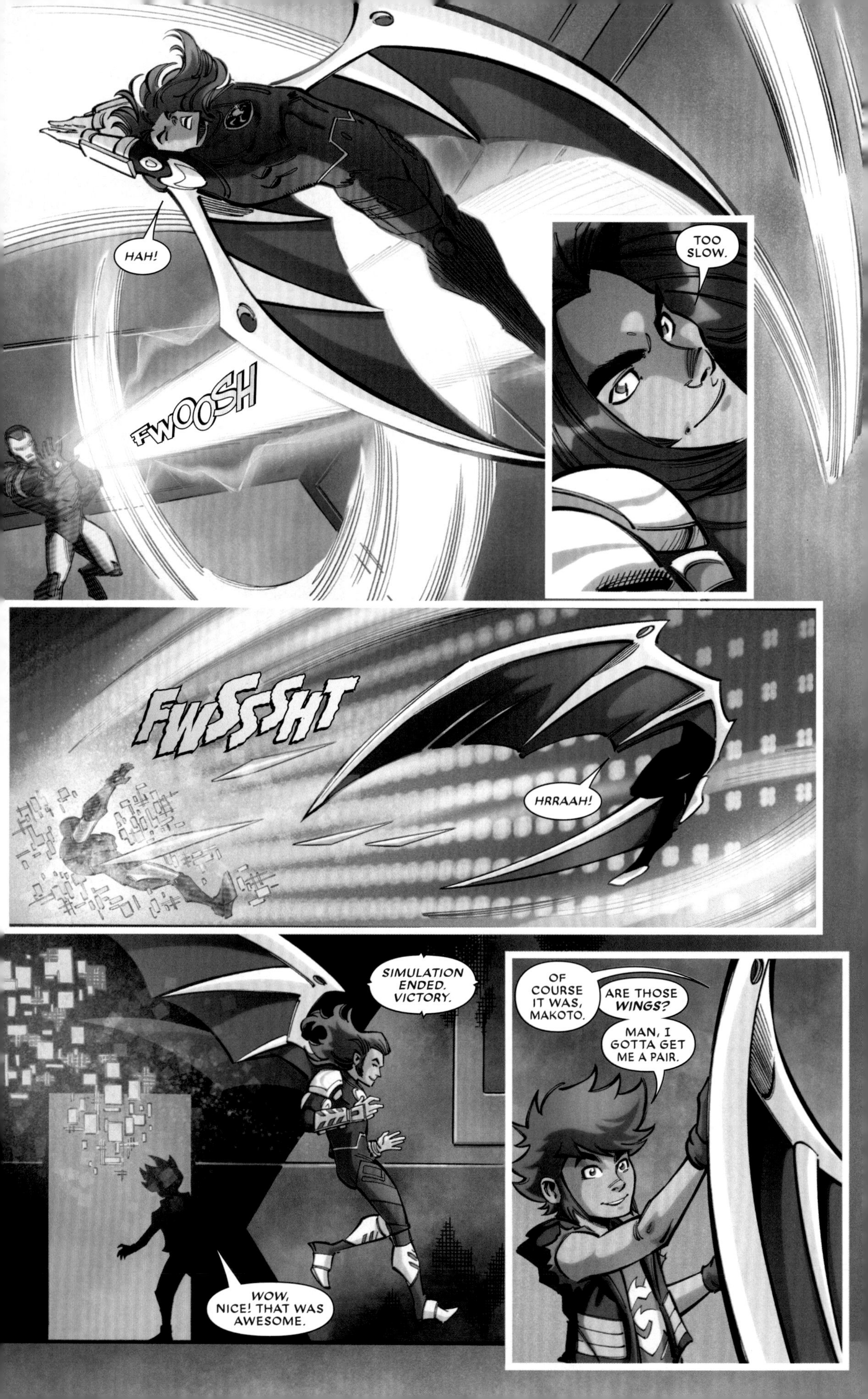
HAH!
FWOOSH
TOO SLOW.
FWSSSHT
HRRAAH!
SIMULATION ENDED. VICTORY.
WOW, NICE! THAT WAS AWESOME.
OF COURSE IT WAS, MAKOTO.
ARE THOSE WINGS?
MAN, I GOTTA GET ME A PAIR.

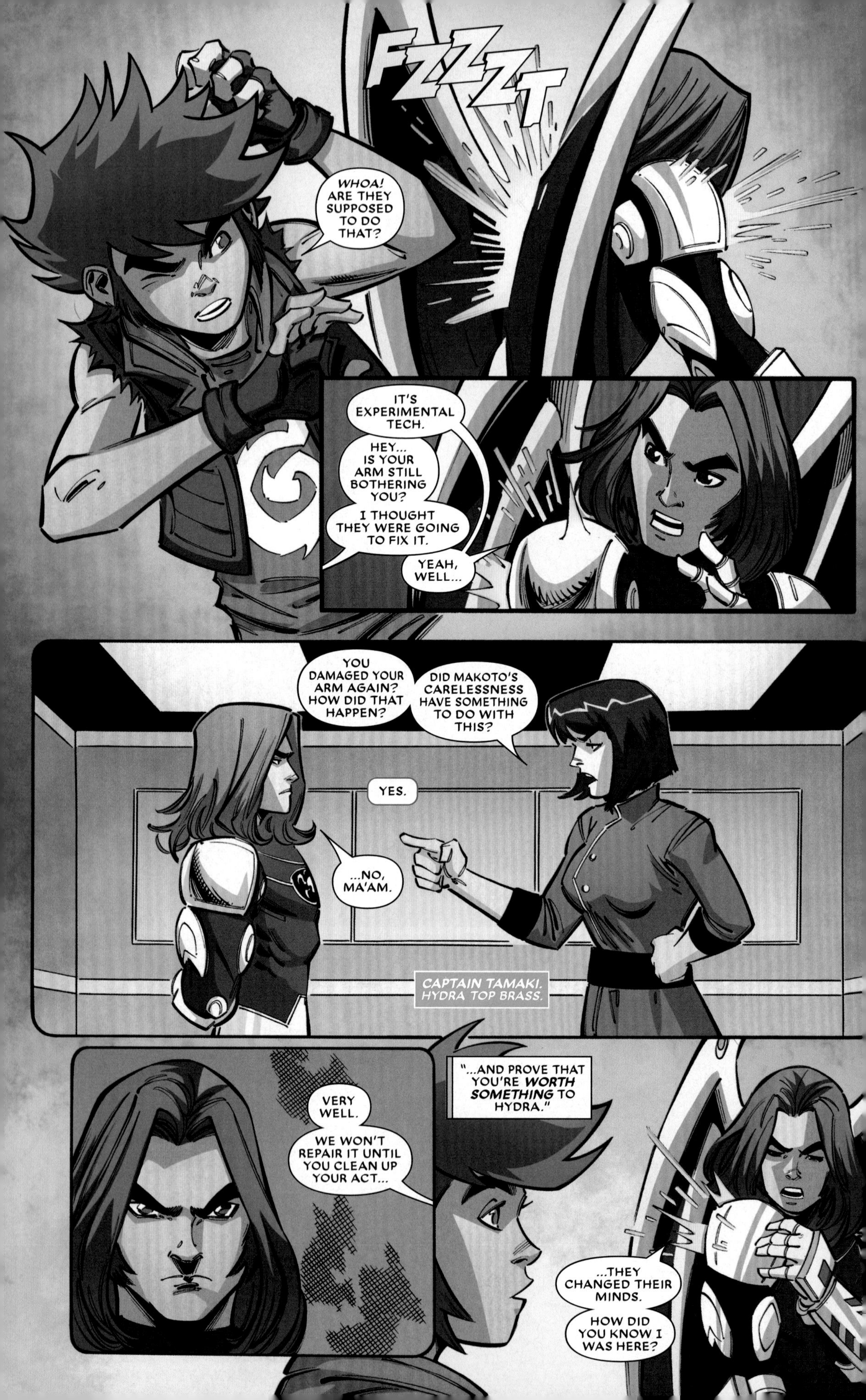
FZZZT
WHOA! ARE THEY SUPPOSED TO DO THAT?
IT'S EXPERIMENTAL TECH.
HEY... IS YOUR ARM STILL BOTHERING YOU?
I THOUGHT THEY WERE GOING TO FIX IT.
YEAH, WELL...
YOU DAMAGED YOUR ARM AGAIN? HOW DID THAT HAPPEN?
DID MAKOTO'S CARELESSNESS HAVE SOMETHING TO DO WITH THIS?
YES.
...NO, MA'AM.
CAPTAIN TAMAKI. HYDRA TOP BRASS.
VERY WELL.
WE WON'T REPAIR IT UNTIL YOU CLEAN UP YOUR ACT...
"...AND PROVE THAT YOU'RE WORTH SOMETHING TO HYDRA."
...THEY CHANGED THEIR MINDS.
HOW DID YOU KNOW I WAS HERE?

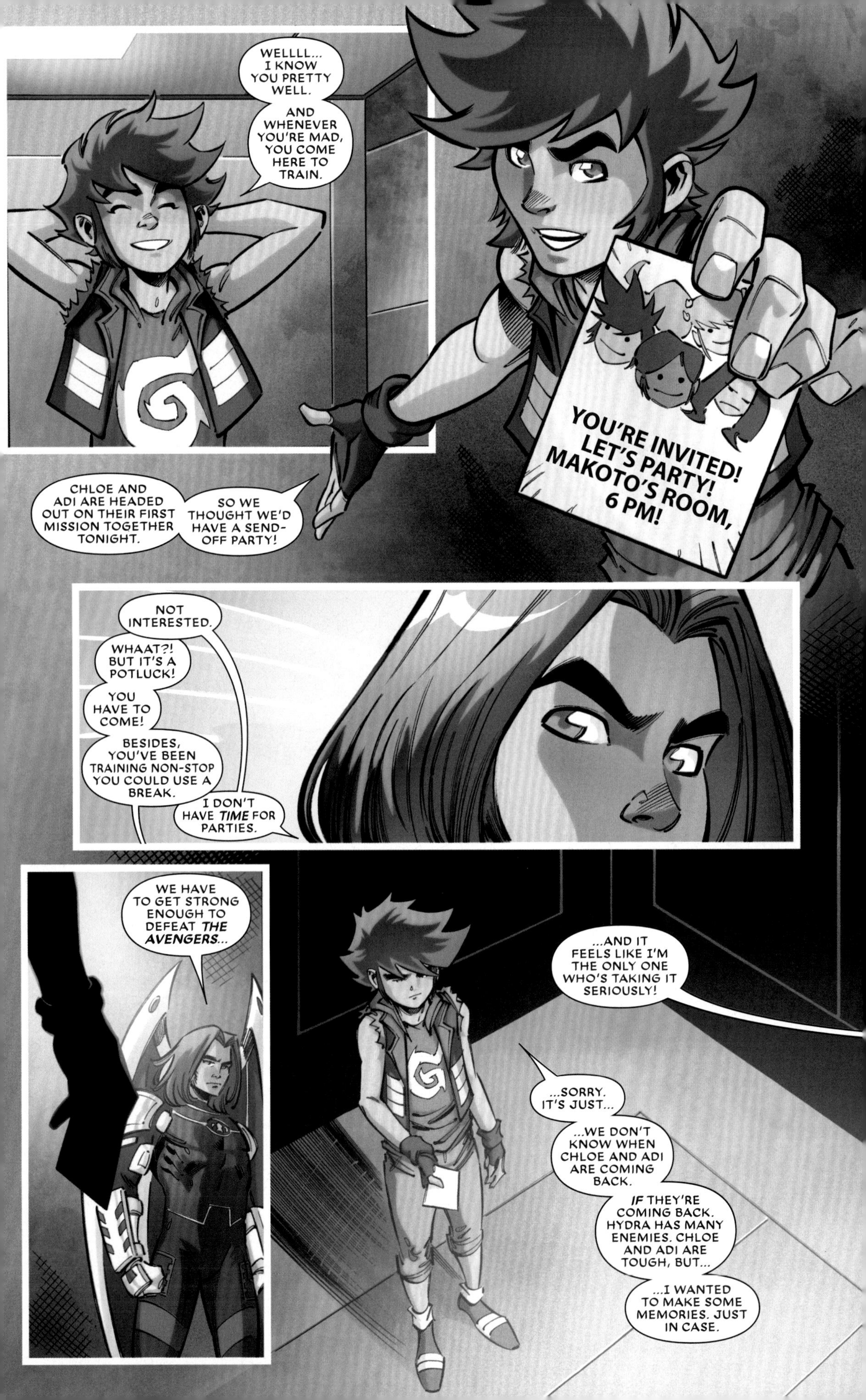
WELLLL... I KNOW YOU PRETTY WELL.
AND WHENEVER YOU'RE MAD, YOU COME HERE TO TRAIN.
YOU'RE INVITED! LET'S PARTY! MAKOTO'S ROOM, 6 PM!
CHLOE AND ADI ARE HEADED OUT ON THEIR FIRST MISSION TOGETHER TONIGHT.
SO WE THOUGHT WE'D HAVE A SEND-OFF PARTY!
NOT INTERESTED.
WHAAT?! BUT IT'S A POTLUCK!
YOU HAVE TO COME!
BESIDES, YOU'VE BEEN TRAINING NON-STOP YOU COULD USE A BREAK.
I DON'T HAVE TIME FOR PARTIES.
WE HAVE TO GET STRONG ENOUGH TO DEFEAT THE AVENGERS...
...AND IT FEELS LIKE I'M THE ONLY ONE WHO'S TAKING IT SERIOUSLY!
...SORRY. IT'S JUST...
...WE DON'T KNOW WHEN CHLOE AND ADI ARE COMING BACK.
IF THEY'RE COMING BACK. HYDRA HAS MANY ENEMIES. CHLOE AND ADI ARE TOUGH, BUT...
...I WANTED TO MAKE SOME MEMORIES. JUST IN CASE.

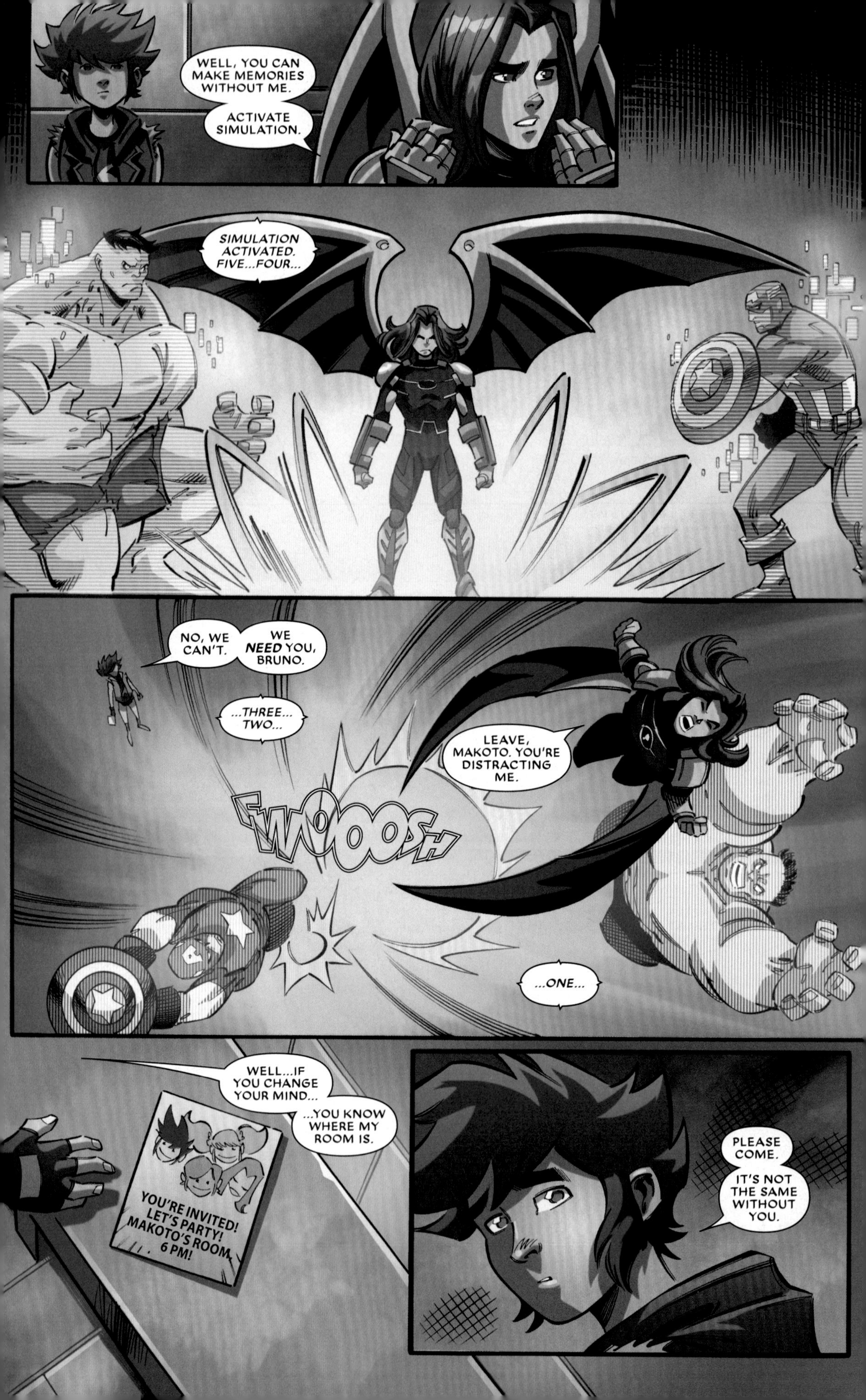
WELL, YOU CAN MAKE MEMORIES WITHOUT ME.
ACTIVATE SIMULATION.
SIMULATION ACTIVATED. FIVE...FOUR...
NO, WE CAN'T.
WE NEED YOU, BRUNO.
...THREE... TWO...
LEAVE, MAKOTO. YOU'RE DISTRACTING ME.
FWOOOSH
...ONE...
WELL...IF YOU CHANGE YOUR MIND...
...YOU KNOW WHERE MY ROOM IS.
YOU'RE INVITED! LET'S PARTY! MAKOTO'S ROOM, 6 PM!
PLEASE COME.
IT'S NOT THE SAME WITHOUT YOU.

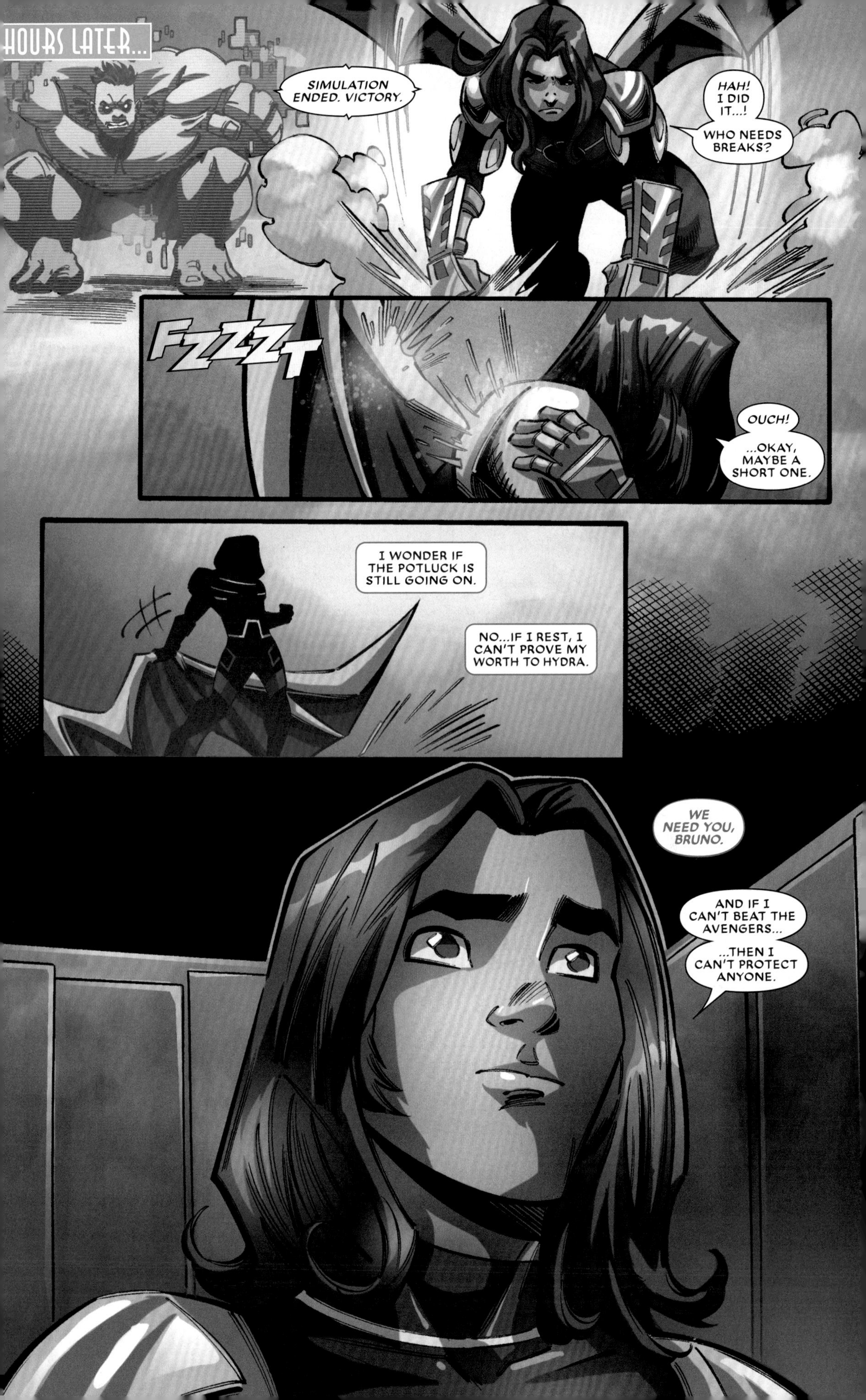
HOURS LATER...
SIMULATION ENDED. VICTORY.
HAH! I DID IT...!
WHO NEEDS BREAKS?
FZZZT
OUCH!
...OKAY, MAYBE A SHORT ONE.
I WONDER IF THE POTLUCK IS STILL GOING ON.
NO...IF I REST, I CAN'T PROVE MY WORTH TO HYDRA.
WE NEED YOU, BRUNO.
AND IF I CAN'T BEAT THE AVENGERS...
...THEN I CAN'T PROTECT ANYONE.

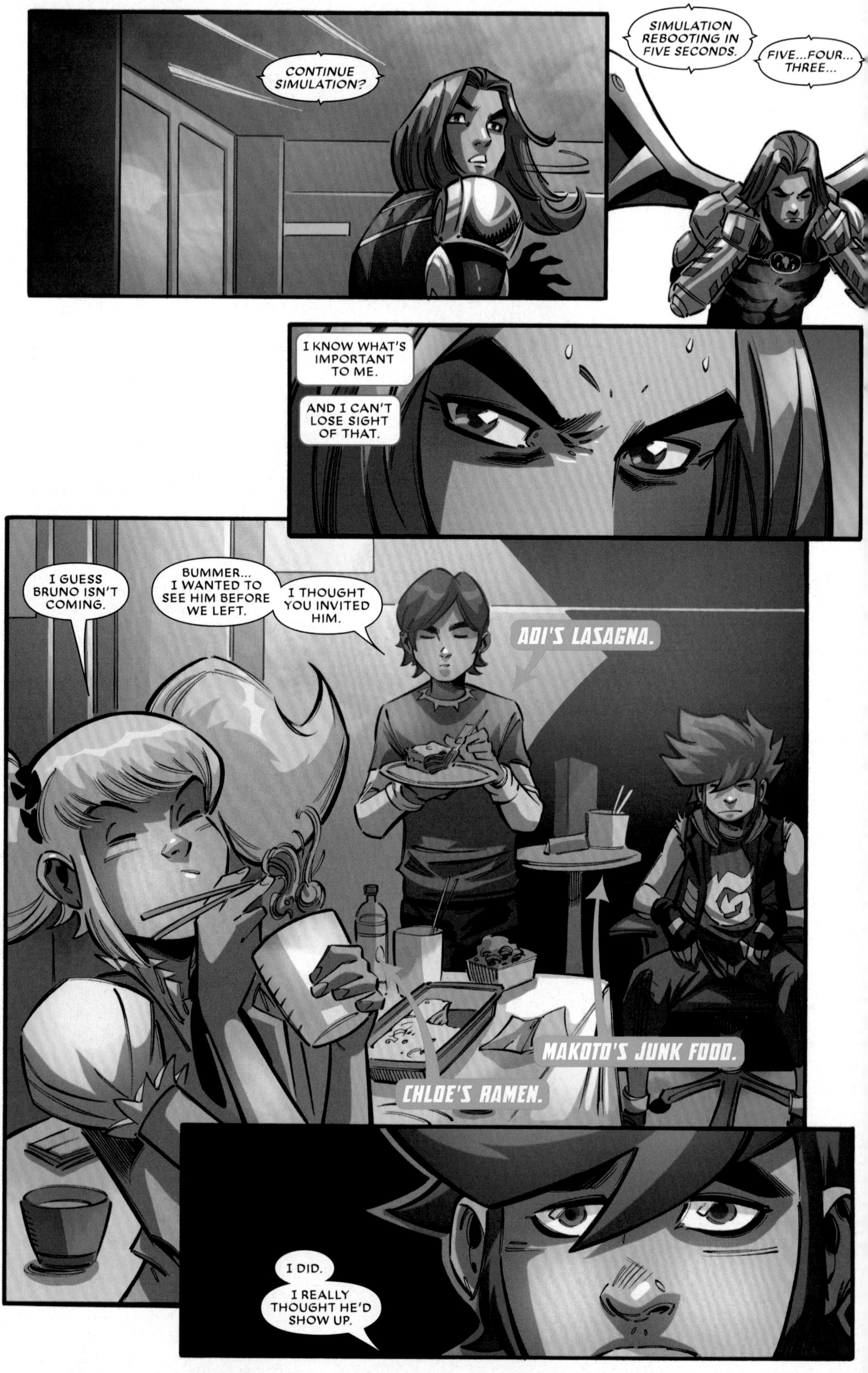
CONTINUE SIMULATION?
SIMULATION REBOOTING IN FIVE SECONDS.
FIVE...FOUR... THREE...
I KNOW WHAT'S IMPORTANT TO ME.
AND I CAN'T LOSE SIGHT OF THAT.
I GUESS BRUNO ISN'T COMING.
BUMMER... I WANTED TO SEE HIM BEFORE WE LEFT.
I THOUGHT YOU INVITED HIM.
AOI'S LASAGNA.
MAKOTO'S JUNK FOOD.
CHLOE'S RAMEN.
I DID.
I REALLY THOUGHT HE'D SHOW UP.

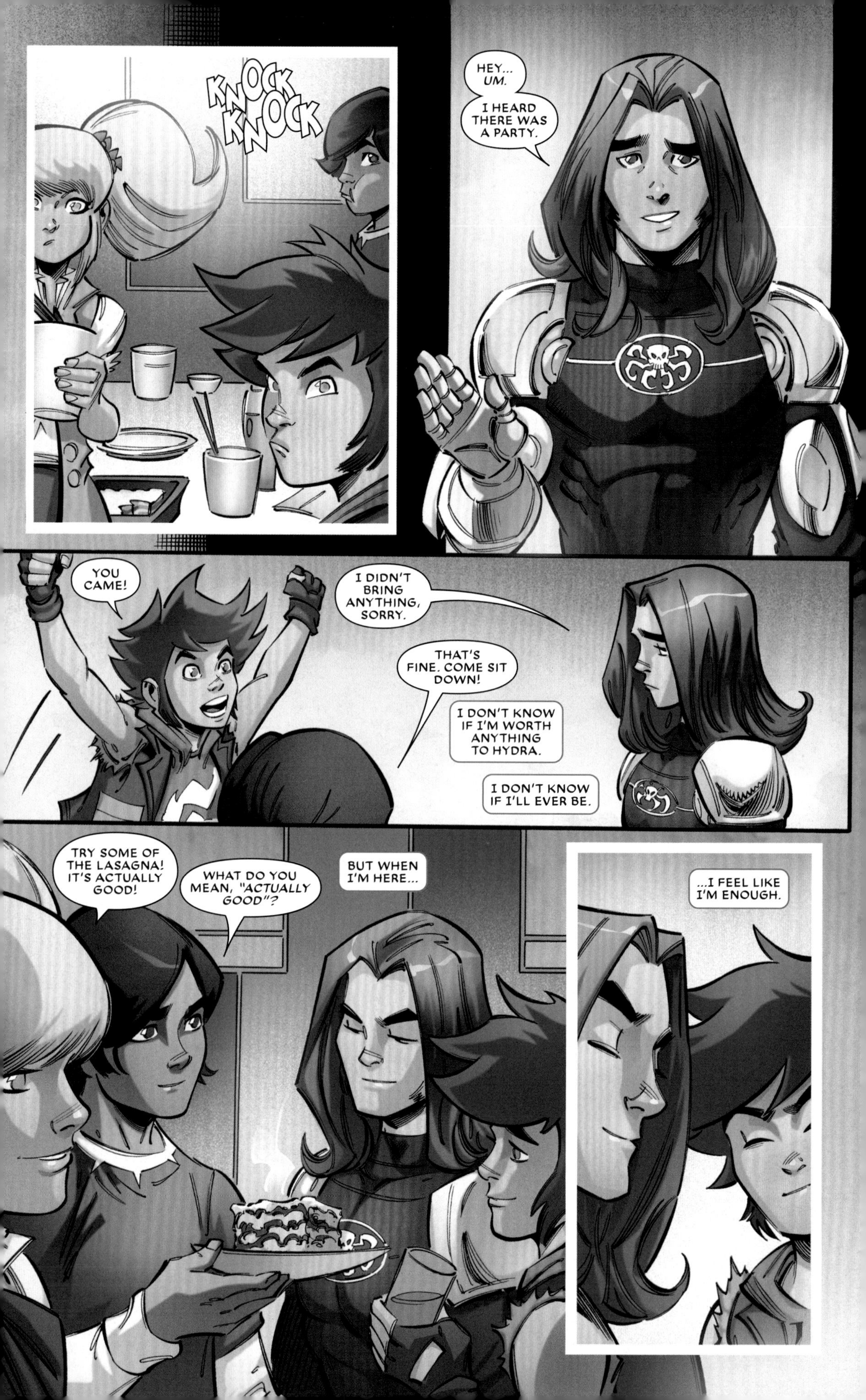
KNOCK KNOCK
HEY... UM.
I HEARD THERE WAS A PARTY.
YOU CAME!
I DIDN'T BRING ANYTHING, SORRY.
THAT'S FINE. COME SIT DOWN!
I DON'T KNOW IF I'M WORTH ANYTHING TO HYDRA.
I DON'T KNOW IF I'LL EVER BE.
TRY SOME OF THE LASAGNA! IT'S ACTUALLY GOOD!
WHAT DO YOU MEAN, "ACTUALLY GOOD"?
BUT WHEN I'M HERE...
...I FEEL LIKE I'M ENOUGH.

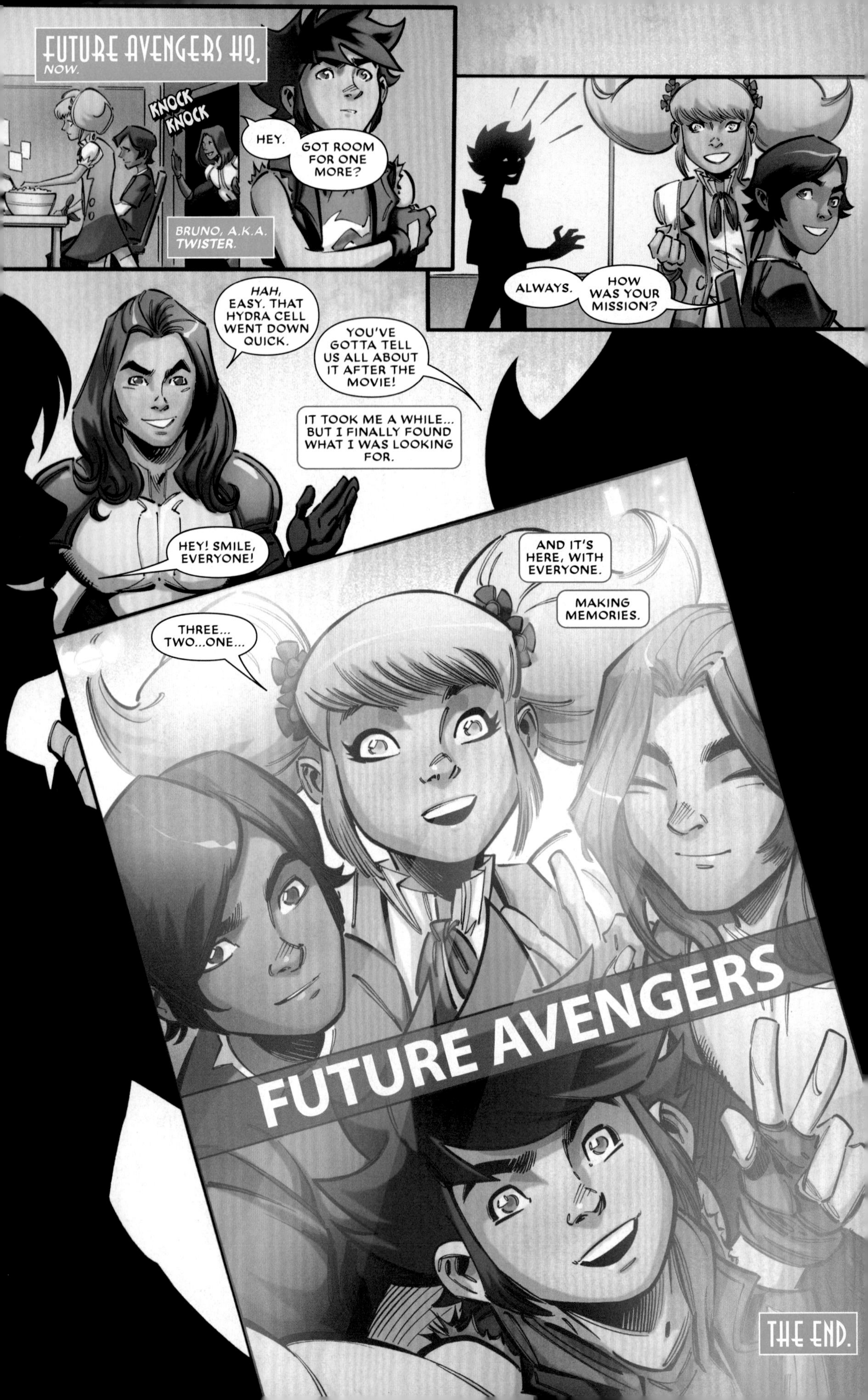
FUTURE AVENGERS HQ,
NOW.
KNOCK
KNOCK
HEY.
GOT ROOM FOR ONE MORE?
BRUNO, A.K.A. TWISTER.
ALWAYS.
HOW WAS YOUR MISSION?
HAH, EASY. THAT HYDRA CELL WENT DOWN QUICK.
YOU'VE GOTTA TELL US ALL ABOUT IT AFTER THE MOVIE!
IT TOOK ME A WHILE... BUT I FINALLY FOUND WHAT I WAS LOOKING FOR.
HEY! SMILE, EVERYONE!
AND IT'S HERE, WITH EVERYONE.
MAKING MEMORIES.
THREE... TWO...ONE...
FUTURE AVENGERS
THE END.

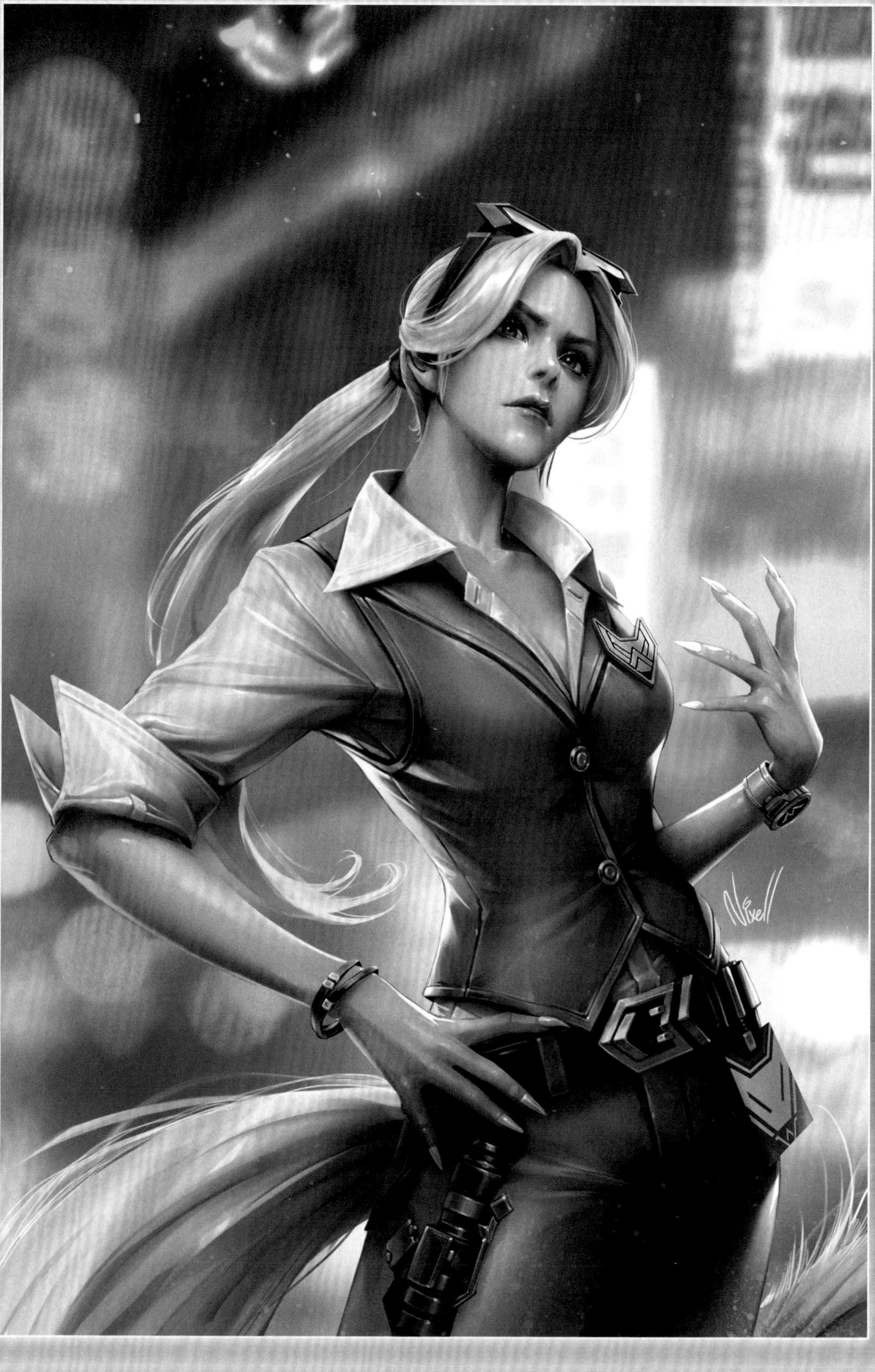
Nixell

WHITE FOX #1 NETMARBLE VARIANT BY **YONGJOON CHO**

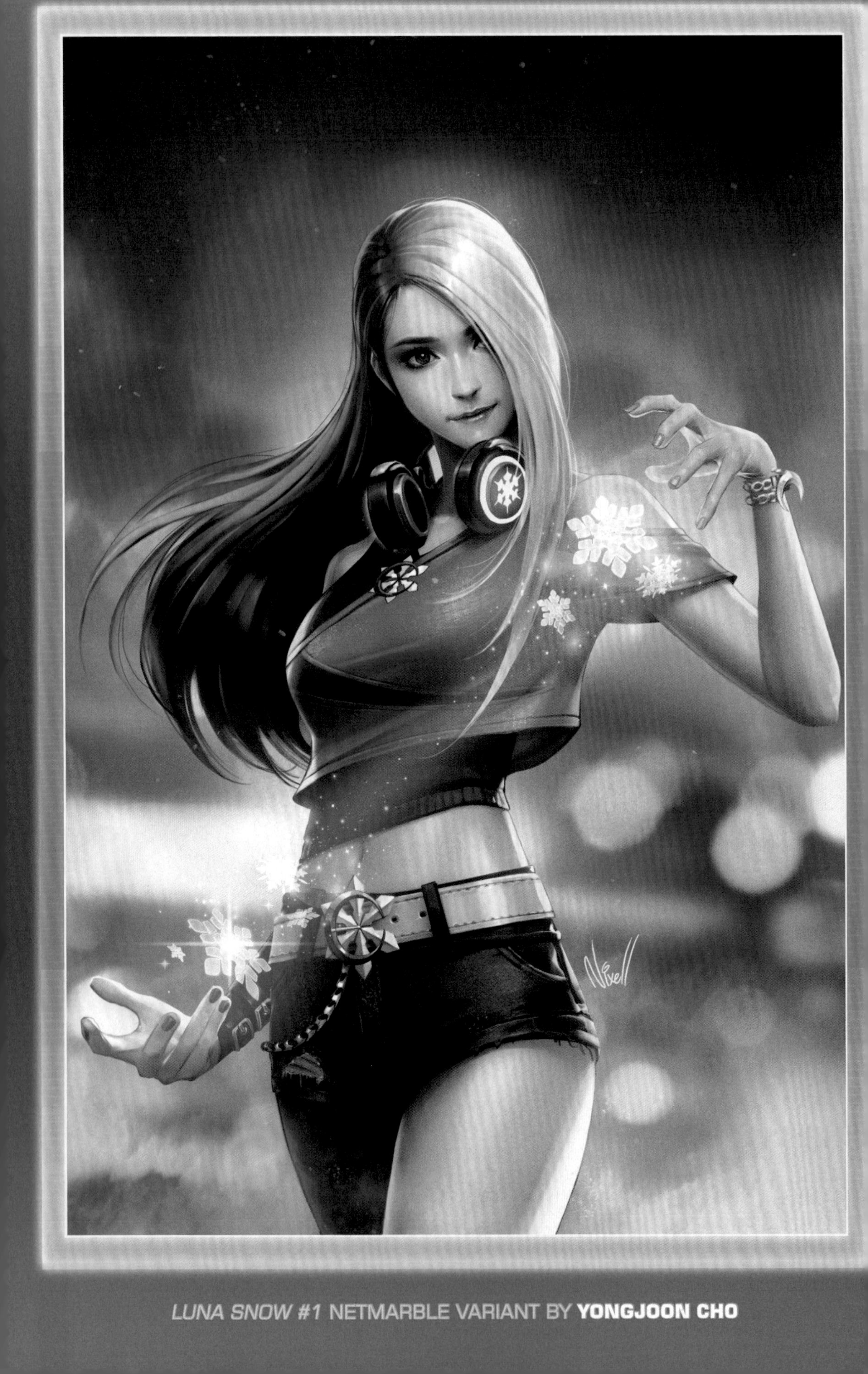

LUNA SNOW #1 NETMARBLE VARIANT BY **YONGJOON CHO**

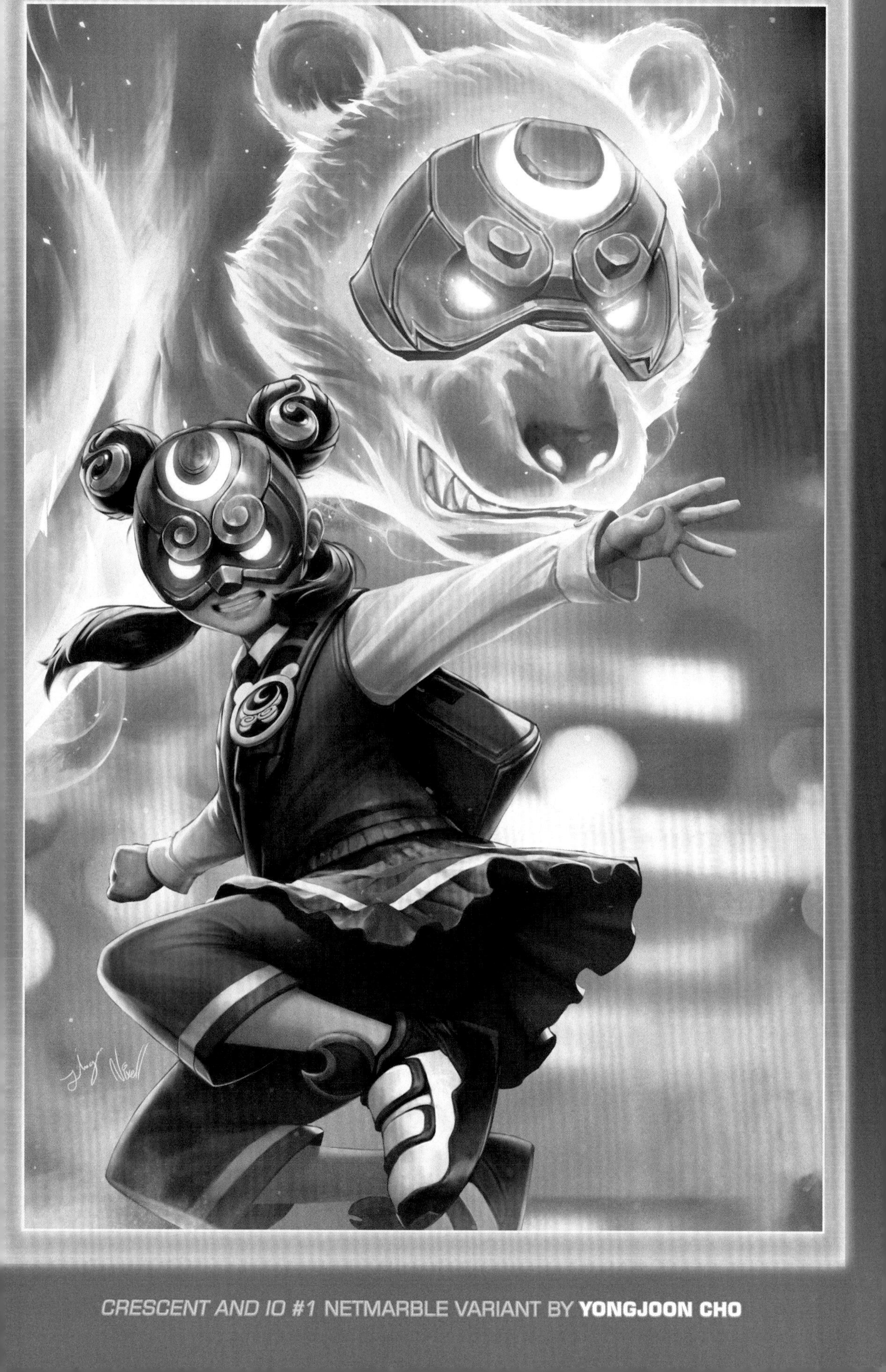

CRESCENT AND IO #1 NETMARBLE VARIANT BY **YONGJOON CHO**

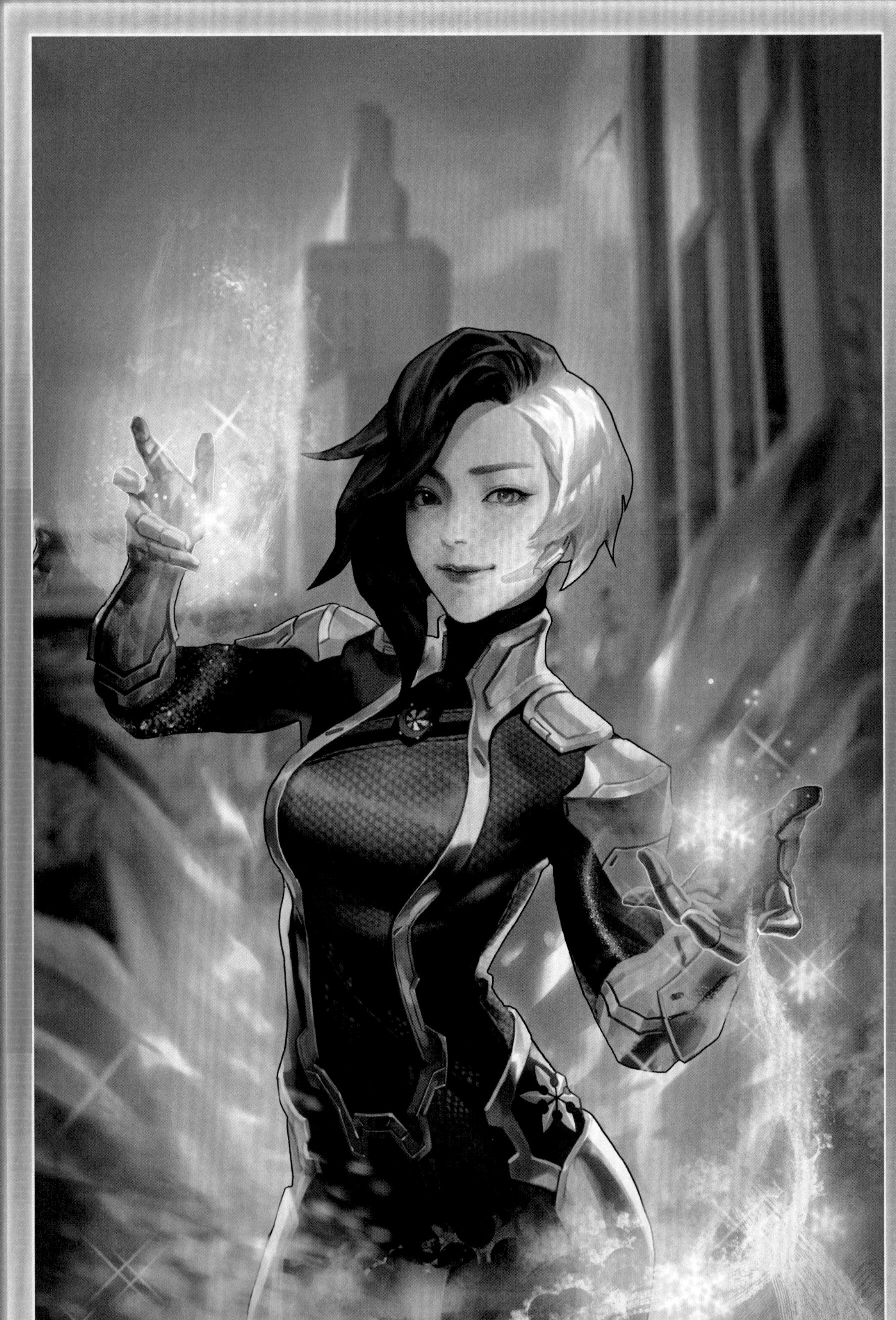

LUNA SNOW #1 VARIANT BY **COAX**

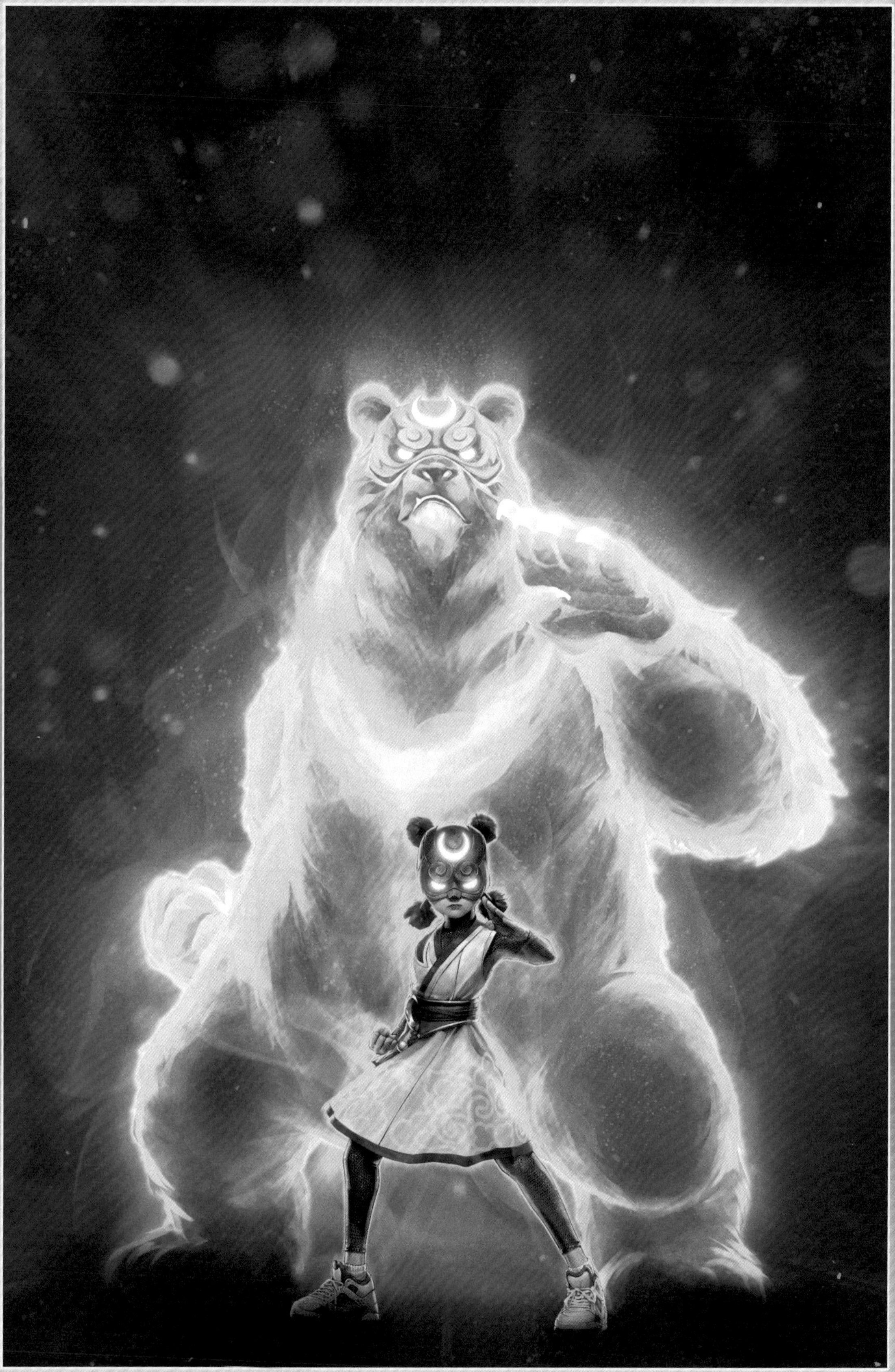

CRESCENT AND IO #1 VARIANT BY **JEEHYUNG LEE**